HTML 4.0

User's Resource

ISBN 0-13-927104-X

90000

9 780139 271045

HTML 4.0

William H. Murray
Chris H. Pappas

Prentice Hall PTR
Upper Saddle River, NJ 07458
http://www.phptr.com

Editorial/Production Supervision: Joe Czerwinski
Acquisitions Editor: Jeffrey Pepper
Editorial Assistant: Christy Schaact
Manufacturing Manager: Alexis Heydt
Cover Design: Design Source
Cover Design Director: Jerry Votta

Prentice-Hall, Inc.
A Simon & Schuster Company
Upper Saddle River, NJ 07458

Prentice Hall books are widely used by corporations and government agencies for training, marketing, and resale.

The publisher offers discounts on this book when ordered in bulk quantities. For more information, contact

Corporate Sales Department, Phone 800-382-3419;
FAX: 201-236-714; e-mail: corpsales@prenhall.com
Or write:
Prentice Hall PTR, Corp. Sales Dept., One Lake Street, Upper Saddle River, NJ 07458

Printed in the United States of America

10 9 8 7 6 5 4 3 2 1

ISBN 0-13-927104-X

Prentice-Hall International (UK) Limited, *London*
Prentice-Hall of Australia Pty. Limited, *Sydney*
Prentice-Hall Canada Inc., *Toronto*
Prentice-Hall Hispanoamericana, S.A., *Mexico*
Prentice-Hall of India Private Limited, *New Delhi*
Prentice-Hall of Japan, Inc., *Tokyo*
Simon & Schuster Asia Pte. Ltd., *Singapore*
Editora Prentice-Hall do Brasil, Ltda., *Rio de Janeiro*

To

Dr. Bryan K. Blanchard,

an asset to the educational community

CONTENTS

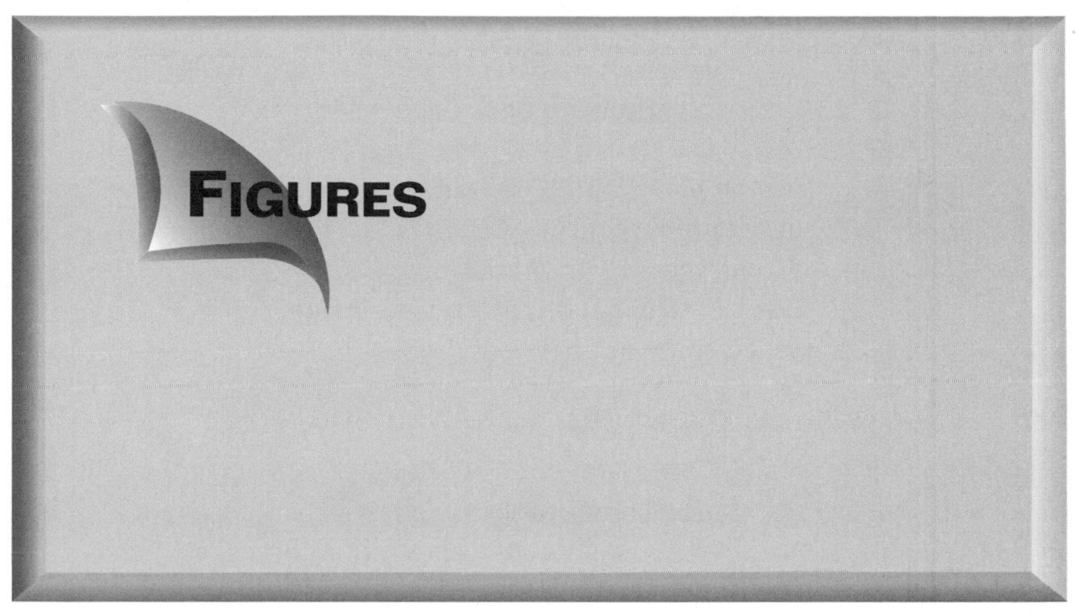
FIGURES

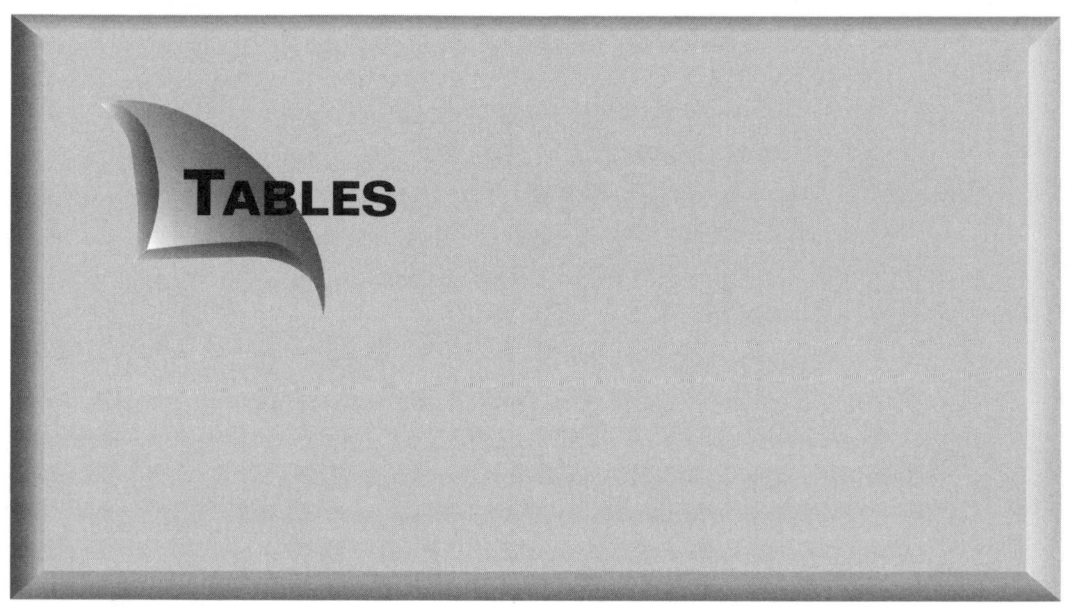
TABLES

Acknowledgments

We would like to take the time to thank all of the fine people at Prentice Hall for their help in the production of this book.

We would like to particularly thank Jeff Pepper for his help and guidance. We have worked with Jeff on numerous books and have always found him to be encouraging, positive, and professional. Jeff seems to have a knack for knowing where the industry is going and getting projects, such as this book, off the ground while other publishers are trying to decide what to do next. If we owe thanks to any individual for our success it is Jeff Pepper. Thanks for all of your help, Jeff!

–The Authors

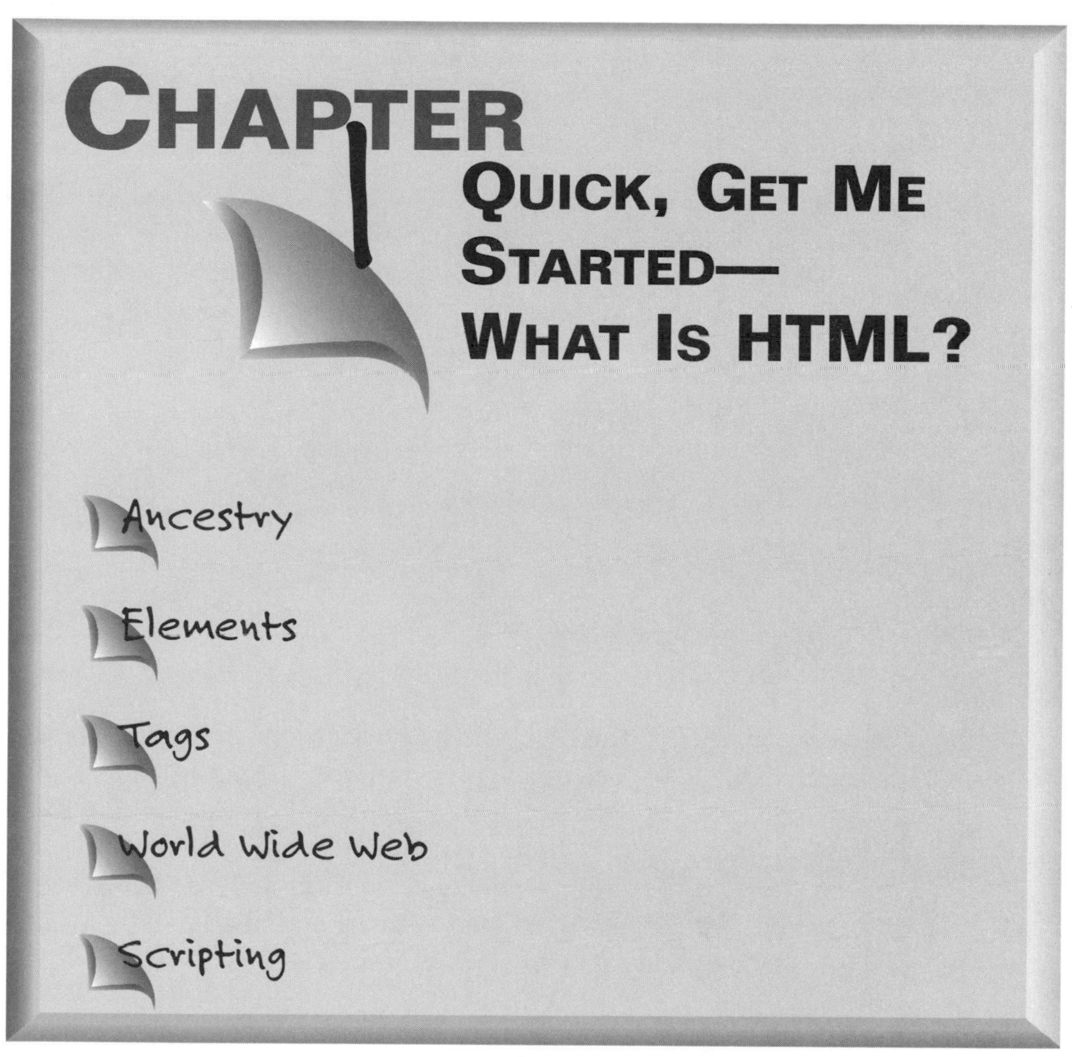

CHAPTER 1
QUICK, GET ME STARTED—WHAT IS HTML?
Ancestry
Elements
Tags
World Wide Web
Scripting

From IBM to grandmother, everybody is getting into page development on the WWW (World Wide Web–a *hypertext*-based system of presenting information over the Internet). It's the visually exciting way to say to the world, "I've arrived!" For many, the big excitement in constructing Web pages is in using the easy-to-learn protocol of HTML.

Hypertext

Is an online document that has words or graphics containing links to other documents. Usually, selecting the link area onscreen (with a mouse or keyboard command) activates these links.

HTML is even more interesting when you know how it came about.

HTML Ancestry

It all began at CERN, the high-energy physics laboratory in Geneva, Switzerland. CERN's scientists disseminated research papers and other documents throughout the nucleus of buildings on the CERN campus, and they shared their statistics throughout the world. In doing so, they encountered problems of time delay. This problem was addressed by *Tim Berners-Lee*, who devised a a simple set of protocols for sharing materials over interconnected TCP/IP networks worldwide.

TCP/IP

Is an abbreviation for Transport Control Protocol/Internet Protocol, a set of protocols that applications use for communicating across networks or over the Internet. These protocols specify how packets of data should be constructed, addressed, checked for errors, and so on.

Tim broke his solution down into two parts: HTTP (HyperText Transfer Protocol) and HTML (HyperText Mark-up Language). HTTP defines how information is sent or received, providing a simple way for users to request and receive files over the Internet. HTML defines the visual presentation of the material on the receiving end.

The fledgling Internet was seen more as a library than as a Virtual Reality Mall. Accordingly, the original definition of HTML included only as much output display control as would be needed by the typical scientific journal article. HTML was never intended to support the variety of display potentials presented by today's multitasking, object-oriented operating systems like UNIX and Microsoft Windows. Nor was it ever designed to create wild multimedia sites that incorporated graphics and animation.

Because HTML's protocols were succinct and complete, the scientific community promptly accepted them and adopted HTML as their electronic typesetter. Scientists were particularly excited about HTML's ability to create links to other pages of information, making the documents much more alive than a static piece of paper.

SGML

Actually, HTML is a subset of an even larger page-display protocol definition known as SGML (Standard Generalized Mark-up Language). The scientists at CERN used SGML for highly technical and legal documentation. SGML is still used by large organizations that maintain libraries of frequently referenced documentation.

SGML flavoring lingers to this day within the formal HTML standard with its insistence on document structures, the separation of content from formatting, and the use of logical tags. Tags are the special control characters–namely the left and right angle control brackets: < >–that separate HTML mark-up from ordinary text.)

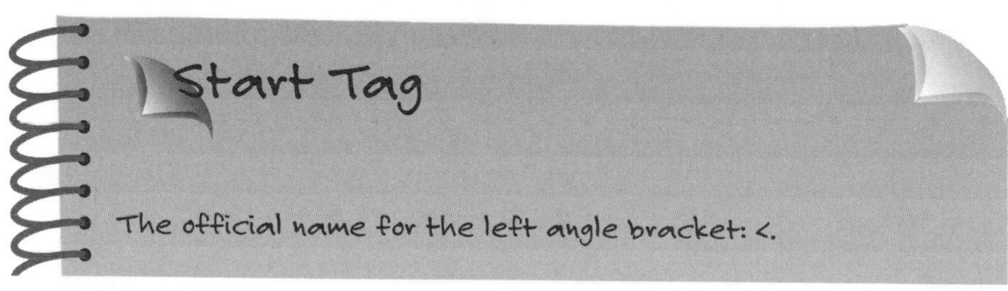

Start Tag
The official name for the left angle bracket: <.

The official name for the closing tag which usually terminates the Start Tag's control attribute. End Tags use the forward slash immediately after the left angle bracket, </, followed by the closing tag moniker and the right angle bracket, as in the HTML mark-up </B>, which is used to cancel BOLD formatting.

DTD

All documents that can be marked up with the same hierarchy of elements are said to belong to a certain *document type*. Rather than describe a set of tools to mark up documents, SGML defines the structure of a particular type of document in what is called *document-type definition* (DTD). HTML 4.0, code-named *Cougar,* is an example of an SGML DTD.

SGML in HTML

The most prominent throwback to SGML, still incorporated in today's state-of-the-art HTML 4.0, is the set of tags <H1> through <H6> used to generate a six-level outline format. Today's users employ these tags as a quick way to format headings with varying degrees of emphasis. Some tags, such as <B> for bold and <EM> for emphasis, may appear to be two different ways of saying the same thing, and indeed some *browser*s treat them as such. Technically, however, <B> is font specific, whereas <EM> provides more leeway in formatting the document.

Browsers

Such as Netscape Communicator and Internet Explorer 4.0—are programs that give you the ability to browse the World Wide Web. Some browsers offer additional functionality, such as FTP and e-mail support.

With the explosion in popularity of the Internet, the browser market skyrocketed in 1995, and so, too, did the availability of new HTML tags. However, the SGML throwbacks are still the quickest and easiest way to create tables of contents and indices automatically.

Realizing the tremendous profit potential of this new electronic medium, Netscape and Microsoft locked into a perpetual battle to give their customers "The De Facto Standard" in Web browser capabilities. Fortunately the W3C (World Wide Web Consortium–*http://www.w3.org/*–which technically oversees HTML revisions) stepped in to maintain some sort of compatibility across platforms. One of the exciting protocols to come out of W3C meetings is the cascading style sheet. Cascading style sheets make it possible to specify particular fonts, point sizes, and text placement for a wider variety of HTML elements.

What Is an Element?

An *element* is any HTML tag or tag pair that is parsed and treated as a unique item on a page. An element is not an object unless it is named with an ID attribute. Some examples of elements are headers, paragraphs, lists of items, or tables. Elements can contain plain text, or other elements, or both.

More on Tags

HTML tags, as mentioned earlier, mark the elements of a file for your browser. Tags are usually paired. For example, the start tag <H1> for a level-one header definition is followed by an end tag </H1>. End tags look just like start tags except for the addition of a forward-slash (/) symbol immediately after the left angle bracket.

Some elements may include an *attribute*, which gives additional information, inside the start tag. For example, files in GIF or JPEG format can use top-, middle-, or bottom-edge alignment, if the appropriate attribute is included with the image-source HTML code.

One final note: HTML tags are *not* case sensitive, so <H1> = <h1>. (Well, there are a few exceptions, which we'll document throughout the book.)

What Is an HTML Document?

Technically, an HTML document is nothing more than a combination of HTML tags placed inside a standard ASCII text file. This means that you can create an HTML file using Windows Notepad, or Emacs or Vi on UNIX architectures, or even BBEdit on a Macintosh platform. If you are running the latest edition of a popular software suite such as Corel Office or Microsoft Professional, then you own a WYSIWYG (What You See Is What You Get) word processor capable of generating and visually displaying HTML documents!

So If It's So Easy, What's the Catch?

There's only one snag to your actually taking a completed HTML document and flashing it on every monitor from here to Moscow–money (unless you are a student). You see, you need someone (a *host server*–and for students, well, let the institution take it out of your tuition) willing to store your multimedia-punched front page, to pay for the electricity running the system, to pay for the hardware connection to the Internet, and to pay a tech support person to keep everything static free and running clean.

The great news is that some communities operate what is called *FreeNet*, a community-based network that provides free Internet access. If all else fails, well, then you'll have to subscribe to a service such as AOL (America Online) or a local service provider. These services usually charge two separate rates, one for personal and another for business Web Page accounts.

OK—Here's a Quick HTML Document

Whether you are using Assembly Language, Ada, Java, Perl, or C++, every language, beyond its formal description, has an industrywide accepted list of language-specific DOs and DON'Ts. HTML is no exception. Even a minimal HTML document should contain certain standard HTML tags–mainly a head and body text. The head contains the title, while the body encapsulates the actual text to be displayed. The body can contain multiple paragraphs, lists, tables, graphics, and other elements.

Browsers, like compilers, expect an HTML document to be in a certain form. This standard form comes directly from the SGML and its sibling, HTML specifications. The simplest, properly formed HTML document you can create looks very similar to the following code listing:

```
<HTML>
<HEAD>
<TITLE>My First HTML Document</TITLE>
</HEAD>
<BODY>
<H1>Hello World!</H1>
<P>This is my first paragraph letting the world
know that I am ready to begin my cottage industry.
<P>OH, and make my first MILLION!
</BODY>
</HTML>
```

<HTML>

The first tag in the listing, <HTML>, flags the browser to the fact that it is parsing an HTML-encoded file format. HTML files always contain an **.html* file extension (or for systems using the 8-letter filename, 3-letter file-extension format, an **.htm* extension).

<HEAD>

The <HEAD> tag identifies the first part of your HTML-encoded document, which contains the document's title. The title is shown as part of your browser's window.

<TITLE>

The <TITLE> tag defines your document's title and broadcasts its content in a global context. Your browser displays the title in an area separate from the document text. Choosing your document's <TITLE> is a little more important than it may initially appear, since this is what is displayed on someone's hotlist or bookmark list and what is referenced when search engines are used. Always choose a <TITLE> that is unique, descriptive, and pulls those Web surfers right down onto your Web page.

<BODY>

The largest portion of your HTML document is encapsulated within the <BODY>, </BODY> tag pairs and contains the information displayed by the browser. The tags described below are used within the <BODY>, </BODY> tags.

<H1>—Level Header

As mentioned earlier, HTML has a six-level throwback to its SGML progenator. Tags used for these levels are <H1> through <H6> and </H1> through </H6>, respectively. Each level is displayed using a larger and/or bolder font than is used by the browser for displaying normal text.

<P>—Paragraph

Browsers ignore carriage returns embedded within the <BODY> of an HTML document. This means that you need not concern yourself with how long each line of your text is. Any text formatting you want must be accomplished with an appropriate HTML tag. So, for example, the two lines in the source file:

```
<P>This is my first paragraph letting the world
know that I am ready to begin my cottage industry.
```

are seen as one continuous line and will be formatted based on the browser's current screen width. From the browser's point of view, the source file could have been entered as follows:

```
<HTML> <HEAD> <TITLE>My First HTML Document</TITLE>
</HEAD> <BODY> <H1>Hello World!</H1> <P>This is my
first paragraph letting the world know that I am ready
to begin my cottage industry. <P>OH, and make my first
MILLION! </BODY> </HTML>
```

and the visual display interpretations would be identical. Browsers also condense multiple spaces embedded within an HTML document down to a single space.

You may be wondering why the sample HTML document contains no </P> end tags. This is because browsers understand that a start <P> tag indirectly indicates that a previous paragraph is terminating.

Note, however, that a </P> end tag exists but is traditionally used only when the encapsulated paragraph (<P>, </P>) requires a certain attribute, such as centering, as in this reworked example:

```
<P ALIGN=CENTER>
<P>This is my first paragraph letting the world
know that I am ready to begin my cottage industry.
</P>
```

A Word about HTML Document Formatting

Since browsers ignore carriage returns and extra spaces, you can use these to visually format your HTML document. For example, you should separate a heading from its associated body with a blank line. Use extra blank lines to separate document sections. All of this will go a long way toward streamlining any edits or modifications the document may need over time.

Some Common File Types and Their Extensions

Spectacular multimedia enhancements made possible by HTML 4.0 have changed Web pages forever. Throughout this book you will learn how to add images (in their various formats), sounds, even animation. The various types of files you can use are listed below by name and file extension.

Table 1–1: *Common File Types and Their Extensions*

File Type	File Extension
Plain ASCII text	.txt
HTML document	.html (or, for 8.3 formats, .htm)
GIF image	.gif
TIFF image	.tiff (or, for 8.3 formats, .tif)
X Bitmap image	.xbm
JPEG image	.jpeg (or, for 8.3 formats, .jpg)
PostScript file	.ps
AIFF sound file	.aiff (or, for 8.3 formats, .aif)
AU sound file	.au
WAV sound file	.wav
QuickTime movie	.mov
MPEG movie	.mpeg (or, for 8.3 formats, .mpg)

Quick, Tell Me—How Does the Web Work?

We can view the World Wide Web (WWW) in terms of three parts: (1) the server that is hosting (storing/connecting to the Internet) your HTML document, (2). the surfer or end user viewing your HTML document, (3) the protocol making the bidirectional communication possible.

It Gives Every Type of Computer World Access!

The Web is *platform independent*. This means that you can access the Web regardless of whether you're running on a low-end PC, an Apple Mac, an expensive Silicon Graphics Workstation, a VAX Cluster, or a multimillion-dollar Cray Supercomputer!

Web Browsers—the Electronic Sears Catalog

A Web browser, as mentioned earlier, is a program that you use to view pages–sometimes called *Web clients*–on the World Wide Web. A vast diversity of Web browsers are available for just about every type of architecture you can imagine. The most important types are GUI (graphical-user-interface-based) systems, such as X11, Windows, and Mac platforms. There are even text-only browsers available for simple dial-up UNIX connections.

Full-Color Shopping at Your Fingertips

A key feature of Web browsers is their ability to display both text and graphics in full color on the same page, using a simple URL address, followed often by nothing more than consecutive mouse clicks. If you are just jumping onto your Internet surfboard for the first time, you may not be aware that in its fledgling state, the Internet was accessed by nonstandard, confusing, command-line, text-only protocols. Of course, today's state-of-the-art rendition reacts to simple mouse clicks and is much more interesting with its new sound and even streaming video capabilities. Even 3D virtual-reality simulations are possible with VRML (Virtual Reality Markup Language).

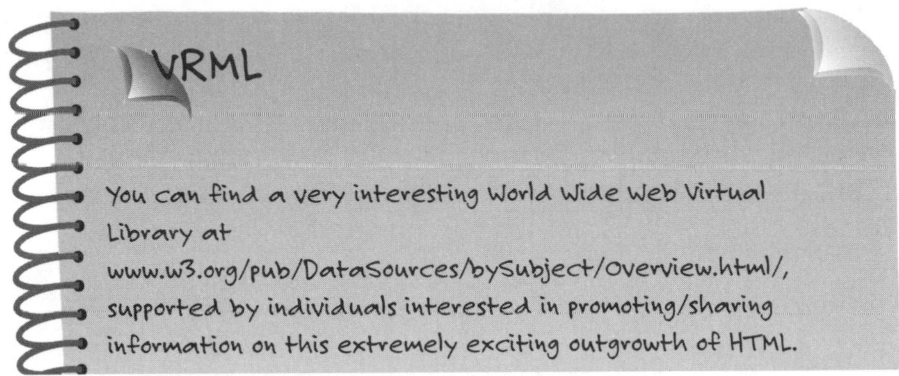

VRML
You can find a very interesting World Wide Web Virtual Library at
www.w3.org/pub/DataSources/bySubject/Overview.html/,
supported by individuals interested in promoting/sharing information on this extremely exciting outgrowth of HTML.

Info, Info Everywhere

The very name, World Wide Web, indicates that the information you are downloading may be distributed throughout the entire globe. Since the information available occupies vast amounts of disk storage, particularly when it includes images, multimedia, and streaming video, no computer yet built could house this bit explosion in one physical location.

Actually, this distributed diversity of data-storage repositories works to your advantage. Were this information stored in a single location, imagine the chaos generated by a downed mainframe! The Web is so successful in providing so much information because that information is distributed globally across thousands of Web sites. And the best part about the interconnection is that if, for any reason, one leg of the information route is interrupted, an alternate Web link takes over.

Full Bidirectional Communication

An exciting aspect to Web interaction is that you can "talk back," whereas a radio or television broadcast, for example, is only one-directional output.

Moreover, with today's HTML your document's display instructions are not limited to text only but can include graphical and auditory elements and can communicate back to the server.

Web Browser Characteristics

While there is only one HTML 4.0 standard, it is not true that there is only one visual interpretation of this standard among all the various browsers. Each Web browser displays HTML elements differently. Complicating matters further, not all browsers support all of the HTML 4.0 code standard! Fortunately, any HTML code that a browser does *not* understand, it usually just ignores.

The unwarned can spend endless hours, even days or weeks, perfecting and tweaking the visual aspects and technical content of their company's Web page, only to find that on an unfriendly browser it looks like a mosaic. Hence these words of advice (from the NCSA General Internet HTMLPrimerAll.html document):

> "Code your files using correct HTML. Leave the interpreting to the browsers and hope for the best."

What Is a URL?

When a Web surfer, or end user, or *client* (the system being used by the Web surfer) makes a request to a server, the request is expressed in terms of the HTTP protocol mentioned earlier and a *URL* (Universal Resource Locator). A URL specifies the location and name of a World Wide Web resource such as a Web site or an HTML document:

URL

A Universal Resource Locator consists of a protocol name, a colon (:), two forward-slash characters (//), a machine name, and a path to a resource using a single forward slash as a separator. URLs can also specify more than just Web page addresses. For example, you can retrieve a document by preceding the URL with ftp://, or File Transfer Protocol, instead of http://, HyperText Transfer Protocol.

The server in turn processes the request and, again using HTTP protocol, transfers the requested information back to the client. It is the server's responsibility to tell client the type of document being transmitted. The document is usually defined as a *MIME* (Multipurpose Internet Mail Extension–an enhancement to Internet e-mail that allows for the inclusion of binary data such as word processing programs, graphics, and sound). The client must then process the information before splashing it on the surfer's screen.

MIME

Designed as a means for embedding complex binary documents within an e-mail message. MIME types consist of a main type and subtype. For example, plain text is ëtext/plain', but ëimage/gif' specifies an image stored in GIF format. A browser encounters the MIME protocol and deciphers the document's type and subtype. The browser then decides how it wishes to handle the document. It may choose to process it internally, or it may invoke an external program to decipher the information.

Some elements of the displayed document are fixed, such as titles, paragraphs, lists, and so on, but are considered live or *dynamic*. These dynamic elements display more current information, such as a 'hit counter' telling you how many other Web surfers have surfed this page before you.

What Is Scripting?

Now that you have a general overview of HTML and browser capabilities, you may be wondering whether there's any more to all this than just displaying formatted text and multimedia images. The answer is Yes. Welcome to the world of *scripting*.

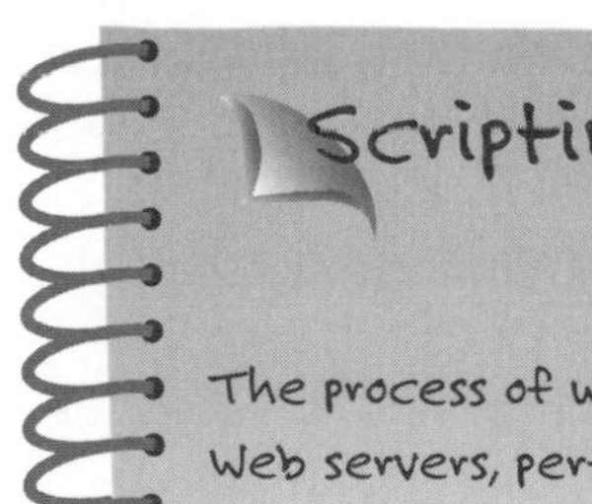

Scripting

The process of writing a script. Scripts are executed by Web servers, performing functions such as HTML document searches and forms processing.

CGI

One of the earliest scripting languages was CGI or, Common Gateway Interface. Its most common application is in forms processing. CGI allows you to create pages for users as individual requests come in, and you can customize pages to match the incoming information.

The user usually fills out a form and clicks on a submit button. Then the user's browser sends the server a request that includes the information the user entered into the form. The server sends this information on to another program for actually processing and responds with the appropriate output at the client or user end. Depending on the kind of server your site resides on, you can write CGI programs in C++, Perl, even AppleScript.

If you don't want to go to the trouble of writing complex programs to create pages with server-side interaction, you can purchase products like Microsoft's FrontPage Web site editing program. It incorporates *bots*, which are small programs that attach themselves to the host server. Bots can process forms, provide timestamps, and serve as streamlined site-specific search engines.

SCRIPT Tags

HTML page programming takes place via SCRIPT tags, which tell script-aware browsers that a script will follow. Within these SCRIPT tags are HTML tags. This approach can be extended to do far more complex things, such as creating *cookies*.

Cookies store small amounts of information about a user's preferences on a user's machine and use that information to create customized pages on subsequent visits. You can customize most aspects of Web pages and even the browsers.

Perl

Perl, which combines C syntax and the power of UNIX regular expressions, is undoubtedly the most common language used for scripting CGI in UNIX environments. It is possible to write simple programs in Perl with a minimum of effort.

JavaScript and JScript

Netscape Version 2.0 is credited with the introduction of JavaScript. Immediately, Microsoft Internet Explorer 3.0 countered with its own flavors, called JScript and VBScript, based on the easy-to-learn Visual Basic. The good news is that JavaScript and JScript are evolving toward one another, but various browsers still respond in nonuniform fashion.

These languages provide HTML developers with additional programming horsepower that enables them to make browsers do new and different things. Not everything has to take place on the server end; the client can take on more of the responsibility of processing.

VBScript

Offering Visual Basic programmers the programming enhancements of a scripting language, VBScript came bundled with Microsoft's Internet Explorer 3.0. While JavaScript and JScript have a strong C- or Java-based aroma, VBScript offers Visual Basic programmers the familiarity of their popular language. VBScript also easily integrates Microsoft's ActiveX controls in a Web environment.

Plug-Ins and ActiveX

Netscape is originally credited with developing the first plug-ins, Microsoft with developing ActiveX controls. The idea behind both is that the controlling software is loaded onto the user's computer (client), and then the Web page includes another file that contains the specific instructions or content.

While there are significant structural differences between plug-ins and ActiveX controls, their basic purpose on the page is basically the same. Like a Java applet, they add additional features and functionality to a Web page without directly affecting the host page. They also create a bidirectional communication between the end user and the plug-in.

Java Applet vs. Java Application

Java applets are programs that will run only when hosted by a Web browser, while Java applications are standalone programs that are designed to run on any system and need no Web browser or Internet connection.

The downside to both technologies is that they add to the download time of the Web page. In addition, neither technology really provides interaction with other elements on the page. Some ActiveX controls provide features like tooltips or pop-up menus, but, like plug-ins, these items are operated directly by the control and have no ability to go beyond the feature itself.

What's New in HTML 4.0

In the HTML 4.0 project, code-named Cougar, the W3C has again undertaken to set the standard that will divide the mark-up of content from the appearance of a Web page. The Cougar protocol separates the physical style from content mark-up by placing more reliance on style sheets. (Style sheets specify style information whose parameters will govern the formatting of an entire document.)

HTML 4.0 is being authored by David Raggett and Arnaud Le Hors, and it continues to recognize frequently used tags from older versions of HTML. If it didn't, we would be looking at all kinds of problems when different browsers accessed pages that exploited its new features.

HTML 4.0 isn't really that different from the previous versions of HTML. The key changes can be summed up by the word *dynamic*. HTML 4.0 will now allow the user to manipulate and access the text and image elements directly. The Web page has become dynamically updatable, and the properties are easily accessible from code. This might seem like no big deal, as most operating systems have boasted this for years, but in Web pages it's quite a major undertaking.

The updated standard, however, does more than simply incorporate a few new tags and attributes. While most of the tags from previous versions remain, the new dynamic ability to manipulate and access elements with a scripting language forms the unique cornerstone of HTML 4.0. For this reason both Netscape and Microsoft have christened this new HTML version *Dynamic HTML*.

Both Netscape Communicator and Internet Explorer 4.0 have changed the structure of Web page display by exposing their browsers to these new dynamic HTML capabilities. For example, with advancement of dynamic or movable images, shoppers can now slide pictures of their purchase items into an image of a shopping cart. These are new features of the Dynamic HTML language itself, but they depend upon the browser to display the results. You can't expect the HTML 4.0-specific parts of a page to do much in Navigator 3 or Internet Explorer 3. As with all new developments in HTML, the browser must provide support before the page can perform as intended. The following seven features highlight the exciting potential of this latest HTML version:

- Dynamic Fonts–allow you to create your own fonts that others can download, similar to image files. This adds pizzazz to a Web page by making it more eye appealing and unique.
- Absolute Positioning of Elements–allows you to manipulate the *x*, *y*, and *z* coordinates of objects on a page, placing each item where you want it, rather than letting the browser decide.

- Cascading Style Sheets–add even more page format control, are accessible to scripting languages, and allow for a consistent look by applying fonts, colors, and element positioning to multiple pages.
- Canvas Mode–allows the developer to view the HTML-driven page full screen, instead of in the frame of the browser window.
- Dynamic Redraw–allows real-time updating of any element on a page, instead of the time-delayed approach of redrawing the page whenever the user has made a selection.
- New Event-Handling Techniques–event capturing allows events to be passed along from one object to another. It also allows the capturing of events not supported by one object, from another object.
- Document Object Model–allows the JavaScript language to program the formatting and positioning properties for elements on a page.

What You Need to Get Started

All you need in order to create an HTML document is a text editor capable of saving files in ASCII format and a browser such as Netscape's Communicator or Microsoft's Internet Explorer. With a quick click of your mouse and an already established Internet connection, you can download the latest versions of both these browsers to your system via the following addresses:

For Netscape Communicator 4:

www.home.netscape.com/comprod/mirror/index.html

For Internet Explorer 4.0:

www.microsoft.com/ie/ie/htm

All of the examples and figures for this book were created using a PC running Windows 95 and using Windows Notepad Text Editor for generating the HTML documents. As mentioned earlier, however, HTML is a hardware- and platform-independent language. For this reason you can easily create, view, and test the same HTML documents on a UNIX or Apple Macintosh machine and its associated operating system.

Should you choose to purchase one of the more popular HTML editors coming onto the market, such as Microsoft's FrontPage, you'll discover a more "point-'n'-click" approach to visually creating your Web pages. These programs work very much like paint programs, only the graphics primitives you place are actually HTML elements and attributes.

These products, as you are graphically designing the page, are simultaneously generating the required HTML tags. All of this is fine, as long as the product is designed to give you everything you would like from your Web page. However, it is suggested that you stay with a plain text editor for the purposes of this book, as there are some tricks and techniques that even the most powerful HTML editors cannot generate.

Interesting Sites to Visit

www.cern.ch–the consortium created in 1994 in conjunction with CERN, the European Laboratory for Particle Physics in Switzerland. CERN was the group that gave birth to the Web in 1989.

www.corel.com/products/graphicsandpublishing/–CorelDRAW! is a high-end vector art program that comes in a bundle by the same name along with Photo-Paint, Dream 3D (a 3D rendering program based on Ray Dream Designer), and Presents (a multimedia presentation program); it allows you to export an entire page as HTML.

www.fractal.com/–provides excellent painting capabilities such as oil, watercolor, and chalk.

www.cyberdog.apple.com/–provides a versatile tool that includes a Web browser, using Apple's OpenDoc technology.

www.hwg.org/–The HTML Writers Guild is an international organization of World Wide Web page authors and Internet publishing professionals. It provides several levels of paid memberships offering benefits such as mentoring programs, educational classes, access to a job board, and software discounts!

www.htmlhelp.com/–This site offers a collection of HTML tips, tricks, and hacks covering both document authoring and Web server management, presented in a question-and-answer format.

www.browserwatch.iworld.com–a browser that offers breaking news in the browser and plug-ins industry, plus browser usage statistics and a rich library of plug-ins and *ActiveX* components.

ActiveX

Is an integration technology developed by Microsoft to add new features to the Internet Explorer Web browser. ActiveX allows programmers to extend Web browser functionality with the programmer's own code. If you consider a Web browser as a miniature operating system, you can see why programmers would love to extend the browser's capabilities.

www.nyu.edu./pages/wsn/subir/lynx/platforms.html/–*Lynx* is a full-featured World Wide Web browser designed for both the UNIX and VMS platforms, using cursor-addressable, character-based terminals or emulators. This is a text-based browser frequently used in universities, libraries, and other environments where affordable access is needed to bring the information of the World Wide Web to as many individuals as possible.

www.developer.netscape.com/index.html/–This Netscape site's DevEdge provides communications, tools, support, and marketing assistance to speed the planning, development, and deployment of Internet and *Intranet* solutions.

Intranet

An internal network that uses Internet technology. Many companies now describe the network they use for intra-company communications as an Intranet.

www.microsoft.com/sitebuilder/–This site provides access to Microsoft's in-depth resources for developing Web sites using Microsoft technology. The Site Builder Network accesses a multilevel library of technical information, products, technologies, services, and ideas and support for using the latest Internet technology, such as the new Dynamic HTML 4.0, ActiveX controls, and Java *applets*.

Applet

A progam, written in Java, with a single or limited function. Many Windows and Win95 special-function programs are called applets, and, from that usage, simple Java programs are also called applets. An application, by contrast, is a program that performs a specific type of work, such as a word processor. Also, applications are standalone products capable of running under an operating system disconnected from the Internet/Intranet, while an applet is to be downloaded by a browser which then executes it.

www.w3.org/pub/WWW/–led by Tim Berners-Lee, director of the W3C and creator of the World Wide Web. This platform-independent, vendor-neutral consortium works with the global Internet/Intranet community to produce freely available specifications and reference software.

www.w3.org/pub/WWW/TR/REC-CSS1/–accesses the document specifying level 1 of the cascading style sheet mechanism (CSS1).

www.w3.org/pub/WWW/MarkUp/DOM/–a site providing an overview of materials related to the document object model *(DOM)*.

DOM

Is a platform-independent, language-neutral interface, allowing programs and scripts to dynamically access and update Web page structure, content, and display style.

www.w3.org/hypertext/WWW/Addressing/Addressing.html–a site dedicated to defining the various types of URLs available, as well as explaining *URIs* and *URNs*.

URI

Or Universal Resource Identifier—Incorporates not only URLs but also URNs (Uniform Resource Names) and URCs (Uniform Resource Citations). URNs and URCs will have wider use in later versions of HyperText Transfer Protocol.

www.yahoo.com/Computers/World_Wide_Web/–This site links to more than 2,500 pages of HTML documentation. Here you can access multiple sites concerning Internet technology developments such as HTML, CGI, Java, ActiveX, *VBScript*, *VRML*, in addition to resources for page layout, design, programming, and browser technology updates.

VBScript

Developed by Microsoft, VBScript is similar to JavaScript Web page scripting language, only it is based on what some consider to be the easiest programming language to learn/use—BASIC.

VRML

Or Virtual Reality Modeling Language—is a language that supports the display of 3D objects in HTML documents.

www.ncsa.uiuc.edu/SDG/Software/Mosaic/NCSAMosaicHome.html/–accesses a Web browser developed by the National Center for Supercomputing Applications (NCSA) at the University of Illinois in Urbana-Champaign.

www.home.netscape.com/try/comprod/mirror/client_download.html/–accesses Netscape's Composer, the WYSIWYG editor bundled with the Netscape Communicator suite.

www.microsoft.com/ie/ie40/–accesses FrontPad, the WYSIWYG Web page editor used in Microsoft Internet Explorer 4. FrontPad is a streamlined version of Microsoft's *FrontPage*, which you can download for free!

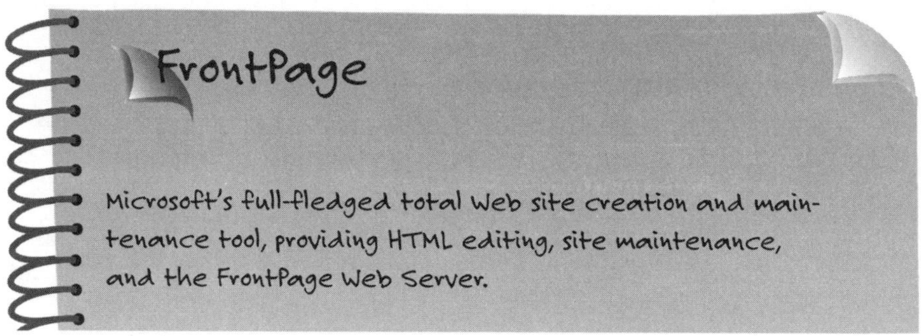
FrontPage
Microsoft's full-fledged total Web site creation and maintenance tool, providing HTML editing, site maintenance, and the FrontPage Web Server.

www.adobe.com/prodindex/pagemill/overview.html/–accesses Adobe's PageMill, a powerful WYSIWYG Web page editor. Adobe is the genius behind PageMaker and PDF (Portable Document Format).

In addition, the following Usenet newsgroups provide friendly, conversational interchange, where you often find a compassionate ear ready to discuss and help solve just about any HTML question you could conceive.

- alt.html
- comp.infosystems.www.authoring.misc
- comp.infosystems.www.browsers.ms-windows
- comp.infosystems.www.browsers.mac
- comp.infosystems.www.browsers.misc

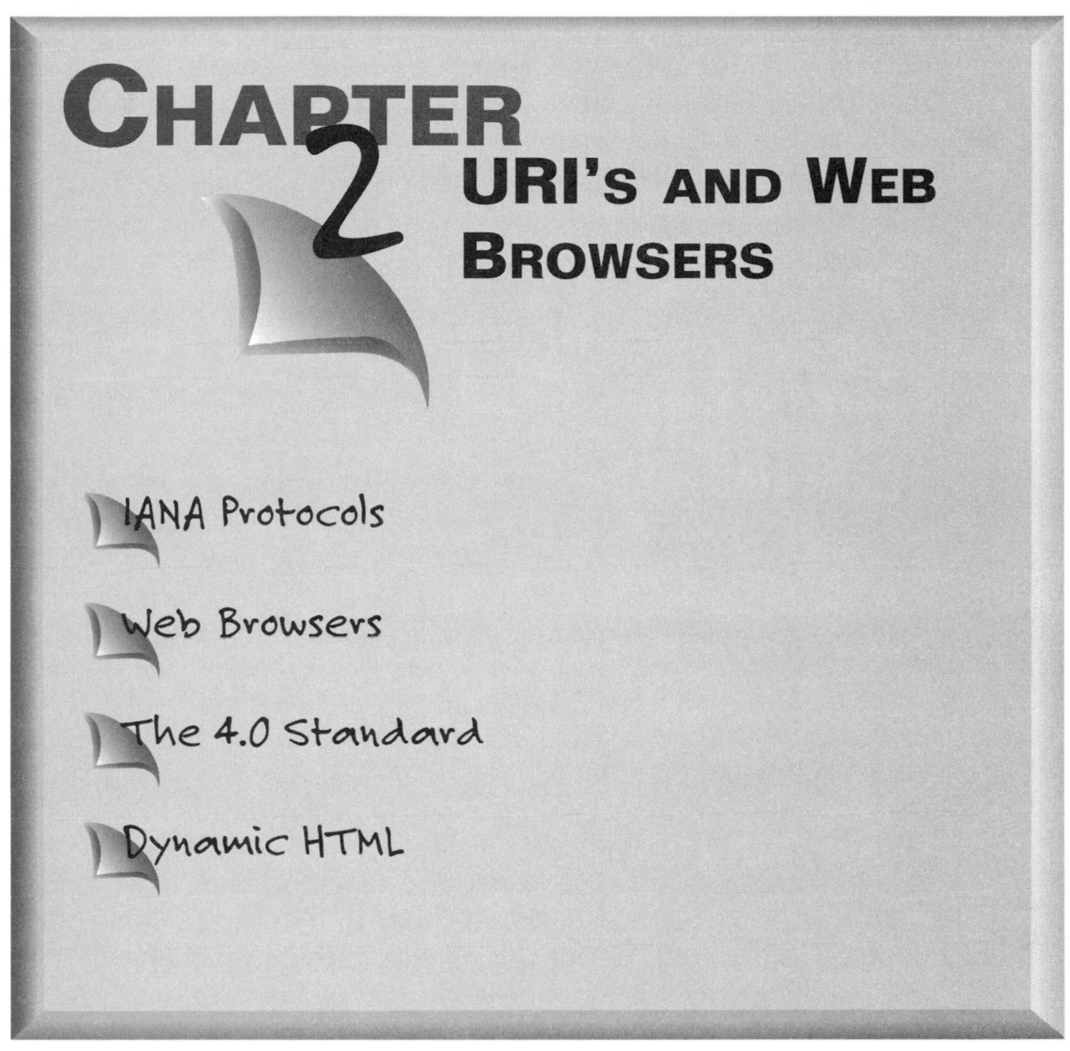

In the last chapter you learned a little about HTML's history, what a browser is, and what is new in Dynamic HTML 4.0. In the next chapter you will learn how to build your first fully featured HTML document. But before you start doing that, you need a few more fundamentals under your belt.

First, you need to understand the *schemes* or Internet protocols as registered with the Internet Assigned Numbers Authority.

Second, you need to understand HTML 4.0 browser compatibility–and this theme will run throughout the remainder of the book. In an ideal world every browser would interpret identically and faithfully each and every detail of the HTML standard, but unfortunately we do not live in an ideal world. For this reason, you need to be aware of the issues in how to design a Web page and how it will be interpreted by two of the most popular Web browsers (those developed by Netscape and Microsoft).

Understanding IANA Protocols

The IANA (Internet Assigned Numbers Authority) accepts applications for and standardizes protocols, sometimes called *schemes*. These protocols define an algorithm for accessing a resource and the rules or syntax for representing the protocol. The next section briefly describes the protocols used most often within Web page links.

URI Protocols

The string of characters that identifies the precise location of a resource available on the World Wide Web is known as a URI (Universal Resource Identifier). In order to be upward compatible, the URI syntax must not only encompass current protocol standards for accessing data on the Internet, such as http, ftp, and gopher access, but also allow for new recognizable extensions to the protocol as they become available.

Technically, URIs are the umbrella category that also includes URLs (Universal Resource Locators) and URCs (Uniform Resource Citations). The most common of these are the URLs used to locate Web pages. You can think of a URL as a pointer to a filename in some directory or subdirectory on a Web server. A typical URL looks like this: *http://www.webserver.com/~me/index.html.*

URLs can do much more, though, than point to a specific Web page file. They can also point to ftp, newsgroup, and gopher sites and to other resources using protocols other than HTTP. The example shown in the preceding paragraph is known as an *absolute* URL, because it specifies the syntax to be used to make the connection. The

URL syntax also identifies the request for the resource as complying with the Internet Protocol and specifies the path to be followed in locating and retrieving the file. An indirect or relative URL, such as somefile.html, instructs the Web browser to search for the file somefile.html in the same directory as the resource located at ~me/index.html.

While all of these examples use URI/HTTP protocols, the URI standard can access other types of resources. The URI protocol consists of four arguments. The first argument specifies the protocol type, as in http, and is followed by a colon and double forward slash (://) (although not always–see news: and mailto: below). The second argument references the actual Internet node being accessed. The third argument identifies the server's file path, and the fourth argument is optional and represents URI-specific parameters (these are usually passed to a CGI script for processing).

HTTP:// PROTOCOL

The HTTP protocol syntax, as discussed above, looks like this: *http://<hostserver>:<optional_port>/<filepath>?<searchstring>*

You rarely see or need the :<optional_port> setting, as this has a default. The question mark and <searchstring> are optional. If they are omitted, so too is the single forward slash (/). Additional forward slashes may be used to separate references in a hierarchical manner.

FTP:// PROTOCOL

Unlike HTTP, FTP (File Transfer Protocol) protocol details a request for a specific file from an ftp file server. The protocol includes options for a username and password. Very often ftp sites are set up to receive anonymous requests. This means that if you do not know the username or password, you can simply respond with the username *anonymous* and your Internet e-mail address will satisfy a request for a user password. A typical ftp request looks like this: *ftp://ftp.server.com/~me/mypix.gif*

However, the path for the ftp can use a rather sophisticated syntax, as in: <cwd1>/<cwd2>/<cwd3>/<myfile.ext>;type=<atype>, where cwd1/2/3 represent arguments passed to the change-directory command followed by the name of the file to retrieve. The type must be either a (for ASCII format), i (for binary format), or d (for list format), identifying the type of transfer.

FILE:// PROTOCOL

The simplest scheme is file://. This protocol can be used only to access files on a hard drive and not to reference any file across the Internet. This simplest of protocols looks as follows: *file://<hostserver>/<filepath_and_name>*. The hostserver represents a fully qualified domain system name, and filepath_and_name is the directory/subdirectory path to the file residing on the hostserver. If the hostserver name is omitted, the filepath_and_name is resolved using the current URL. Remember, the file protocol cannot include any Internet access protocols, such as ftp, or any other access method, such as gopher.

GOPHER:// PROTOCOL

Webster defines a gopher as "an errand boy, assistant, or the like, who is sent to fetch coffee, cigarettes, etc." On the Internet, a gopher is a protocol that provides an indexing of the information available from the World Wide Web. This text-based scheme looks as follows: *gopher://<hostserver>:<optional_port>/<gopher_path>*. The optional_port is usually omitted. If the gopher_path is omitted, the slash is optional. A simple gopher access would look like this: *gopher://mysystem.com.*

NEWS: PROTOCOL

A popular pastime for Web surfers is accessing newsgroups–collections of like-minded individuals who organize discussions, materials, and links to other topic-related sites under individual category names. You can find a newsgroup on virtually any topic or area of interest you can conceive. The news: protocol is used to access either the newsgroup itself or an article from the newsgroup in what is called *Usenet* form (Usenet is the collection of discussion groups available via the Internet).

To access a newsgroup directly, the URL syntax looks like this: *news:<newsgroup_id>*–for example alt.philosophy. (By the way, notice the absence of double forward slashes. This was not an oversight, as the news: protocol does not comply with the Internet protocol.) Accessing a particular article requires a slightly different syntax, as in: *news:<message_id>*–for example, *news:myfile197.frm@webserver.com.* Don't be surprised, however, if a message_id access fails. News articles do not exist forever; they regularly expire and are deleted. Any message_id of interest should be downloaded (assuming you have the legal permission to do so) to your Web page for continued access.

MAILTO: PROTOCOL

The next time you want to send someone an e-mail, why not try using the mailto: protocol. If your browser supports mailto: URLs, then when a link that contains one is selected, the browser will prompt you for a subject and the body of the mail message. When you are done, the browser will send that message to the appropriate address. Some browsers, however, do not support mailto: and produce an error if a link is attempted. The general form for a mailto URL is: *mailto: mailto:<internet e-mail address>*, as in *mailto:someone@webserver.com.* If your e-mail address contains a percent sign (%), you will have to use the escape character %25 in its place. Percent signs are special symbols to URLs. Notice, also, that like news:, mailto: URLs do not meet the Internet protocol standard requiring the use of double forward slashes (//).

Punctuating URLs

Sometimes a URL address contains nonstandard symbols. A normal URL address consists of upper- or lower-case letters, numbers, and a dollar sign ($), dash (-), underscore (_), period (.), plus sign (+), and tilde (~). Whenever you need to use any other symbols, you need special URL escape codes to keep them from being misinterpreted as part of the URL itself.

A URL escape sequence begins with the percent sign (%) and a two-digit hexadecimal value obtained from the ISO-Latin-1 character set (this is a superset to what most people already know as the ASCII character set). In ISO-Latin-1, %2 represents a forward slash, %3f a question mark, and %20 a single space.

If you have never used a Macintosh computer, then you are probably unaware that the subdirectory names on a Mac can contain spaces. For this reason an http:// address might look like this: *http://webserver.com/root/My Sub directory/index.html.* If you were to put this URL within quotation marks in a Web page link tag, it might work. However, because spaces are considered special characters to the URL, some browsers misinterpret them and may have problems recognizing the pathname correctly. To guarantee compatibility within all browsers rewrite the URL using the URL escape sequences, as in: *http://webserver.com/root/My%20Sub%20directory/index.html.* Obviously you want your Web page accessed as easily as possible–hint, leave out the spaces!

Nodes

As previously discussed, hypertext refers to a way of preparing and publishing documents that enables readers to select their own paths through the information. Hypertext has two fundamental components: nodes and hyperlinks. You can view a *node* as a unit of information, such as a Web page. It is small enough to manage and stand on its own. A *hyperlink* is a navigation tool that enables the user to jump to a new node, and this link is usually embedded within the currently displayed text. A hyperlink is text you find on a Web site which can be "clicked on" with a mouse which in turn will take you to another Web page or a different area of the same Web page. Hyperlinks are created or "coded" in HTML. They are also used to load multimedia files such as AVI movies and AU sound files. A collection of nodes connected by hyperlinks is called a *web*.

File Paths

There is much debate on certain Usenet newsgroups about the presence or absence of a *trailing slash* in URIs. Since the majority of the World Wide Web is hosted by UNIX environments, the slash has two functions. In one case, it acts as a separator between directories and files and specifies the path from the root to sub- to subsubdirectories, followed by the file name itself. However, the second use of the forward slash is to represent the root directory itself.

While the URI protocol follows the UNIX convention of using a slash as a separator, a URI is not a UNIX filename. Using the forward slash as a URI separator works on all operating systems, including MS-DOS, Windows, and Macintosh. In this syntax the forward slash is considered a separator of components of a hierarchical name known as a *url path*. The slash in front of the url path is not considered a part of the path itself. Instead, it is viewed as terminating the <webserver>:<optional_port> part of the protocol, and it flags the beginning of the url path. For example, a *url path* specifying a directory, returns the count of accesses to all documents under that directory–not just the index.html file for that directory (should it exist). Here are some example *url paths* one might query on:

/
: returns count of accesses to all web documents

/index.html
: returns count of accesses of index.html file, either directly or indirectly via an access for a directory.

/~foo
: returns count of accesses to all of user foo's web documents.

Arguments

When a URI contains optional arguments, they must be preceded by a question mark (?). As the browser is not inherently capable of processing this optional information, it typically passes them on to a CGI script. If there are multiple arguments, they are separated with a plus sign (+), as in:

```
<A HREF="/cgi-bin/ascript?argument1+argument2">run a_script
```

The <webserver> substrings the request and passes argument1 and argument2 to the script. Often this approach is referred to as a query, because it is how browsers communicated search keys in an earlier version of searches called ISINDEX searches. Although state-of-the-art searches are done using forms, this syntax of encoding arguments is still used, and you should be aware of it if you are going to use CGI scripts.

Web Browsers—Meeting the Standard

In the last chapter you learned about the W3C (World Wide Web Consortium) and the HTML 4.0 (Dynamic HTML) standard. You also learned that problems and differences always arise when HTML standards change or are updated. At the time of this writing, both Netscape and Microsoft have released versions of their browser with Dynamic HTML support. At this point you need to learn more about the issue of compatibility between these two browsers as they attempt to implement the HTML 4.0 standard and also about how they handle current HTML standards.

Web Publishing

There are two main factors in the evolution of HTML. The first involves the Web page design problem of keeping up with the technological changes in document production. The second involves the appearance of the documents. The HTML Working Group segment of W3C is made up of leading industry hardware and software manufacturers who are intimately aware of the symbiosis between the two ends of the spectrum. The group has incorporated the following eight goals into the latest HTML standard:

- Support for interactive documents and the Rich Forms technology
- Script-driven dynamic Web pages
- Easy frame modifications
- Extended child or nested-window control
- Improved multimedia display capabilities
- Increased support for multiple fonts and international characters
- Digital signature script security
- A standardized mechanism to provide information about a Web page to Web search engines and to monitor programs that control a Web page's display content

One Attempt at Meeting the HTML 4.0 Standard

The following discussion highlights the more important enhancements made to Netscape Navigator 4 as Netscape attempts to meet the challenge of the HTML 4.0 protocol standard.

Page Elements

On the browser end is something called an *element object array*, which provides access to **plug-ins**, **embeds**, **applets**, and **forms** (elements placed in a document so that they can be used by the recipient on another computer) and is accessible to scripting languages.

The new HTML 4.0 standard extends this static enumeration by providing dynamic content using two new tags, **<LAYER>** and **<ILAYER>**. Both may be moved, positioned, and hidden and their content and order changed within the *z* of *x-y-z* ordering, while the main Web page is displayed. Normal HTML elements such as headings and images normally do not have these capabilities unless they are placed within a **<LAYER>** element. The new tags also provide special properties enabling parent-child navigation. Layers are flexible enough to allow creation of a page where the contents can be changed dynamically by code running in the browser.

In particular, Netscape 4 accesses the contents of the user's selections within a document as a simple string, using the getSelection function. The browser can even search for text within the page using the new find function. Although displayed content cannot be changed outside a layer, this is not generally a problem, owing to the flexibility of layers.

Dynamic Event Capture

Netscape Communicator 4 incorporates the latest Project Cougar (HTML 4.0) requirement for a browser to provide dynamic event selection for all objects, which can be bound to script code in order to allow the construction of completely interactive Web pages.

Using the Event object, Netscape Communicator 4 returns information about all the scriptable events that are occurring in the browser via event capturing. The captureEvents function instructs the document or window to capture events originally destined for a contained element. Depending on the system's security settings, this ability to capture events is extended to capturing events in other documents loaded into a <FRAMESET>. Each captured event can be handled or routed to the original element with a routeEvent function call.

Some examples are the new key-press and mouse events, which greatly enhance a document's interactivity. However, they are usually restricted to elements like the document, links, and, in special cases, images.

Style Sheets

From the very beginning, long before many of the come-lately competitors, Netscape browsers adopted the use of styles and style sheets. Needless to say, Netscape Communicator 4 implements full support for the latest CSS1 standards (Cascading Style Sheets Level 1). The latest enhancement to style-sheet definitions includes the new positioning properties and–once defined–the styles that can be accessed via scripting languages in order to provide dynamic Web page interactivity.

Netscape Communicator 4 includes proprietary JavaScript Style Sheets (JSS). Like the CSS, JSS provides absolute positioning to some elements and gives access to the style properties of most of the elements on a Web page using a separate style language specific to JavaScript. A JavaScript delete function allows programmers to remove objects, properties, or elements from the Web page document. While Netscape Communicator 4 does support the <SPAN> and <DIV> tags, <DIV> does not provide any events and so is not compatible with dynamic pages that use any <DIV>-generated events.

The HTML 4.0 standard includes a requirement for support of the SRC and TYPE attributes in a <SCRIPT> tag. This approach allows the script to be downloaded separately from the hosting document. Netscape Communicator 4 processes the <SCRIPT> tag with the SRC attribute, using an implementation of a JavaScript interpreter. This approach allows a signed (secure) script to be imported into a Web page. Under development as this text is being written is the replacement of the LANGUAGE attribute with TYPE.

Since Dynamic HTML 4.0 is a superset of the earlier nondynamic HTML standard, many of the example programs and discussions of HTML 4 are still valid and will work under earlier versions of popular browsers. The accompanying two figures are designed to entice you into downloading or purchasing the latest version of Netscape Communicator 4 by showing you the new visual interface and discussing some of its new capabilities. Figure 2–1 illustrates the now familiar Netscape Navigator browser main window.

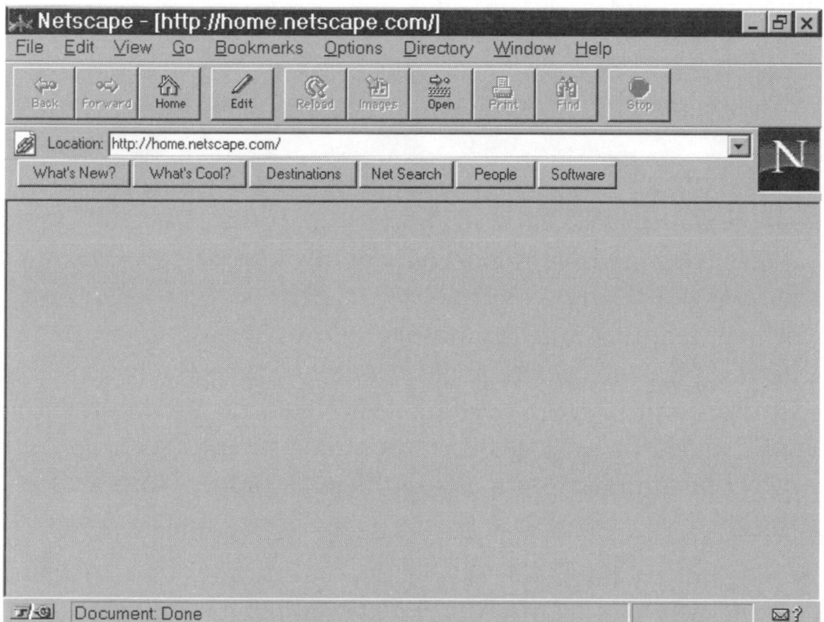

Figure 2–1: *Standard Netscape Navigator browser window*

Figure 2–2 shows how you can set up Netscape Communicator 4 with its new floating-dockable toolbar. Notice the streamlined main menu options list, the cleaner, uninterrupted "button bar." Netscape Navigator 4.0 is the newest version of Netscape's world-leading software for browsing information on intranets or the Internet.

Navigator has been updated and improved for greater ease of use. Plug-ins (small programs that add functionality to Navigator) are now downloaded and installed automatically so they work right away without any user configuration. New information-management tools simplify access to favorite sites and provide one-click access to Internet searches.

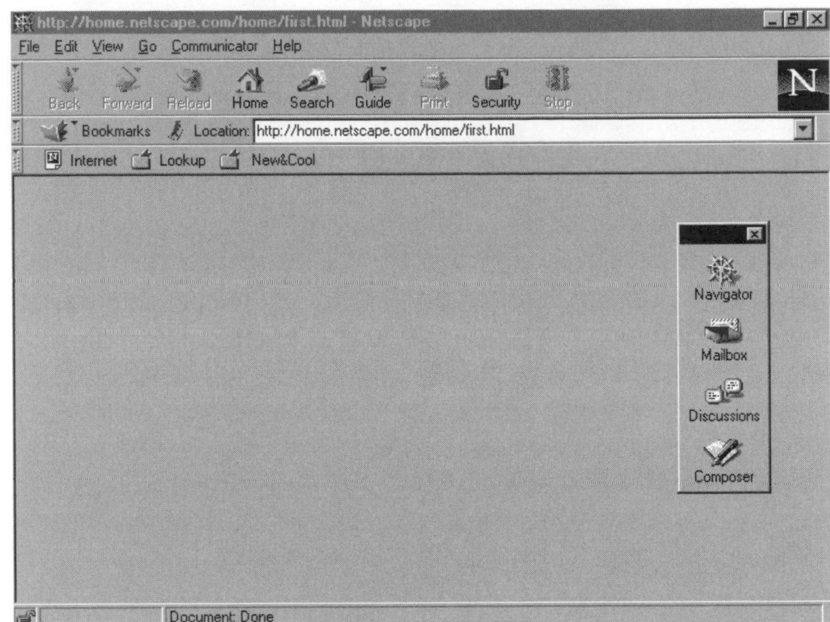

Figure 2–2: *The new Netscape Navigator 4 browser window*

Powerful new features and technology allow developers to create visually exciting, fully interactive pages. Users can directly manipulate and move images and Java applets. Like all Netscape Communicator components, Navigator includes open standards-based security features to protect information such as credit card numbers and personal financial data.

You can customize Navigator 4.0 to access Intranet and Internet information the way you want. You can customize its toolbar to suit your personal preferences. You'll find that bookmarks for marking favorite sites are more powerful and easier to use. Access to the Internet's most powerful search engines is simple and quick: the new Search button links directly to them. A single click takes you to Netscape Guide By Yahoo. The Places button takes you directly to this Internet site directory. Thanks to Dynamic HTML, you'll find dynamic, interactive, visually rich pages that are faster and easier to access.

You can encrypt sensitive data. Netscape's SSL 3.0-based security is integrated throughout Navigator 4.0. Data encryption in Navigator 4.0 protects information as it is transmitted over the Internet.

With Navigator 4.0 you can view and listen to multimedia information without becoming a multimedia expert. Navigator 4.0 comes pre-installed with the most popular multimedia plug-ins. SmartUpdate automatically configures and installs new multimedia plug-ins. It supports interactive 3D with the Cosmo Player VRML 2.0 rendering engine.

You can access other documents, such as Microsoft Excel spreadsheets, from Navigator 4.0. Support for ActiveX documents (OLE) allows Navigator 4.0 users to link directly to other ActiveX applications, such as Microsoft Office, from within a Navigator window.

Not to be outdone, of course, Microsoft has packed Internet Explorer 4.0 with its own set of visual candy. Figure 2–3 shows the extremely familiar Internet Explorer 3.0 main window.

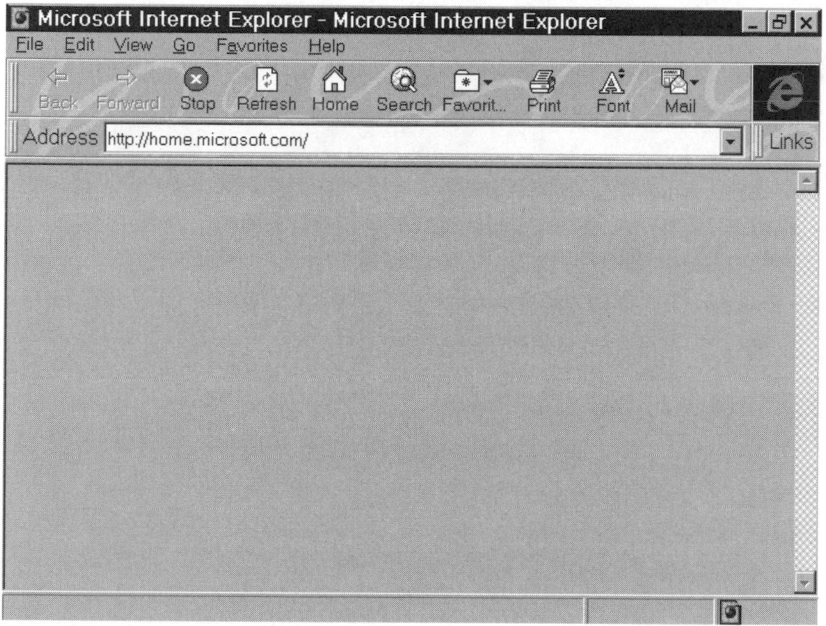

Figure 2–3: *Internet Explorer 3.0 main window*

At the time of this writing Microsoft and Sun Microsystems were heading into a court battle to decide just what should and should not be a part of Windows 98 and its interconnection with Internet Explorer 4.0. Currently, Internet Explorer 4.0 beta includes an option for what Microsoft calls its Active Desktop, seen in Figure 2–4.

The simplest way to describe the *active desktop* is to say that your Windows wallpaper can now be an *active* Web page. The possibilities are virtually unlimited; you can select and connect–live–to any information source of interest: stock quotes, latest sports scores, RealVideo broadcasts, even the Home Shopping Network!

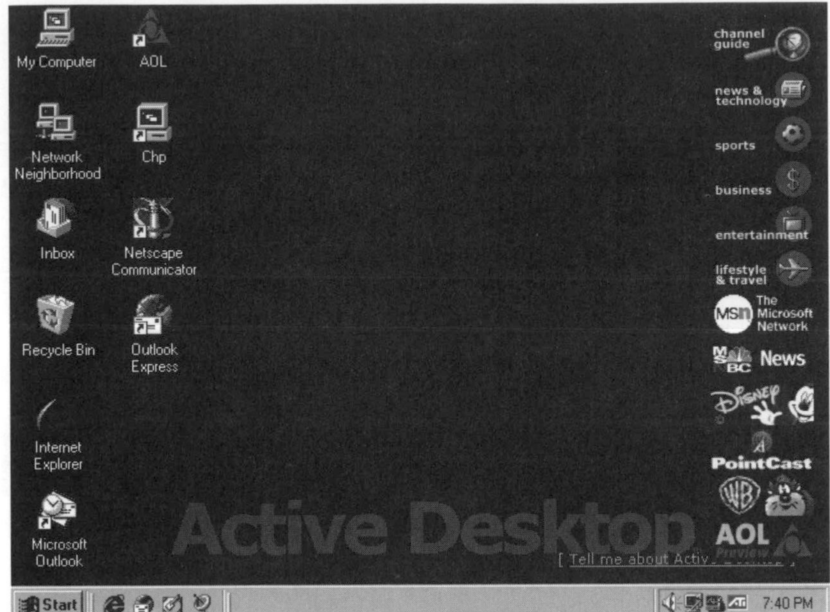

Figure 2–4: *Internet Explorer 4.0 Active Desktop*

Internet Explorer 4.0 itself has a newer, cleaner, up-to-date look, as seen in Figure 2–5.

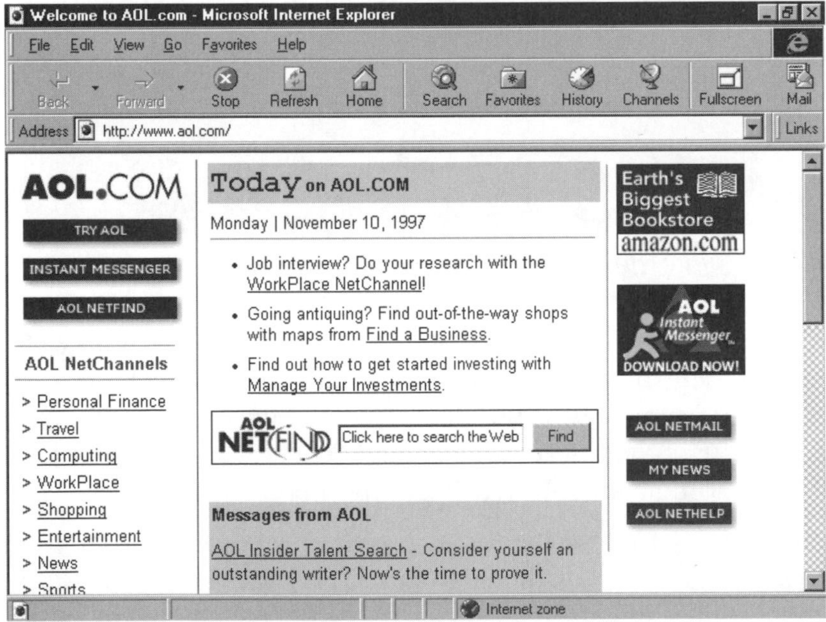

Figure 2–5: *Sample Internet Explorer 4.0 main window*

The crisp, clean appearance has been achieved by removing the 3D-button image around each of the control icons. Notice that both Netscape Navigator 4 and Internet Explorer 4.0 offer a Fullscreen option, as seen in Figure 2–6.

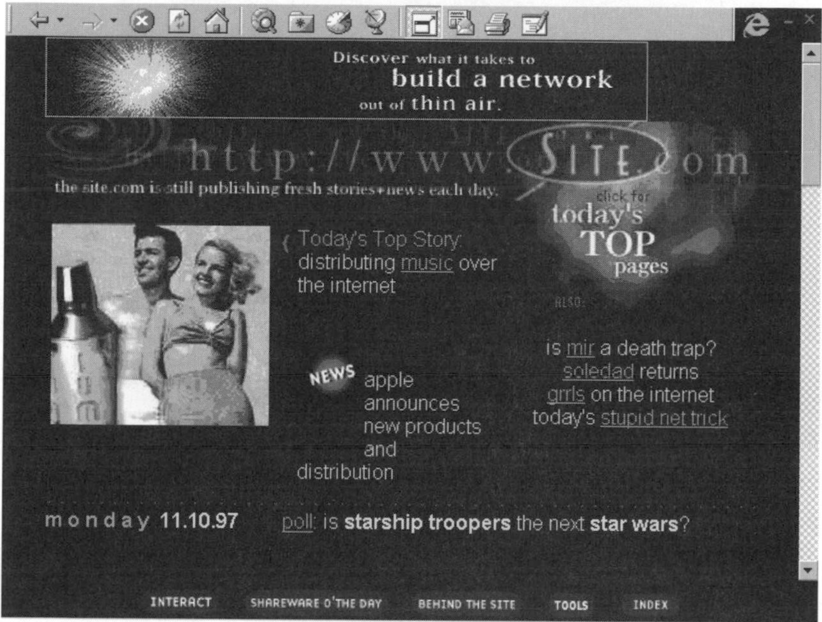

Figure 2–6: *Internet Explorer 4.0 Fullscreen mode*

If you are like most Internet surfers, you'll greatly appreciate the extra screen real estate provided by this large-screen display format.

Of course there is much more to Windows 98 and Internet Explorer 4.0, such as the addition and relocation of various features and their visual presentation. For example, the Settings group now has an additional Active Desktop Utility to manage this new capability, as seen in Figure 2–7.

The choice is yours–the new frontiers of Netscape Navigator 4 or the exciting enhancements to Windows 98 and Internet Explorer 4.0. However, regardless of which way you go, incompatibilities in the interpretations of the HTML 4.0 standard will continue, at least for the near future.

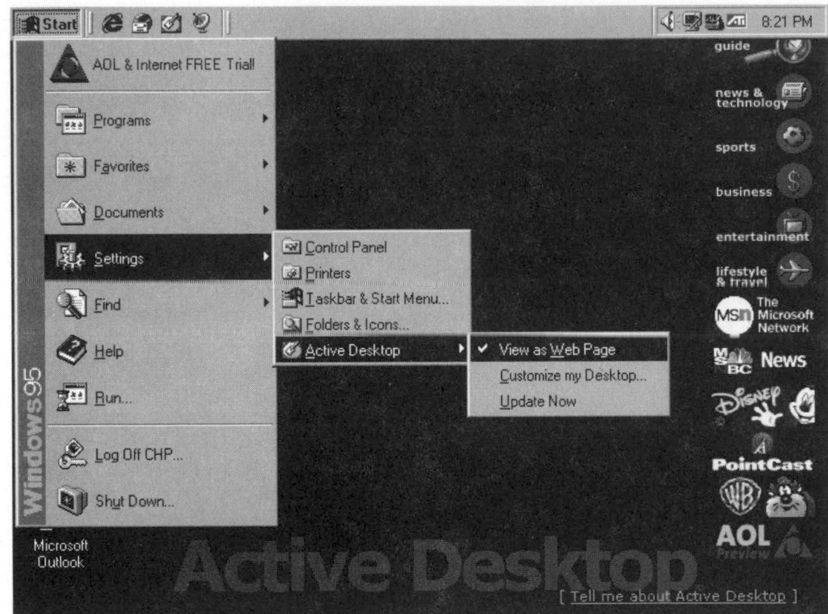

Figure 2–7: *The new Settings Active Desktop utility*

Dynamic HTML 4.0 Browser Compatibility

The new 4.0 browser technologies allow Dynamic HTML to support a much richer multimedia Web content. Some of these technologies are common to both browsers, but others remain unique to either Microsoft or Netscape. The four HTML features listed below are common to both browsers, though some of their specific support differs in the implementations:

- Cascading Style Sheets
- Document Object Model
- JavaScript
- Shockwave

The discussions that follow provide an overview of these common concepts and describe how to work around the implementation differences in building browser-compatible Web pages.

Cascading Style Sheets

Cascading Style Sheets are used to define the appearance of content on Web pages. Much of the visual impact of Dynamic HTML is based on these new settings, and fortunately they are defined in the same way in both the Microsoft and Netscape browsers.

Cascading style sheets can set attributes such as font size, color, leading, and margins as well as arbitrary positions for elements on the page. The settings can be grouped into external style sheets, which can be referenced by multiple Web pages.

Cascading style sheets have the ability to override earlier definitions in trickle-down fashion. This allows global style properties to be used across many Web pages, yet still be customized for individual pages or tags.

Document Object Model

Common to both 4.0 browsers is the Document Object Model concept, which provides scripting access to Web page elements. The actual Microsoft and Netscape object models are different, making it a challenge to write JavaScript that works in both. We describe below how to accomplish this.

Using Netscape Navigator 4

Netscape Navigator 4 supports scripting access to specific collections of HTML page elements, such as layers on the page. The layer collection includes areas bounded by a <LAYER> tag and areas positioned using CSS attributes. Elements within those collections can be accessed by index, name, or ID. Changes to layer position, visibility, and clipping appear instantaneously on the page.

Using Microsoft Internet Explorer 4.0

Microsoft's Internet Explorer 4.0 also supports scripting access to all HTML page elements, including style-sheet properties. Page elements are reflected as objects contained in a document, while all collections and elements can be accessed by index, name, or ID. Changes to object properties appear instantly on the page.

SWITCH-HITTING

Whenever you wish to access an object in either browser, when the page is loaded a reference variable can be set to the syntax for whichever browser is being used. Then, by building references to objects, one script can be used in both browsers.

JavaScript

As far as scripting languages go, both Netscape and Microsoft have agreed on a JavaScript standard, pending a final agreement through the ECMA standards body. Unfortunately, the browsers' event-handling models are different, in fact are reversed. For example, clicking on a hypertext link would cause the following event handlers to be called:

Netscape	**Microsoft**
1. Window	1. Link
2. Document	2. Layer
3. Layer	3. Document
4. Link	4. Window
5. Default event handler	5. Default event handler

How Events Are Handled

The discussions that follow highlight how each 4.0 browser attempts to capture and handle events.

NETSCAPE EVENTS

Netscape's Navigator 4.0 uses an event-capturing model, instead of an event-bubbling model. Events, rather than being generated by the bottommost object in the hierarchy and then bubbled up, are generated at the top of the object hierarchy and then fall through to events lower in the hierarchy.

The window is first given the opportunity to handle the event before it falls through to the document object and then any layer objects that might exist. The target of the event is the last to process the event before it falls off the bottom and is handled by the default event handler. A limited number of page elements can generate and process events. For example, onMouseOver is handled only by images and links.

MICROSOFT EVENTS

Microsoft's Internet Explorer 4.0 uses the event-bubbling model. That is, the object associated with where the event happened receives the event first. This object can then choose to process the event or pass it along to its parent object.

An unprocessed event continues to bubble up the document structure until it falls off the top and is processed by the default event handler. If an object chooses to process an event, it can stop the event immediately or choose to continue bubbling it up.

Microsoft allows individual page elements to generate and process events. Even simple HTML tags such as <H1> or <BLOCKQUOTE> can now generate and process mouseOver, mouseOut, and onClick events. This allows a lot more interaction and feedback to be built into a Web page.

CROSS-PLATFORM EVENTS

The simplest way to generate scripts that will work in both browsers is to avoid passing any events to parent event handlers, since the passing order is reversed in the two browsers. Simply handle each event with a single function. In addition you could use only those events defined for the Netscape browser, since they will work with Microsoft's browser as well.

Browser-Specific Dynamic HTML 4.0

We list here those features of Dynamic HTML that are generic to Netscape's and Microsoft's browsers and that won't work on the competing product.

Netscape

The following capabilities are specific to Netscape Navigator 4.0 and will not work with Microsoft Internet Explorer:

- <layer> tag
- JavaScript style sheets
- Bitstream fonts

Microsoft

The following capabilities are specific to Microsoft Internet Explorer 4.0 and will not work with Netscape Navigator 4.0:

- Direct animation controls
- Data binding
- VBScript
- OpenType fonts

If you are concerned about these differences, see the documentation that Microsoft and Netscape provide or log on to their Web sites for the latest details.

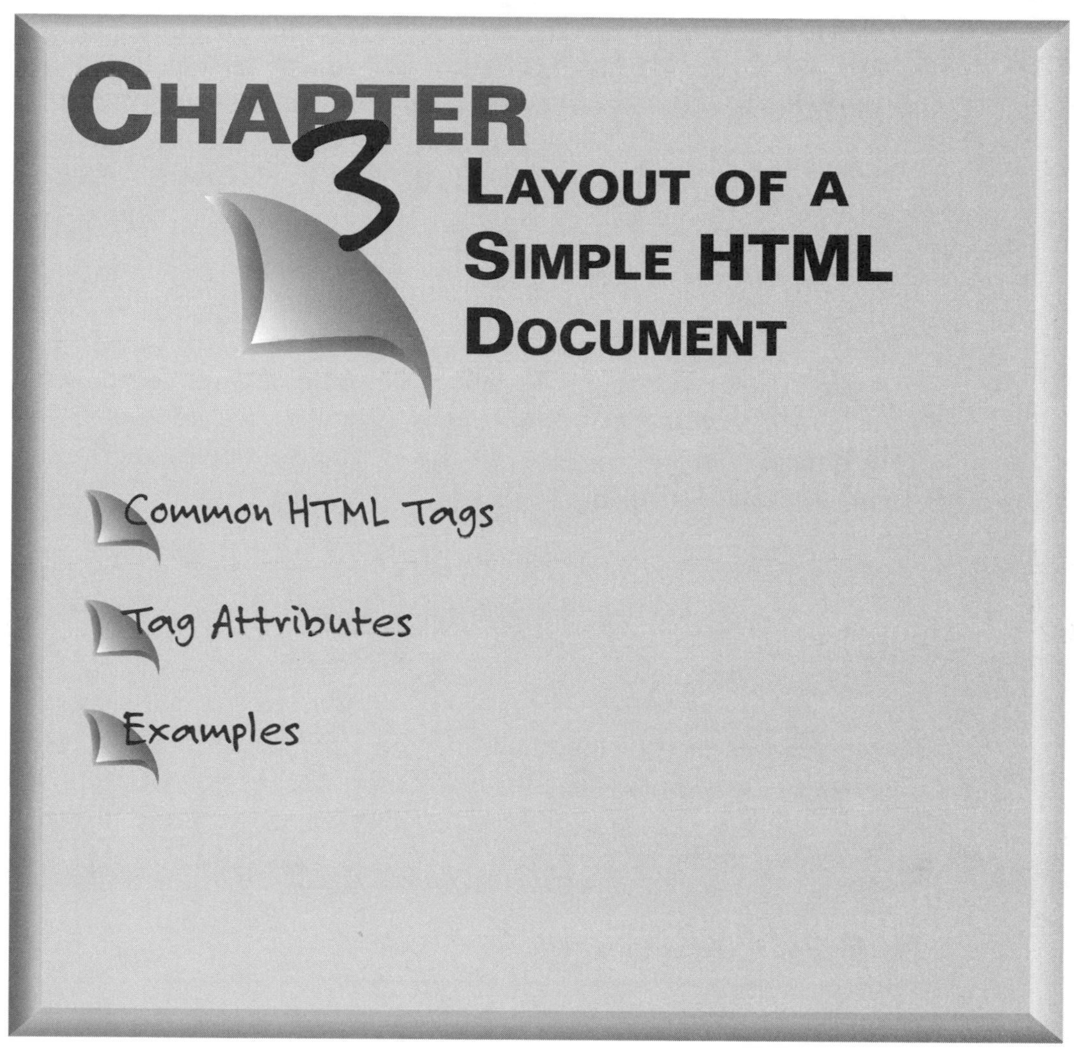

Introduction

The beauty of HyperText Mark-up Language is that it does not require a complicated compiler and endless years of mastering language syntax, all of which can be rendered obsolete by some new programming technology that sends us back to college. The real secret behind HTML is that there is no secret! Everything is right out there in the open, simply waiting for the right interpretation. HTML documents are just a stream of plain characters waiting to be produced by virtually any text editor capable of generating pure ASCII file output format.

Learning to use HTML requires you to master two fundamentals: the order in which characters occur, and the way in which they are used to produce the desired results. Although browsers are somewhat forgiving–you can still see acceptable results even if certain statements have been omitted or misused–the best way to use HTML is to understand and work within its defined boundaries. The focus of this book is not on what makes it easy for *you* to design an HTML document, but rather on what makes your HTML document consistent and easy to access for the *end user.*

In this chapter you will learn about the fundamental components of an HTML document and its overall structure. We hope you may begin to appreciate, along the way, the eloquence, upgradability, and ease of use HTML provides.

This Chapter's HTML Tags

Seven tags are used in conjunction with a basic introductory Web page design. These tags, together with short description of each, are listed in Table 3–1. You'll see how the developer uses these tags and their various attribute options.

Table 3–1: *New tags relating to styling*

Tag	Description
<HTML>	Flags the document as using HTML format
<HEAD>	Marks the beginning of the document header
<BODY>	Contains all the embedded tags defining content display control. Legal attributes include: ALIGN, BGCOLOR, TEXT, BACKGROUND, LINK, ALINK, VLINK
<H1...H6>	Level 1 through Level 6 header style, font, and point size
<P>	Flags the beginning of a paragraph
 	Intraparagraph formatting for a line break

Content versus Controls

HTML's first fundamental is that it always separates *content* from the *controls* that act on the content. The content is visually similar to the text on this page; it is displayed in the browser window. The controls, sometimes called *mark-up* or *tags*, appear in the HTML document between pairs of angle-brackets <> and do not display in your browser's window. These tags define header, graphical, hyperlink, and list formats, controlling *how* the content appears onscreen.

Visiphones, Bulletin Boards, and Infomercials

A note of caution before beginning: remember your target audience. Ask yourself who will be viewing your Web page. How will they view it–on what hardware/software platforms? Are you generating a professional business gateway viewed by corporate-only UNIX sites, or an informal granny-online page that the grandkids will access with everything from ancient Commodore computers (basically text-only displays–using the text-only *Lynx* browser) to University Vax-clusters to high-powered Sun workstations? The answers to these questions will determine which HTML components you do or do *not* use to generate navigable display pages.

Your First Home Page

The meaning of the term *home page* can vary. If you're reading and browsing the Web, you may think of the home page as the Web page that loads when you start up your browser or when you choose the browser's Home button. Each browser has its own default home page. Within your browser, you can change the default home page that launches every time you start your daily surf sessions. If you're publishing pages on the Web, however, then "home page" has an entirely different meaning. The home page is the first or topmost page in a hierarchy of pages used to cover all the information on your Web site.

Your home page often resembles a stylized high-level outline enumerating the content of your presentation and consisting of a list or table of contents or a set of icons. Just remember, you do *not* design your page based on what it looks like on your computer system and your browser. You *do* design it to have clear, well-structured content so that it is easy to read and understand in most browsers.

<HTML>, <HEAD>, and <BODY> Required

The <HTML>, <HEAD>, and <BODY> tags, while not yet *required* tags, could easily become standard in the near future. Tools may also emerge that need these tags. Therefore, you should not consider creating an HTML document without them, even though most browsers can navigate around their nonexistence. If you get into the habit of including them now, you won't have to worry about updating your files later.

<HTML> AND </HTML>

The <HTML> start tag identifies the beginning of the HTML document; its ending tag </HTML> defines the end of the HTML document; and together they encapsulate everything that is supposed to be parsed as HTML. All the text and HTML commands in your HTML document should go within the beginning and ending HTML tags, as in:

```
<HTML>
… content and embedded tags here …
</HTML>
```

Theoretically, any content following the </HTML> end tag is ignored by the browser.

<HEAD> AND </HEAD>

The <HEAD> tag marks the beginning of the document header. The header of the document is where global settings are defined and is contained within the <HEAD>, </HEAD> tag pair, as in:

```
<HTML>
<HEAD>
… embedded head tag items here …
</HEAD>
</HTML>
```

This is where you put one or more tags used exclusively within the header portion of an HTML document. It is also an ideal place to include scripting-language function definitions. In addition, the <HEAD> tag pair defines page-level information about the HTML document and can include its title, base URL, index information, next-page pointer, and possible links to other HTML documents. Some of the most commonly used tag pairs that can be embedded within the <HEAD> tag pair are <TITLE>, <LINK>, <META>, <SCRIPT>, and <STYLE>. There can be only one <HEAD> tag pair per document. It must follow the opening <HTML> tag and precede the <BODY> tag.

With special HTTP protocol access, headers serve yet another important purpose. They allow search engines to get some basic information about the page title, file format, last modified date, and any keywords, all without examining the document further.

<TITLE> AND </TITLE>

Browsers use a page's title for bookmarks or hotlist programs, while other programs use the title to catalog the Web page. Most browsers display the title within their title-bar area. <TITLE and </TITLE> tags always appear embedded within the page <HEAD> tag pair:

```
<HTML>
<HEAD>
<TITLE>My Specific, Unique, Search-Engine-Ready Title</TITLE>
… embedded head tag items here …
</HEAD>
</HTML>
```

<BODY> AND </BODY>

The remainder of your HTML document, including all text and other page elements, such as links and pictures, is encapsulated within the <BODY> tag pair. There can be only one <BODY>, and it must follow the <HEAD> tag. Here you add the text you want displayed in the main browser window, add tags and attributes to modify that text, create hyperlinks to other documents, and so on. The completed HTML minimal template now looks like this:

```
<HTML>
<HEAD>
<TITLE>My Specific, Unique, Search-Engine-Ready Title</TITLE>
… embedded head tag items here …
</HEAD>
<BODY>
Nothing less than the most thought-provoking, visually
enticing eye candy and memorable quotables you have ever
laid eyes on goes here!
</BODY>
</HTML>
```

When loaded into Netscape 4, the HTML document defined above looks like Figure 3-1.

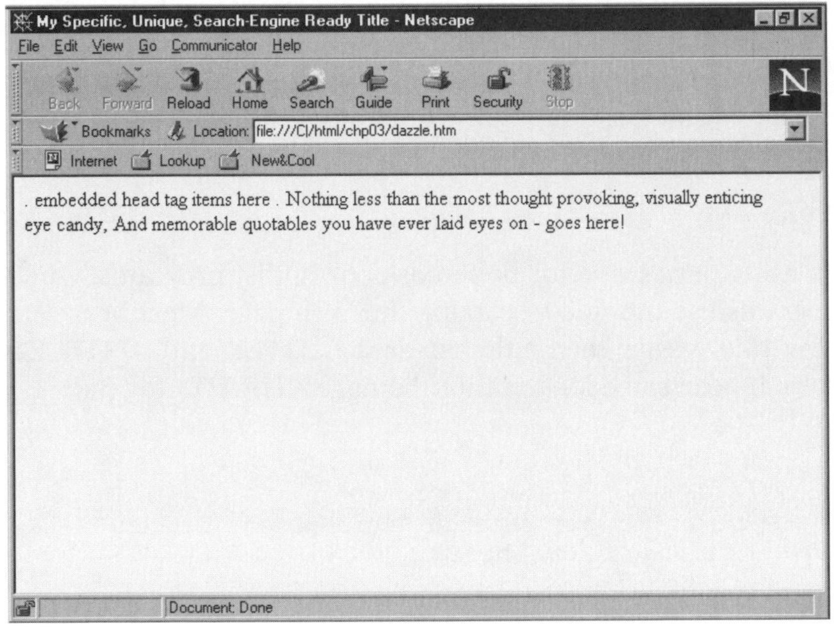

Figure 3–1: *Example HTML document viewed in the Netscape browser*

This display is anything *but* "visually enticing," although somewhat thought provoking. A few characteristics are worth noting. First, notice that the Netscape browser placed the title "My Specific, Unique, Search-Engine-Ready Title" at the top of the window.

Examples of good <TITLE>s occupying this position include:

1. *Ford Escort Online Catalog*
2. *Jim Henson and the Muppets*
3. *Current Movie Reviews*
4. *NYC Opera Ticket Sales Information*
5. *PC Magazine Printer Reviews*

Each of these has one or more *keywords* which a properly launched search engine can lock onto. The following selections, by contrast, are found on the one-thousand-three-hundred-and fifty-third page of your search engine's hit list:

1. *Index of Titles*
2. *The Decade We Live In*
3. *My Personal Home Page*
4. *Musical Instruments*
5. *The Time, Date, and Place of America's Most Important Historical Events*

These <TITLE>s are vague, ambiguous, and general. Perhaps the most robust end user could find them, but most of us wouldn't live that long!

Look again at Figure 3–1. Notice also that the line spacing of the <BODY> text does *not* match that of the HTML document. By default, browsers simply wordwrap text unless special formatting tags are embedded within the <BODY> of your document.

The good news is that you can easily improve even this simple document's pupil punch by changing the color of the text, background, and so on. The following are legal <BODY> attributes:

- TEXT
- BGCOLOR
- BACKGROUND
- LINK
- ALINK
- VLINK

<H1>...<H6> and </H1>...</H6>

Every well-written newspaper article, book review, or catalog and every professionally laid out photo album originates in a good outline. That outline, though it may exist only in the creator's mind, is the most important production step after selection of the main topic. Clever, unique, and logical headings help organize and map any presentation including that of a Web page. HTML defines six levels of headings for this purpose. The tags used are <H1> through <H6> and their respective end tags </H1> to </H6>.

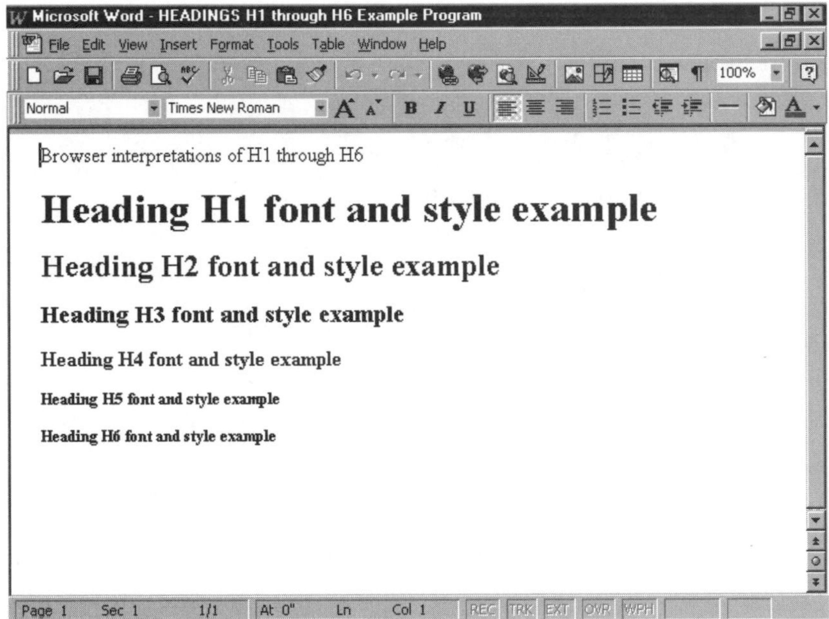

Figure 3–2: *Sample HTML document viewed from within Microsoft Word 97*

Although browsers vary in the size and style of type they assign to the six heading levels, every browser follows the basic rule of giving the biggest and boldest style to <H1> and the smallest and least significant to <H6>. These six heading styles indicate the relative importance of different parts of your page, much as this book does by using different levels of headings to visually organize its contents.

The following HTML document will be loaded into Microsoft Word and the Netscape and Internet Explorer browsers so that you can compare their interpretations (see Figures 3–2, 3–3, and 3–4, respectively).

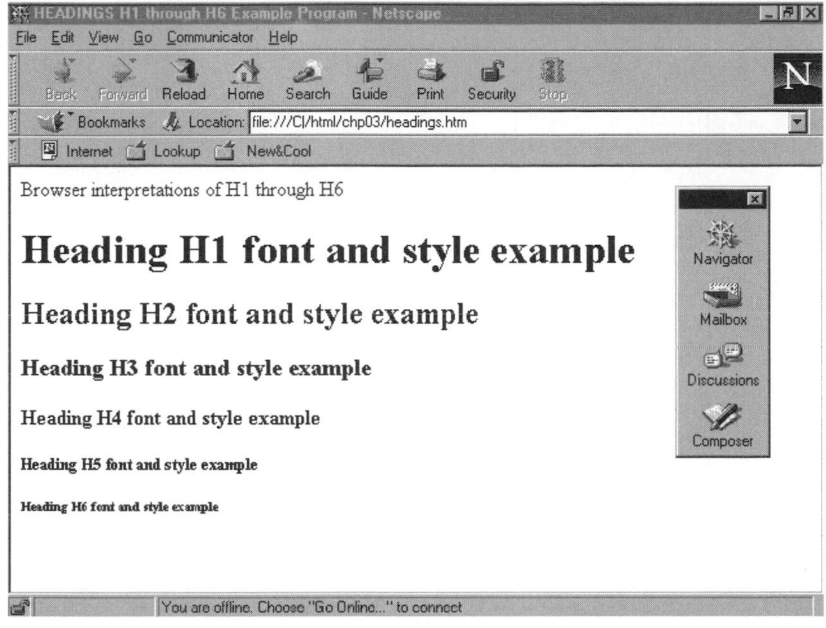

Figure 3–3: *Sample HTML document viewed from within Netscape Navigator*

```
<HTML>
<HEAD>
<TITLE>HEADINGS H1 through H6 Example Program</TITLE>
</HEAD>
<BODY>
Browser interpretations of H1 through H6
<H1>Heading H1 font and style example</H1>
<H2>Heading H2 font and style example</H2>
<H3>Heading H3 font and style example</H3>
<H4>Heading H4 font and style example</H4>
<H5>Heading H5 font and style example</H5>
<H6>Heading H6 font and style example</H6>
</BODY>
</HTML>
```

Notice that each heading is placed on a new line, and any material following it is placed on the next new line. For this reason, you should *not* use heading tags to create emphasized text within the document. In the next section you will learn how to use HTML tags for this purpose.

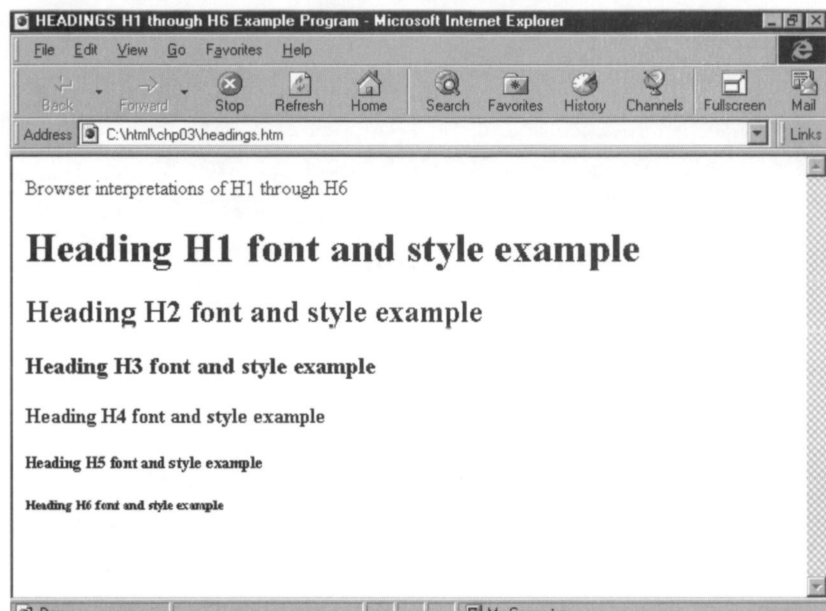

Figure 3–4: *Sample HTML document viewed from within Internet Explorer 4.0*

In the examples given here you will notice an extreme and atypical similarity in HTML tag interpretations. You might expect both Microsoft Word 97 and Internet Explorer to display similar results, but here even Netscape's browser seems to agree. The point: depending on which tags you sample, and which browser software you test, you may conclude you've designed the perfect cross-platform Web page when in fact you have not. Examples will be given to demonstrate this throughout the book.

<P> and </P>—Paragraphs

Paragraphs are defined with the <P> and </P> tags. Beginning with HTML 3.2, paragraph tags were given the attribute ALIGN, where alignment types include LEFT, CENTER, and RIGHT. Remember from Chapter 1 that the end tag </P> is optional, since every new start tag <P> indirectly flags the end of one paragraph and beginning of the next. The HTML document shown below demonstrates how to use these attributes.

```
<HTML>
<HEAD>
<TITLE>Paragraph Formatting Example</TITLE>
</HEAD>
<BODY>
The following examples demonstrate paragraph format-
ting and alignment.
<P> ALIGN=RIGHT>This way to page two ...</P>
<P> ALIGN=CENTER>-- Separator Bar Section --</P>
<P> ALIGN=LEFT>Normal default mode positioning</P>
</BODY>
</HTML>
```

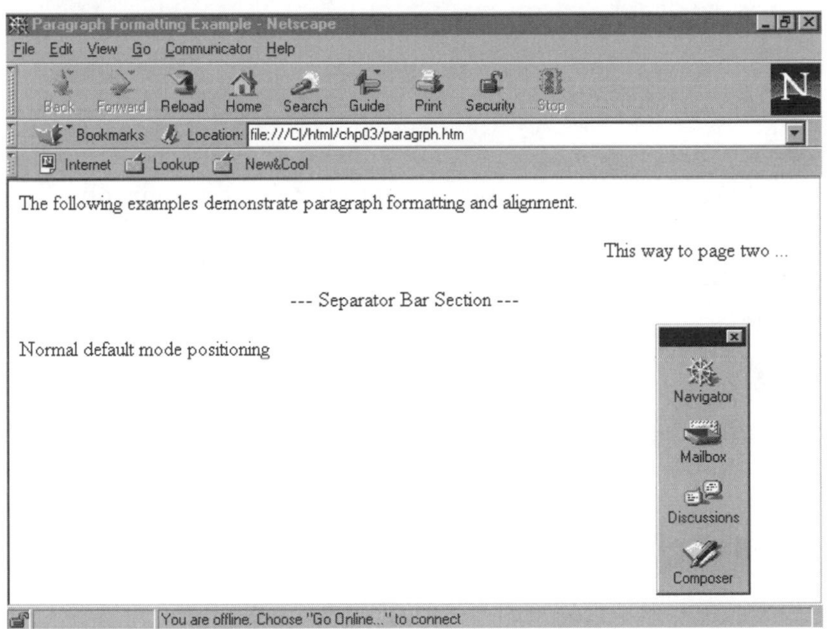

Figure 3–5: *<P> ALIGN=RIGHT/CENTER/LEFT> example*

—Line Break

Line spacing within a paragraph differs in a subtle way from line spacing between paragraphs or line breaks. The <BR> tag forces text to begin on a new line but maintains a line-spacing point size consistent with intraparagraph formatting. Interparagraph line spacing has a slightly larger point size and is proportioned to the font and style chosen for the next paragraph section.

The following HTML document highlights these subtle differences.

```
<HTML>
<HEAD>
<TITLE>Paragraph Formatting Example</TITLE>
</HEAD>
<BODY>
The following examples demonstrate paragraph and
line-break formatting. Notice that the interparagraph
spacing uses a higher point size.
<P>The following section demonstrates the similarity
in line spacing within a paragraph whenever the
line-break tag is used.
</P>
<P>Now the section is repeated only this time using
<BR>the line-break tag to separate the sentences.
</P>
</BODY>
</HTML>
```

Notice that there is less space within than between paragraphs (see Figure 3–6).

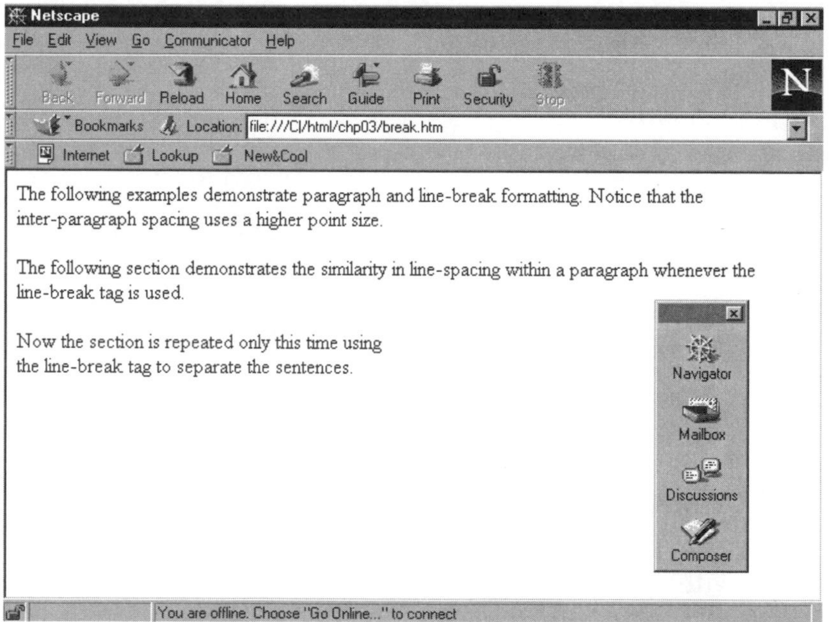

Figure 3–6: *Inter- versus intraparagraph line spacing using <P> and <BR> tags*

Easy Visual Enhancements

This section demonstrates a few of the attributes available within the <BODY> tag pair for quickly spicing up your first Web page.

BGCOLOR

You use the BGCOLOR attribute within the <BODY> tag pair to establish the background color of an HTML document. The color can be specified using a color's proper name, a hexadecimal value, or an RGB value.

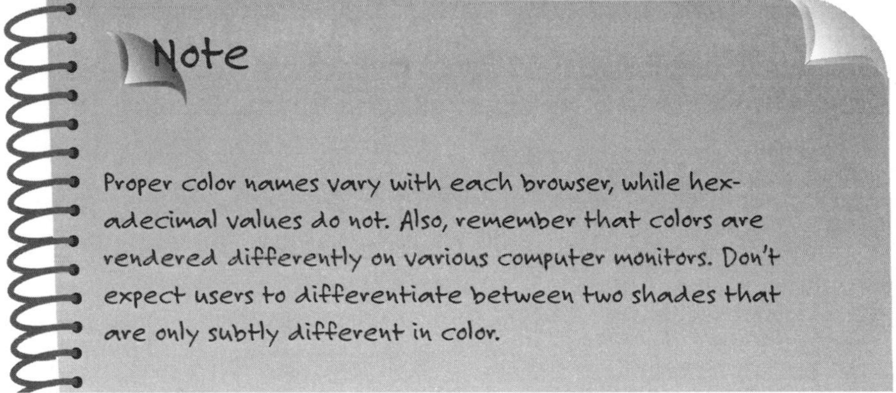

Note
Proper color names vary with each browser, while hexadecimal values do not. Also, remember that colors are rendered differently on various computer monitors. Don't expect users to differentiate between two shades that are only subtly different in color.

For example, White equals #FFFFFF, Red #FF0000, Green #00FF00, Blue #0000FF, Magenta #FF00FF, and so on. See the TEXT description below for an example.

TEXT

The <BODY> TEXT attribute lets you control the color of all the page's body text that isn't a link, including headings, body text, text inside tables, and so on. The following HTML document creates a page with a black background and white text:

```
<HTML>
<HEAD>
<TITLE>Background and Text Color Example</TITLE>
</HEAD>
<BODY BGCOLOR="#000000"TEXT="FFFFFF>
This page displays white text on a black background.
</BODY>
</HTML>
```

Figure 3–7 uses Microsoft Word 97's ability to preview HTML documents to display the example file.

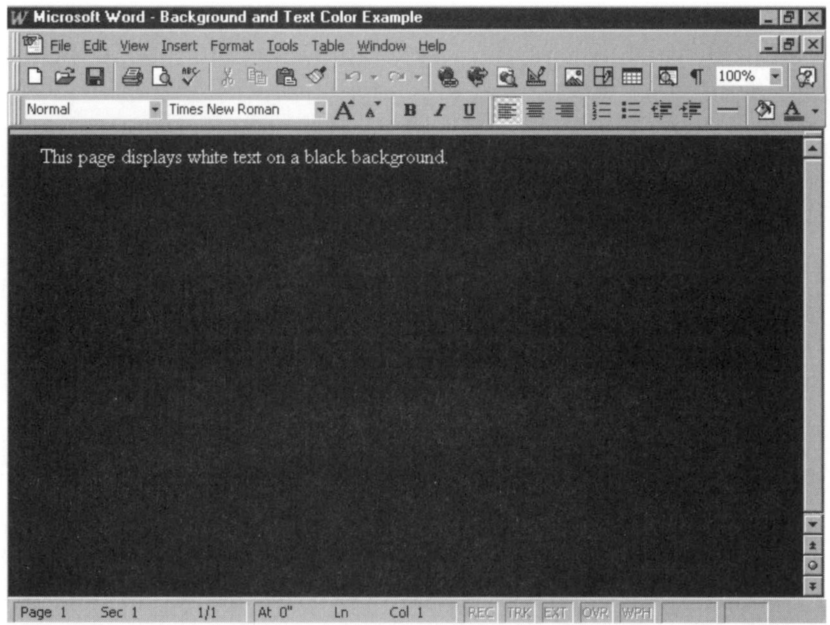

Figure 3–7: *Sample HTML document using the BGCOLOR and TEXT attributes*

The following sixteen colors are recognized by both Netscape Navigator 4 and Internet Explorer 4.0:

AQUA	GRAY	NAVY	SILVER
BLACK	GREEN	OLIVE	TEAL
BLUE	LIME	PURPLE	WHITE
FUCHSIA	MAROON	RED	YELLOW

BACKGROUND

You can easily create more visually impressive backdrops by using the <BODY> tag pair's BACKGROUND attribute. BACKGROUND allows you to import an image as a background for your pages rather than using a solid background.

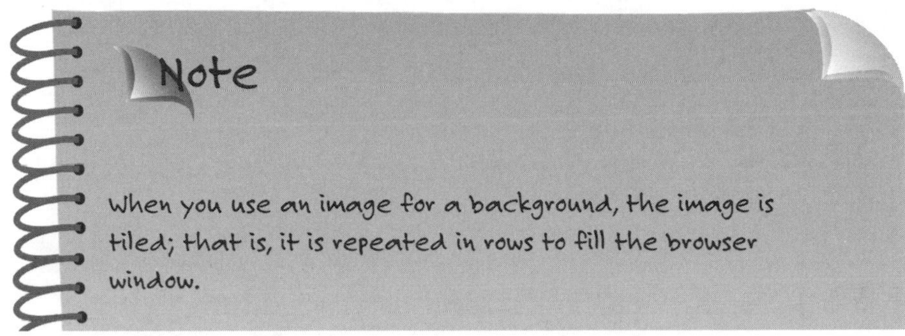

Note
When you use an image for a background, the image is tiled; that is, it is repeated in rows to fill the browser window.

Creating a tile background involves selecting or making a pattern that flows smoothly from one tile to the next–as when you're hanging patterned wallpaper! Your goal is to have the edges meet cleanly, showing no seam. The following example borrows this type of image from the Windows 98 selection of wallpapers.

```
<HTML>
<HEAD>
<TITLE>Image Background Example</TITLE>
</HEAD>
<BODY BACKGROUND="RR.gif">
This page displays a Birthday-paced background.
</BODY>
</HTML>
```

Figure 3–8 uses Internet Explorer to render this Birthday background image, repeatedly tiled in a continuous flow.

LINK, ALINK, and VLINK

The three <BODY> attributes, LINK, ALINK, and VLINK, allow you to define the colors used.

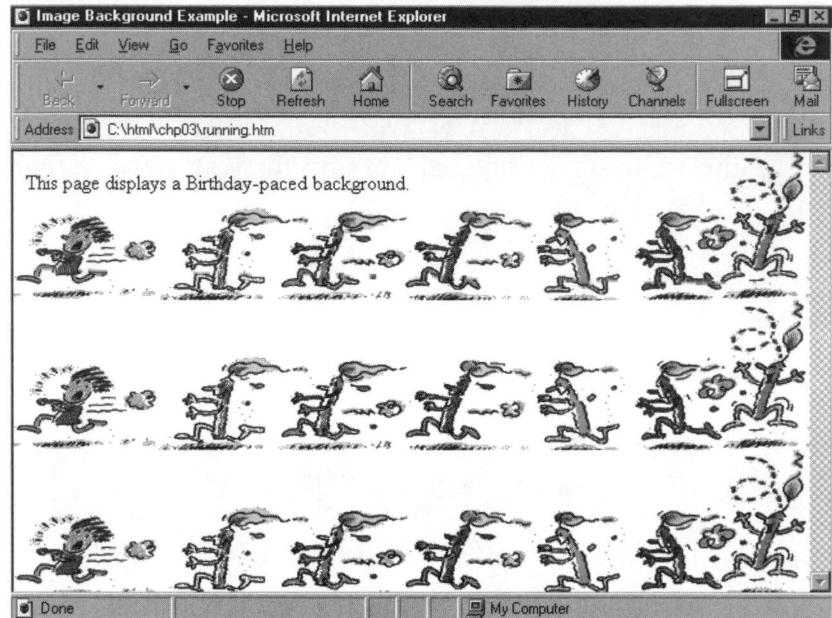

Figure 3–8: *Internet Explorer rendering a fun Birthday BACKGROUND*

LINK — Sets the color of an active hypertext link. Hypertext links are active only while the mouse is clicked on the link.

ALINK — Sets the color of the hypertext links that *have not* yet been visited.

VLINK — Sets the color of the hypertext links that *have* been visited.

All three attributes use the same color-coding options described for the BGCOLOR and BACKGROUND attributes, meaning that you can use color-constant names like WHITE or a hexadecimal RGB value. Since these attributes are legal only for the <BODY> of your HTML document, their syntax is straightforward:

```
<BODY LINK="BLUE" ALINK="YELLOW" VLINK="RED">
```

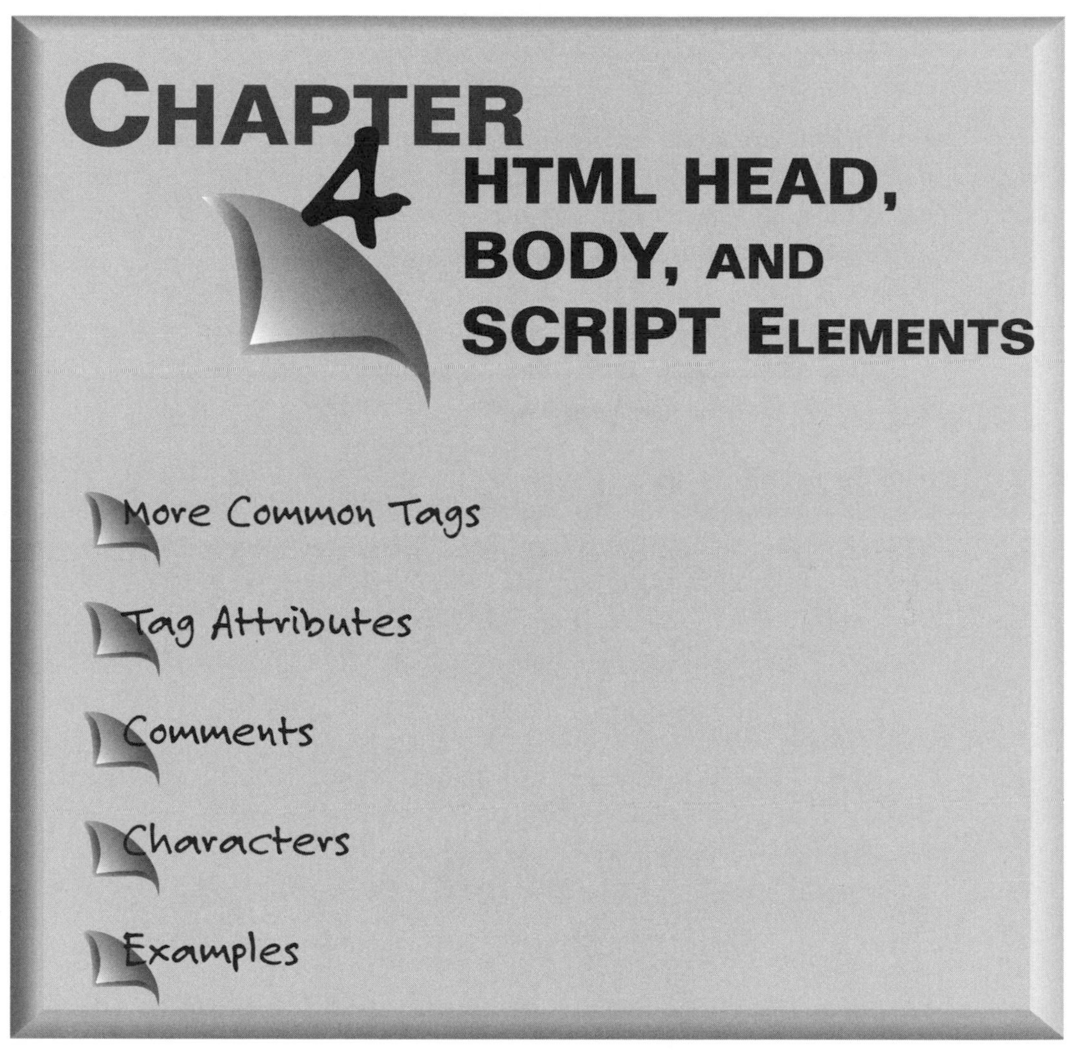

Introduction

Learning and using HTML is addictive! One reason is that you can edit directly into an existing document each new structure, tag, or attribute you learn about. In this chapter you will learn more about the behind-the-scenes proper structure for an HTML document. You'll also pick up a few tricks for avoiding inevitable syntax problems *before* you have them. For example, you'll learn how to put quotation-marks within an HTML syntax that uses quotation-marks to flag the end of a string.

This Chapter's HTML Tags

Seven tags are used in conjunction with a basic introductory Web page design. These tags, together with a short description of each, are listed in Table 4–1. You'll see how these tags are used with the various attribute options available to the developer.

Table 4–1: *New tags relating to simple HTML documents*

Tag	Description
<BASE HREF>	Defines your home page address
<LINK>	Defines hotlinks; attributes include HREF, ID, MEDIA, REL, REV, TARGET, TITLE, TYPE
<STYLE>	Flags the use of style sheets, discussed in greater detail in Chapter 12
<ISINDEX>	Old-style HTML search-engine parameters
<SCRIPT>	Defines the script portion of an HTML document, attributes include LANGUAGE, SRC, TYPE, ONLOAD, ONUNLOAD
Lang	Defines the HTML document base language
Dir	Defines the scan direction for specified language: LTR or RTL
<NOSCRIPT>	Defines document section to be used when <SCRIPT> is not supported
<META>	Special browser instructions, attributes include HTTP-EQUIV, NAME

Comments

Adding comments to your documents is as good an idea in HTML as it is in C/C++, FORTRAN, COBOL, and the like. Professional programmers define a "good comment" as one that neither insults the intelligence of another programmer nor assumes too much. The general idea here is this: you should comment any portion of your HTML file that, two months later, you would look at and say, "Gosh, what *does* that syntax mean?" or "*Why* does it do it that way?" Good comments can give a document a signature indicating when and by whom the file was created, what support files are needed should the site be shared, and so on.

You start an HTML comment with the following four symbols (no blanks please):

```
<!--
```

and terminate the comment with three consecutive symbols, as in:

```
-->
```

Comments can be single or multiple lines. For example the following two styles are both syntactically correct:

```
<!-- Date: Jan 1 98, Created by: J.R.Williams,
Department: Commercial Resources -->
```

or

```
<!--
     Date:         Jan 1 98
     Created by: J.R.Williams
     Department: Commercial Resources


-->
```

Last Updated

A meaningful piece of information you can add to any HTML document is a "Last updated:" message. This allows frequent visitors to your site to decide if you have anything new to say (beyond what they have previously viewed). Although no HTML tag, attribute, or element applies specifically for update messages, the following <BODY> <P>aragraph example does the trick:

```
<P ALIGN=RIGHT>Last updated: Jan 1 1998 by J.R.Williams</P>
```

Formatting Date and TIME

You have a number of ways to represent dates and times. The general format looks like this:

```
YYYY-MM-DDThh:mm:ssTZ
```

Table 4–2 details each acronym.

Table 4–2: *Explanation of time-format acronyms*

YYYY	A four-digit year
MM	A two-digit month (01 = January, etc.)
DD	A two-digit day of month (01 through 31)
Hh	A two-digit hour (00 through 23) (am/pm NOT allowed)
Mm	A two-digit minute (00 through 59)
Ss	A two-digit second (00 through 59)
TZ	The time zone designator

The time-zone designator is one of the following:

Z	*(UTC (Coordinated Universal Time)), or*
+hh:mm	*(specifies a local time which is hh hours and mm minutes ahead of UTC), or*
-hh:mm	*(specifies a local time which is hh hours and mm minutes behind UTC).*

There can be no variation in the syntax. (Note that the "T" appears literally in the string to indicate the beginning of the time element.) If a document does not know the time to the second, it may use the value "00" for the seconds (and minutes and hours if necessary). Both of the following examples correspond to October 5, 1996, 9:20:10 am, U.S. Eastern Standard Time.

```
1996-10-05T14:20:10Z
1996-10-05T09:20:10-05:00
```

Special Characters

Special characters can mean different things to different people. Some will view the German umlaut as a special character, others will have to deal with the UNICODE standard, and still others will just be plagued with how to get greater-than symbols (>) into an HTML document without ending some tag!

The UNICODE standard was devised to handle—hang on for this one!—the encryption/decryption of **every** known language in the world, including hieroglyphics, along with as-yet undefined mappings for undiscovered languages. UNICODE accomplishes this Herculean task by simply allocating 2 bytes per language symbol instead of the ASCII 8 bits or 1 byte. Naturally, your browser needs to be aware of the byte-size change if it is to properly interpret an incoming file.

Many software/hardware combinations will not allow you to enter all UNICODE characters through simple input mechanisms, so SGML offers character-encoding-independent mechanisms for specifying any character from the document character set.

Numeric Character References

Numeric character references specify the integer reference of a UNICODE character. A numeric character reference with the syntax &#D; refers to UNICODE decimal character number D. One with the syntax &#xH; refers to UNICODE hexadecimal character number H. The hexadecimal representation is a new SGML convention and is particularly useful, since character standards generally use hexadecimal representations.

Named Character Reference

A more intuitive approach to character-set references is the HTML *named character reference*. Named character references replace integer references with symbolic names. For example, the named entity å refers to the same UNICODE character as å. A full list of named character entities recognized in HTML 4.0 can be found on the W3C Web site.

Four named character entities deserve special mention, since they are frequently used to escape special characters:

< — *For text appearing as part of the content of an element, you should escape “<” (ASCII decimal 60) as* ***<*** *to avoid possible confusion with the beginning of a tag (start-tag open delimiter).*

& — *The ampersand character “&” (ASCII decimal 38) should be escaped as* ***&*** *to avoid confusion with the beginning of an entity reference (entity-reference open delimiter). You should also escape ampersand within attribute values since entity references are allowed as attribute values.*

> — *In addition, you should escape “>” (ASCII decimal*

*62) as **>** to avoid problems with older user agents that incorrectly perceive this as the end of a tag (tag-close delimiter) when encountering it in quoted attribute values.*

" *Rather than worry about rules for quoting attribute values, its often easier to encode any occurrence of a quotation mark (") with **"** and to use only single-quotes (' . . . ') for quoting attribute values.*

In summary, then:

Use < instead of the less-than (<) sign.

Use & to represent the & sign.

Use > instead of the greater-than (>) sign.

Use " to represent the quotation (") mark

Note, however, that named character references *are* case sensitive. Thus, Å (upper-case A, ring) refers to a different character than does å (lower-case a, ring).

<BASE HREF>

The <BASE> tag identifies the base URL or home reference for the HTML document. Some older browsers do not support the use of <BASE>, although others will use it as the URL for an actual bookmark. The <BASE> home reference URL is important in case the document is moved. Moving the HTML document alters the relative links. A *relative link* is an incomplete file reference lacking any reference to a server and directory/subdirectory path.

Without a <BASE> reference the browser makes the current HTML document location the base and therefore invalidates any relative links. This is particularly aggravating when a mirror site is the author's fixed drive and the computer is not connected to the Internet at the time the browser starts looking for the original. The syntax for a <BASE> home reference looks like this:

```
<BASE HREF=http://myserver.net/mysubdirectory/myfile.html>
```

The HREF attribute is required and must define a fully qualified URL, and the URL must be where the document is located.

<LINK>

The <LINK> tag must be used within a <HEAD> tag and identifies the destination URL named in a hotlink. A <LINK> can identify a point within the same document or the URL of another document. <LINK>s can also identify the current document's relationship with other documents. This document-specific navigation can also define the rendering of specific collections of HTML nodes into the printed documents. This section describes the legal attributes for <LINK>. These are used extensively, in detail, in subsequent chapters.

HREF

The HREF attribute specifies a URL address identifying the hotlinked resource retrieved whenever the user clinks on the link, as in:

```
<HREF="homeURL">
```

ID

The ID attribute allows you to specify a URL named file reference or text as a hypertext link to another document or to another point in the same document.

MEDIA

The MEDIA attribute defines the destination medium–for example, print, screen, speech, projection, Braille, or all.

REL

The REL attribute defines the hotlinked documents type.

REV

The REV attribute specifies the reverse <LINK> relationship:

```
<LINK REV="/base/base.htm">
```

The <LINK REV> tag attribute tells the browser to go to the previous link in the same document.

TARGET

The TARGET attribute determines where the resource will be displayed–for example, user-defined name, _top, _blank, _self, or _parent, as in:

```
<HREF="URL" TARGET="framename">
```

TITLE

The TITLE attribute specifies a referencing title for the linked resource. Historically, the TITLE attribute defined the title of the document named in the link. However, it can also provide a way to place a browser-invisible string of text in the <LINK>.

TYPE

The TYPE attribute defines the Internet content type.

<STYLE>

The <STYLE>...</STYLE> tag pair is one way to use a style sheet in an HTML document. The <STYLE> element has one attribute: TYPE. The LINK element described above imports the style information from a separate style-sheet document, while the <STYLE> tag allows you to suggest a presentation form within the document itself.

This approach has the advantage that there is only one document downloaded, and it also *works* even if the server on which the page resides has not yet been configured to recognize the style-sheet MIME type–which would preclude transferring an external style sheet. The syntax for a document-level style sheet is the same as for external style sheets discussed in Chapter 12. (*Note:* The language used must be given in the TYPE attribute.)

<ISINDEX>

The <ISINDEX> tag dates back to the original days of HTML, when it addressed the need for searching an HTML document. The <ISINDEX> tag caused the browser to present a default prompt symbol, where the user would enter keywords that would be sent to the server. The server would execute a search and transmit the results back to the user. If the server did not have a search engine that could handle <ISINDEX>, it simply failed. HTML evolved to include a PROMPT attribute which allowed the author of the HTML document to define a user prompt. Since <ISINDEX> requires a server-side search-engine capability, it has fallen into disuse. HTML 4's equivalent uses forms and CGI (discussed in later chapters).

Lang

You add the LANG attribute to specify the language content of your <BODY> The syntax is straightforward:

```
lang = language-code
```

White space is not allowed within the language code. All language codes are case insensitive. The default language is "unknown." Language information can be used to control rendering of a marked-up document in a variety of ways–for example, properly launching a language-specific search engine, selecting the proper typographical glyph for proper font displays, or making sure you use the correct spell-checker dictionary and grammar rules.

The LANG attribute's value is a language code that identifies a natural language spoken, written, or otherwise conveyed by human beings to communicate information to other human beings. Computer languages are explicitly excluded from language codes. These codes consist of a primary code and a possibly empty series of subcodes, as in:

```
language-code = primary-code *( "-" subcode )
```

An example of a language code is "en": English, more specifically "en-US", or the English derivation "en-cockney". Here's another example: "i-cherokee": the Cherokee language spoken by some Native Americans. Two-letter primary codes are reserved for language abbreviations. Two-letter codes include fr (French), de (German), it (Italian), nl (Dutch), el (Greek), es (Spanish), pt (Portuguese), ar (Arabic), he (Hebrew), ru (Russian), zh (Chinese), ja (Japanese), hi (Hindi), ur (Urdu), and sa (Sanskrit). Any two-letter subcode is understood to be a country code.

An element inherits language-code information according to the following order of precedence (highest to lowest). First, with highest precedence, is the LANG attribute set for the element itself followed by the closest parent element that has the LANG attribute set (i.e., the LANG attribute is inherited).

In the following example, the primary language of the document is German ("de"). One paragraph is declared to be in French ("fr"), with an embedded Japanese ("ja") phrase, after which the primary language returns to French:

```
<HTML lang="de">
<BODY>
...German lang here ...
<P lang="fr">...French lang here...
<P>...Interpreted as French again...
<P>...French text interrupted by<EM lang="ja">some
      Japanese</EM>French begins here again...
</BODY>
</HTML>
```

Dir

The dir directive defines the direction, left-to-right or right-to-left, in which the text is processed. The dir element has two attributes: LTR (Left-To-Right) and RTL (Right-To-Left), as in:

```
dir = LTR
```

or

```
dir = RTL
```

Besides specifying the primary language of a document, authors may need to specify the base direction of pieces of text or of the text in the entire document. For example, to insert Hebrew text within an HTML document you would enter the following text:

```
<Q lang="he" dir="rtl">...insert Hebrew phrase here...</Q>
```

In the absence of local overrides, the base direction is inherited from enclosing elements.

<SCRIPT>

The <SCRIPT> </SCRIPT> tag pair marks that portion of an HTML document containing a script-language program, such as VBScript or JavaScript. There must be a start <SCRIPT> tag and an end </SCRIPT> tag, with the script sandwiched between. A main advantage of scripts over CGI, both of which allow for considerable interactive Web page content, is that scripts process on the user's computer instead of on the CGI-based server counterpart. Even more important, the user-processed scripts provide dynamic Web page content even if the server does not support CGI.

HTML documents may contain more than one <SCRIPT> element, and they can be located in the <BODY> as well as in the <HEAD> tag pairs. Scripts are very powerful; they can even allow a document to be modified as it is being parsed–generating, for example, a user-specific index. Great care is needed in designing these types of scripts, as well as testing them to make sure they have consistent and predictable results on the various browsers.

Since scripting languages are not universally understood, some browsers do not recognize any of them. Older browsers will display actual contents of the script, if it is not enclosed even further within a comment block. And should the script contain HTML-specific delimiters such as > or –, look out! Some browsers view these symbols as the end of the comment, resulting in the display of whatever follows within the HTML script. To make certain a browser does not misinterpret a nonrecognized <SCRIPT> element, place the script within a comment, as in:

```
<SCRIPT TYPE="text/javascript">
<!-- beginning of comment block which hides the
script from
      unfriendly browsers
      ...script goes here...
-->
</SCRIPT>
```

The <SCRIPT> tag has three attributes: LANGUAGE, SRC, and TYPE. Changes in the standard from HTML 3.2 to HTML 4.0 wean HTML programmers from the older LANGUAGE attribute in place of the newer TYPE specification. Table 4–3 lists the mark-up tags that can use the <SCRIPT>...</SCRIPT> tags:

Table 4–3: *Mark-up tags that use <SCRIPT>...</SCRIPT>*

<A>	<ADDRESS>	<B>	<BIG>
<BLOCKQUOTE>	<BODY>	<CAPTION>	<CENTER>
<CITE>	<CODE>	<DD>	<DFN>
<DIV>	<DT>	<EM>	<FIELDSET>
<FONT>	<FORM>	<H*>	<HEAD>
<I>	<KBD>	<LABEL>	<LI>
<OBJECT>	<P>	<PRE>	<S>
<SAMP>	<SMALL>	<SPAN>	<STRONG>
<SUB>	<SUP>	<TD>	<TEXTFLOW>
<TH>	<TT>	<U>	<VAR>

LANGUAGE

See the <SCRIPT TYPE="type/scriptlang"> attribute below, which replaces the older <SCRIPT LANGUAGE="scriptlang"> attribute.

SRC

The SRC attribute occurs in the form <SCRIPT SRC="URL">, whcrc URL routes the server to the specified plain-text script code file. An example statement would look like this:

```
<SCRIPT SRC="./Jscripts/AJScript.js"
TYPE="text/javascript"> </SCRIPT>
```

TYPE

Beginning with HTML 4, <SCRIPT> tags use the TYPE attribute instead of the LANGUAGE attribute to define the type of file and its associated language. The syntax for TYPE is:

```
<SCRIPT TYPE="typefile/scriptlang"> </SCRIPT>
```

See the SRC attribute for an example of a complete <SCRIPT> element definition. For reference purposes only, the older LANGUAGE attribute was used in the following syntax:

```
<SCRIPT LANGUAGE="VBScript"> </SCRIPT>
```

ONLOAD

The ONLOAD event attribute may be used with <BODY> and <FRAMESET> elements and is triggered whenever the user finishes loading a window or all frames within a <FRAMESET>.

```
onload = script
```

ONUNLOAD

The ONUNLOAD event attribute may be used with <BODY> and <FRAMESET> elements and is triggered whenever the user removes a document from a window or frame.

```
onunload = script
```

<NOSCRIPT>

The <NOSCRIPT>...</NOSCRIPT> tag pair marks the alternate route for browsers incapable of interpreting <SCRIPT>-language documents. In order to provide content to users of browsers that do not support scripts or that have script support turned off for security purposes, authors should never use the <SCRIPT> element as the sole element of a page without also using <NOSCRIPT>.

<META>

The <META> tag is used to indicate special instructions for the client browser or a server performing a parsing operation. Other text can be included to define the date of creation and so on. Search engines may post information specified by the <META> tag. This section describes the two <META> attributes HTTP-EQUIV and NAME.

HTTP-EQUIV

The <META> tag itself is placed within the <HEAD> in an HTML document and must include the CONTENT attribute. It should also contain either the NAME or HTTP-EQUIV attribute, as in:

```
<META HTTP-EQUIV="REFRESH" CONTENT="3;
URL=HTTP://www.server.net/index.html>
```

You use the NAME attribute whenever an HTML document is to be interpreted by the browser and use the HTTP-EQUIV attribute when interpretation is done on the server end. HTTP-EQUIV directs the browser to make requests of the server in order to execute various HTTP functions within the capabilities of the client. REFRESH is just one value that directs the client to repost the URL named, or the current document if no URL is present–in the example above, after 3 seconds.

This next example uses the HTTP-EQUIV attribute to ensure that when a page is reloaded, after the specified expiration date, it is reloaded from the server instead of a cached copy, guaranteeing the latest edition:

```
<META HTTP-EQUIV="Expires" CONTENT="Mon, 12 Dec 1997
16:23:00 GMT">
```

<META> information can make your information more accessible to spiders and robots for automatic indexing, and more accessible to other programs that you might use to help you manage an HTML document collection.

NAME

Some search engines will describe your site from the first few sentences on the index page. A search engine that is indexing a page with

```
<META NAME="keywords" CONTENT="SCUBA, Diving, Bahamas">
```

would use the words contained within the content to index the page. This is more precise, guaranteeing more direct hits to your site.

If you prefer, you can use the CONTENT attribute to specify the description instead, as in:

```
<META NAME:"description" CONTENT="This site is dedi-
cated to all those dry SCUBA Divers who wish they
were wet in the Bahamas right now!"
```

UNIVERSAL ATTRIBUTES

Any text block–for example, the text between <H1> and </H1> tags–is a candidate for dynamically changing text styles. Simply include the ID, the CLASS, and an event-name attribute. These are described next.

ID

```
ID = AnElementName
```

The ID attribute assigns a documentwide name to a specific instance of an element. Values for ID must be unique within a document. Furthermore, this attribute shares the same name space as the name attribute.

CLASS

```
CLASS = ElementInstance
```

This attribute assigns a CLASS or set of CLASSes to a specific instance of an element. Any number of elements may be assigned the same CLASS name. All CLASS names must be separated by at least one blank. *AnElementName* specified by ID must be unique within a document. *ElementInstance* specified by CLASS may be shared by several element instances.

Class values should be chosen to distinguish the role of the element the class is associated with–e.g., comment, sample, error. These attributes can be used in the following ways:

- The ID attribute may be used as a destination for hypertext.
- Scripts can use the ID attribute to reference a particular element.
- Style sheets can use the ID attribute to apply a style to a particular element.
- The ID attribute can be used to identify OBJECT element declarations.

Style sheets can use the CLASS attribute to apply a style to a set of elements associated with this CLASS or to elements that occur as the children of such elements. Both ID and CLASS can be used for further processing purposes–e.g., for identifying fields when extracting data from HTML pages into a database, translating HTML documents into other formats, and so on

Almost every HTML element may be assigned ID and CLASS information. Suppose, for example, that we are writing a document about Web page design. The document is to include a number of preformatted code samples. We use the FRMT element to format the code samples. We also assign a background color (blue) to all instances of the FRMT element belonging to the class "codesamp."

```
<HEAD>
<STYLE
FRMT.codesamp { background : blue }
</STYLE
</HEAD>
<BODY>
<FRMT CLASS="codesamp" ID="First Section">
...formatted code section goes here...
</FRMT>
</BODY>
```

By setting the ID attribute for this example, we can (1) create a hyperlink to it and (2) override CLASS style information with instance style information. Chapter 12 is dedicated exclusively to understanding HTML styles.

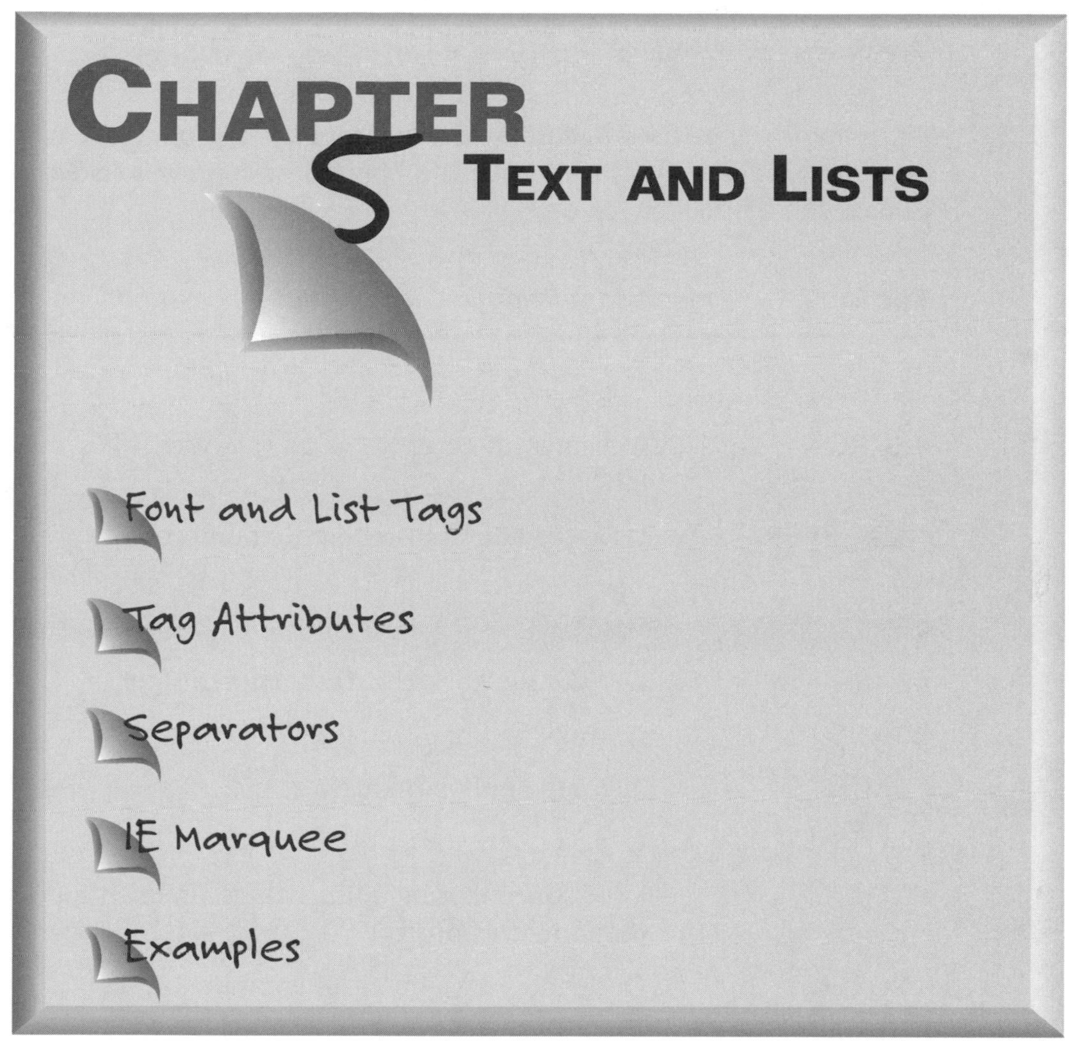

Introduction

The idea behind any well-designed Web page is to, ***convey information!*** One way to create drama and interest and to focus a reader's attention is by enhancing the rendered text–varying the font face, size, and position and using **BOLD**, underline, and *italic*. And since most Web sites are logically related collections of Web pages, an efficient way to convey this relationship is to use lists. The examples in this chapter illustrate thc rendering of some of the textual mark-up elements and list features. You'll see how these tags are used with the various attribute options available to the developer.

This Chapter's HTML Tags

Thirty-two tags are used in conjunction with a basic introductory Web page design. Each tag, together with a short description, is listed in Table 5–1.

Table 5–1: *New tags relating to font characteristics and lists*

<ABBR>	Logically flags an abbreviation
<ACRONYM>	Indicates an acronym (e.g., WWW, HTTP, URL, etc.)
<ADDRESS>	Used for address (frequently rendered as italics)
<B>	Bold
<BASEFONT>	Defines the base HTML document font
<BIG>	Outputs text one size larger
<BLINK>	Netscape only blinking text
<CITE>	Cites a reference or other source
<CODE>	Used for rendering code listings (frequently rendered as Courier)
<CODE>	Designates a fragment of computer code
<DFN>	Indicates that this is the defining instance of the enclosed term
<DFN>	Defining instance of the enclosed term
<EM>	Indicates emphasis
<FONT>	Changes font face, size, and type
<Hn>	Headings
<HR>	Creates a horizontal rule
<I>	Italics
<KBD>	Indicates text to be entered by the user

Table 5–1: *New tags relating to font characteristics and lists (continued)*

<MARQUEE>	Internet Explorer scrolling text
<OL>	Ordered list
<PERSON>	Marks a name for indexing purposes
<Q>	Used for inline quotations
<S>	Strikeout
<SAMP>	Designates sample output from programs, scripts, etc.
<SMALL>	Outputs text one size smaller
<STRONG>	Indicates stronger emphasis
<SUB>	Used for subscripting
<SUP>	Used for superscripting
<TT>	Tele-Typewriter
<U>	Underline
<UL>	Unordered list
<VAR>	Indicates an instance of a variable or program argument

<EM> and <STRONG> are useful in general to indicate emphasis. The other phrasal elements have particular significance in technical documents.

White Space

Since the big brother to HTML, SGML, has a rather unique parsing convention when it comes to the topic of white space, itís worth taking a closer look. SGML discriminates between statement start characters, or line feeds, and statement end characters, or carriage returns. Some architectures use just carriage returns, some just line feeds, and others carriage-return/line-feed pairs for line breaks. You should consider single carriage returns, single line feeds, and carriage-return/line-feed pairs to be single line breaks.

HTML always ignores any line break occurring right after a start tag and any line break right before an end tag. This applies to all HTML elements. With the exception of the PRE element, all leading white-space characters (multiple spaces, horizontal tabs, form feeds and line breaks) following the start tag are always ignored. Multiples of white-space characters are always replaced by a single space. Using the above rendering syntax, the following four examples are rendered identically:

```
<P>
Example highlighting white space and line break parsing.
</P>
```

or

```
<P>
  Example highlighting white space and line break
parsing.
</P>
```

or

```
<P>Example highlighting white space and line break
parsing.</P>
```

or

```
<P>Example    highlighting white space and line break
parsing.</P>
```

The notion of what white space is varies from one language to another. The rule is to collapse white space in script-sensitive ways. For example, in Latin scripts, a single white space is just a space–ASCII decimal 32; in Thai it is a zero-width word separator; and in Chinese a white space is ignored entirely.

These rules can be applied constructively to allow you to use white space to your advantage–for example, to clarify your HTML source with additional white space that will not be rendered by the browser. Consider, for instance, the following HTML document:

```
<P>
This example shows left justification of a paragraph
and a list, with no extra line-spacing for clarity to
the human reader.
</P>
<UL>

<LI>
This is <EM>ITEM 1</EM> .
</LI>
<LI>
This is <EM>ITEM 2second</EM> .
</LI>
</UL>
```

Omitting end tags and using less white space makes the next example easier for a human to understand, yet it is rendered identically by the browser.

```
<P>This example shows a more meaningful HTML document
   format for a paragraph and a list.
<UL>
  <LI>This is <EM>ITEM 1</EM> .
  <LI>This is <EM>ITEM 2</EM> .
</UL>
```

Logical Text Tags

Previous chapters demonstrated several basic page elements and links. With this background, you are now ready to learn more about what HTML can do in terms of text formatting and layout. Table 5-2 describes most of the remaining tags in HTML that you'll need to know to construct your Web page.

Table 5–2: *Text-formatting tags*

<ABBR>	Logically flags an abbreviation
<ACRONYM>	Logically flags an acronym
<ADDRESS>	Used for addresses (frequently rendered as italic). Addresses are often rendered, indented, on their own lines.
<BIG>	Outputs text one size larger
<CITE>	Used for quotations (frequently rendered as italics)
<CODE>	Used for rendering code listings (frequently rendered as Courier)
<EM>	Used for emphasis (frequently rendered as italics)
<Hn>	Headings
<KBD>	Used to represent user keyboard-entry key sequences (frequently rendered as Courier)
<PERSON>	Marks a name for indexing purposes
<Q>	Used for inline quotations
<SAMP>	Used for rendering sample text (frequently rendered as Courier)
<SMALL>	Outputs text one size smaller
<STRONG>	Strong (frequently rendered as bold)
<SUB>	Used for subscripting
<SUP>	Used for superscripting
<VAR>	Defines a variable name (frequently rendered in italic)

Most of the text formatting tags are self-evident. <ACRONYM>, though, needs a little clarification. <ACRONYM> allows authors to clearly indicate a sequence of characters that compose an acronym–for example, "WWW", "NASA", "IRS", and so on. <ACRONYM>s are useful to spell checkers, speech synthesizers, and other browser tools. The content of the <ACRONYM> element defines the acronym itself; often it is used in conjunction with a TITLE attribute to provide the text to which the acronym expands. Here are some sample acronym definitions:

```
<ACRONYM TITLE="World Wide Web">WWW</ACRONYM>
```

The following HTML document uses all of the tags listed in Table 5-2. Figures 5-1(a) and 5-1(b) highlight their various effects:

```
<HTML><HEAD>
<TITLE>Example demonstrating Structured Text.</TITLE>
</HEAD>
<BODY>
<P><H1>Program Demonstrates Structured Text Options</H1></P>
<P>The EM tag <EM>italicizes</EM> text.</P>
<P>The STRONG tag <STRONG>BOLDS</STRONG> text.</P>
<P>The ADDRESS tag formats <ADDRESS>1 Main Street</ADDRESS>.</P>
<P>Putting a <CITE>citation</CITE> within a sentence.</P>
<P>Inserting <CODE>code</CODE> fonts.</P>
<P><SAMP>Sample</SAMPLE> looks similar.</P>
<P>Press <KBD>Enter</KBD> to continue.</P>
<P>Making text <BIG>BIGGER</BIG>.</P>
<P>Making text <SMALL>small</SMALL>.</P>
<P>Lifting things<SUP>up</SUP> a bit.</P>
<P>Dropping them <SUB>down</SUB> a little.</P>
<P>World Wide-Web = <ABBREV>WWW</ABBREV>.</P>
<P><ACRONYM>Acronym</ACRONYM>.</P>
<P><PERSON>Smith,John</PERSON> name indexing.</P>
<P>Please <Q>quote me</Q>.</P>
<P>This is a <VAR>variable</VAR> name.</P>
</BODY>
</HTML>
```

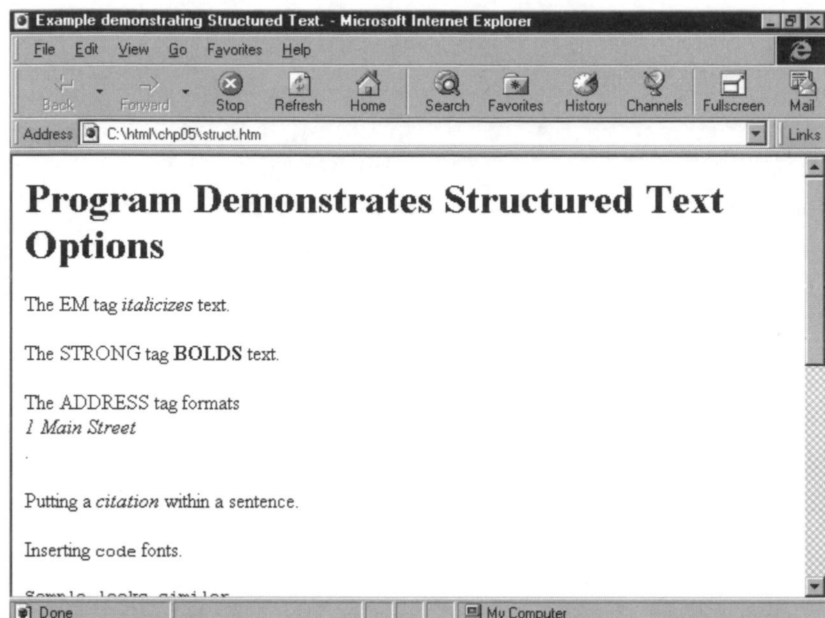

Figure 5–1(a): *Rendered text-formatting attributes*

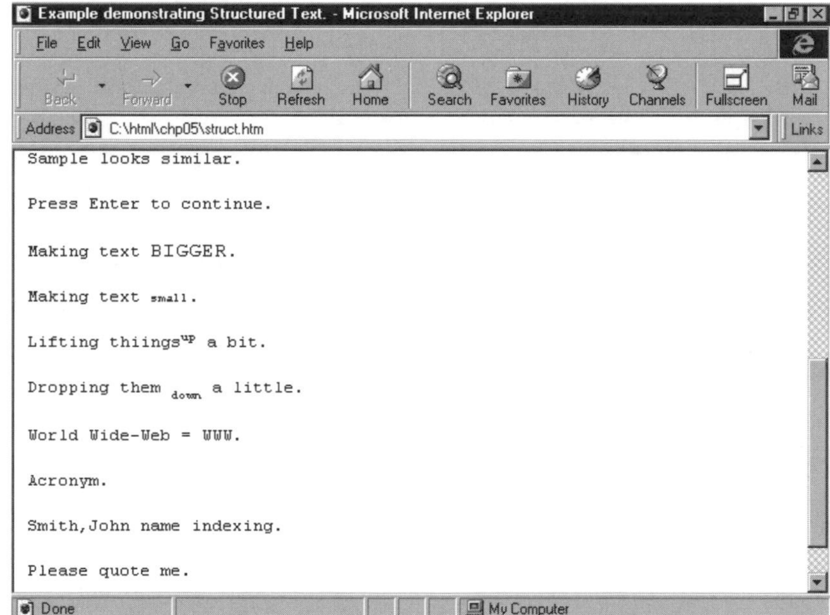

Figure 5–1(b): *Continuation of rendered Figure 5–1(a)*

Physical Text Tags

HTML defines an additional set of tags, some which overlap the logical tags previously defined, for detailing how text is rendered. Table 5–3 lists the physical tag styles available in most popular browsers. (*Note:* <BLINK> is currently available to Netscape browsers only.)

Table 5–3: *Physical tags*

<B>	Bold
<I>	Italics
<U>	Underline
<TT>	Tele-Typewriter
<S>	Strikeout
<DFN>	Definition
<BLINK>	Netscape (simply ignored by other browsers)

The following HTML document, rendered in Figure 5–2, demonstrates how to use physical tags.

```
<HTML><HEAD>
<TITLE>Physical Tags Example</TITLE>
</HEAD>
<BODY>
<P>This is a <B>BOLD</B> word.</P>
<P>This statement uses italics for <I>emphasis.</I></P>
<P><U>This line is completely underlined.</U></P>
<P><TT>Now, U.S. News and World Report, reports...</TT></P>
<P>Parts of this line are <S>struck-out.</S></P>
<P>This line contains a <DFN>Definition.</DFN></P>
<P>This is a Netscape <BLINK>blinker</BLINK>!</P>
<P></P>
</BODY>
</HTML>
```

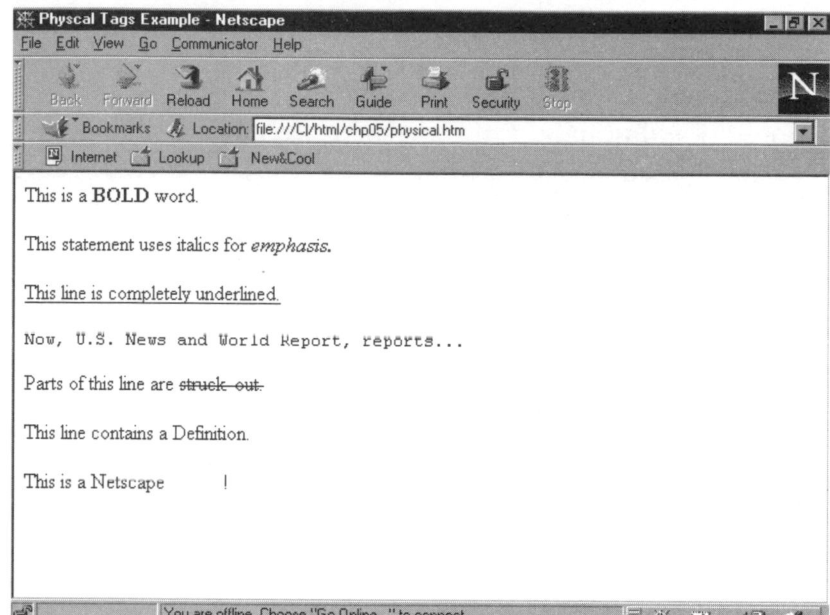

Figure 5–2: *Netscape rendering of physical tag BLINK (hint: it's flashing)!*

Text Formatting

Does anyone remember the days when source code was entered in all CAPITAL LETTERS? Those days are long gone. Nowadays, *everybody* needs to be a typesetter! Even MiXeD CaSe, **BOLD**, *italics*, and underline are no longer visually interesting enough to hold a reader's eye. HTML defines tags that allow you to select a text's font face, color, size, and alignment. This section completes your introduction to Web-page typesetting fundamentals.

Alignment

Three types of alignment are associated with the ALIGN tag: LEFT, CENTER, and RIGHT. The following HTML document, rendered in Figure 5–3, details these options:

```
<HTML>
<HEAD>
<TITLE>Paragraph Alignment: LEFT, CENTER, and RIGHT</TITLE>
</HEAD>
<BODY>
<P ALIGN=LEFT>
LEFT alignment
</P
<P ALIGN=CENTER>
CENTER alignment.
</P>
<P ALIGN-RIGHT>
RIGHT alignment.
</P>
</BODY>
</HTML>
```

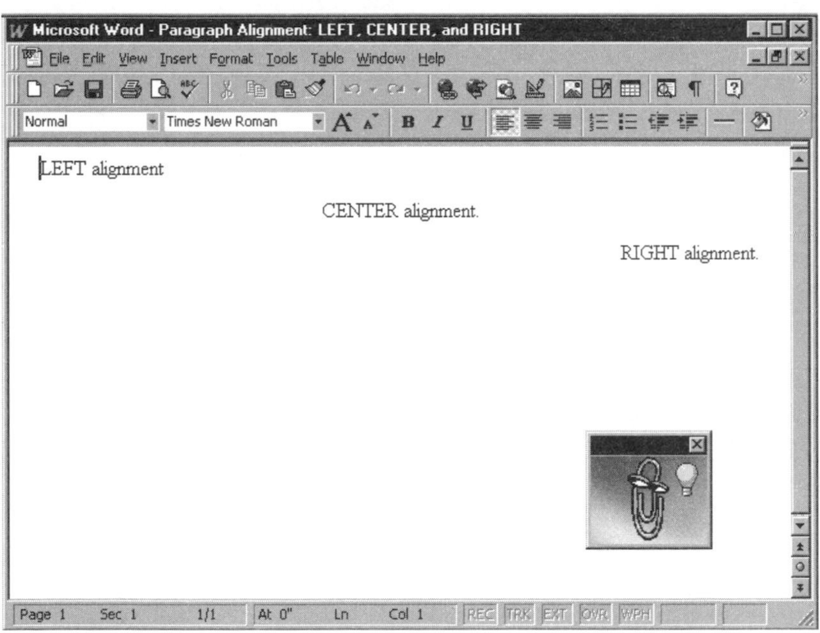

Figure 5–3: *LEFT, CENTER, and RIGHT alignment*

Additional Line Breaks

To add additional line spacing between paragraphs you use the <BR> tag. You should *not* use multiple <P> </P> tag pairs, since by definition a paragraph cannot be empty. Browsers treat multiple paragraph tags in different ways: they may either ignore all but the first tag, insert the extra spaces, or flag the use as an invalid HTML tag. Adding multiple breaks is as simple as adding the following statements within the <BODY> of your HTML document:

```
<BR> <BR> <BR> <BR>
```

CLEAR

The CLEAR attribute is associated with the <BR> tag and allows you to define the textwrapping options around an image. CLEAR forces the browser to render text below the image to the LEFT, CENTER, or first clear RIGHT margin. The syntax for CLEAR is:

```
<BR CLEAR=LEFT | CENTER | RIGHT>
```

<FONT>

The <FONT> </FONT> tag pair allows you to use specific fonts and colors in your pages, just as you can in a printed document. This is accomplished using the <FONT> tag and one of its two attributes, SIZE and COLOR. Some browsers also support a FACE attribute, which is used to specify one or more typefaces to use for the selection. Most browsers allow users to override these settings, so don't count on them to convey content.

SIZE

The SIZE attribute defines the specific or relative size of the contents of the tag. The size is expressed as an integer value from 1 to 7 (the default is 3) or as a relative value from –6 to +6. If a relative value is used, it is added to the current setting for <BASEFONT> (see below). The specific values 1 to 7 render inversely to <H1> through <H6>. Where <H1> is the largest font size, the specific value 1, is the smallest font size. The syntax is:

```
<FONT SIZE=value>… text goes here …</FONT>
```

The following program, rendered in Figure 5–4, uses specific values:

```
<HTML><HEAD><TITLE>Example of FONT SIZE attributes</TITLE>
</HEAD>
<BODY>
<P> <FONT SIZE=1>
Example SIZE = 1
</FONT></P>
<P> <FONT SIZE=2>
Example SIZE = 2
</FONT></P>
<P> <FONT SIZE=3>
Example SIZE = 3
</FONT></P>
<P> <FONT SIZE=4>
Example SIZE = 4
</FONT></P>
<P> <FONT SIZE=5>
Example SIZE = 5
</FONT></P>
<P> <FONT SIZE=6>
Example SIZE = 6
</FONT></P>
<P> <FONT SIZE=7>
Example SIZE = 7
</FONT></P>
</BODY>
</HTML>
```

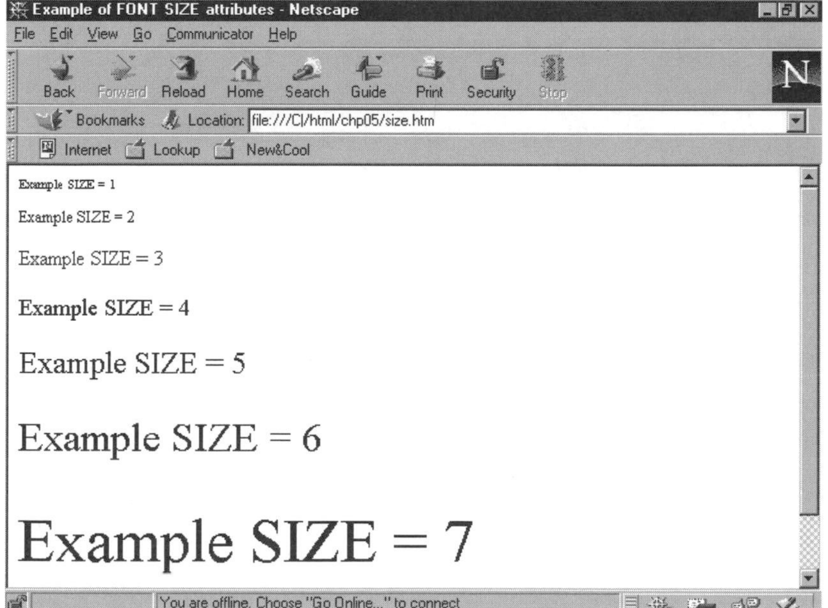

Figure 5–4: *Setting a font's SIZE attribute*

Color

The COLOR attribute defines the color of the text being rendered. There are three forms of color description: a color's name, its hexadecimal value, or an RGB value (described in Chapter 3). The syntax looks like this:

```
<FONT COLOR="BLUE"…text goes here…</FONT>
```

Face

The FACE attribute, an extension to HTML 3.2 also, is supported by most popular browsers. FACE allows you to specify a list of fonts. Whenever the first font specified isn't found, the second one is tried, and so on. If none of the selected fonts exist on the user's system, the default font is used. A sample, rendered in Figure 5–5, looks like this:

```
<HTML>
<HEAD>
<TITLE>Example of FONT FACES</TITLE>
</HEAD>
<BODY>
<P>This is the default font.</P><P> <FONT FACE="arial">
This string is output in arial instead of the default
font.</FONT></P></P></BODY></HTML>
```

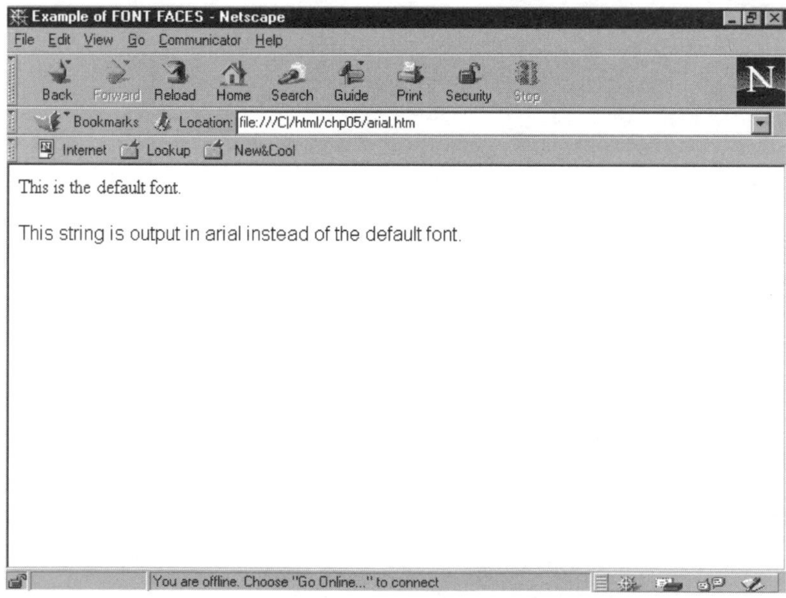

Figure 5–5: *Changing the font's FACE attribute*

<BASEFONT>

You use the <BASEFONT> without a end tag to set the default font size for all text that follows in a document. The default <BASEFONT> size is 3. If a <FONT> </FONT> tag pair is found after the <BASEFONT> setting, the newer <FONT> value is in effect until the closing tag, as seen in the following example (rendered in Figure 5–6):

```
<HTML><HEAD><TITLE>Example of FONT and BASEFONT
</TITLE></HEAD><BODY>
<FONT BASEFONT=0>
<P>This is the BASEFONT of 0.</P><P> <FONT SIZE=7>
This string is output in FONT SIZE 7.</FONT></P>
<P>This text once again defaults to the BASEFONT of 0.
</P></BODY></HTML>
```

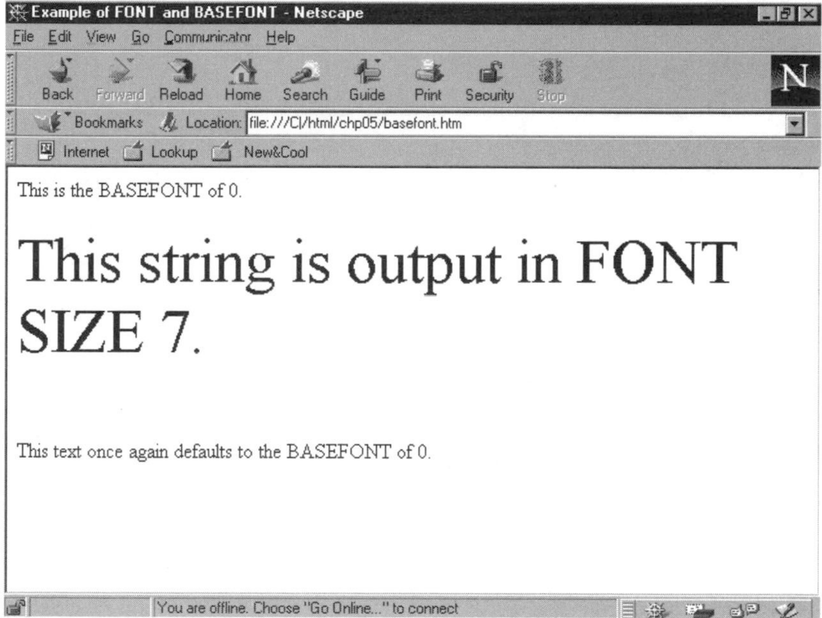

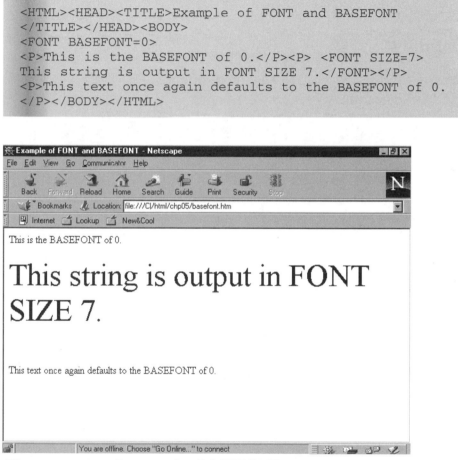

Figure 5–6: *Setting the BASEFONT attribute*

With <BASEFONT> you can use the "relative" version of <FONT SIZE=n>, supplying positive or negative integer values to proportion the rendering to the base font, as in:

```
<BASEFONT SIZE=5>
<P>…text goes here…</P>
<P><FONT SIZE=-2>…two sizes smaller than base font…</P>
<P><FONT SIZE=+1>…one size larger than base font…</P>
```

Visual Bar Separators

One easy-to-apply visual demarcation is known as a *horizontal rule* or *visual separator bar*. This section describes horizontal-rule attributes and is followed by an example HTML document using the various options.

Alignment

Horizontal rules have three alignment options: LEFT, CENTER, and RIGHT. For example:

```
<HR ALIGNMENT=LEFT>
```

Size

You use the SIZE attribute to set the height of the separator, as in:

```
<HR SIZE=5>
```

Width

The WIDTH attribute defines the width of the rule in number of pixels. Calculating this ahead of time for all output display formats can become quite difficult. A simple approach is to use the percent modifier, as in:

```
<HR WIDTH=75%>
```

Color

Though it is not a formal part of the HTML definition, most popular browsers accept a color attribute in an RGB format, as in:

```
<HR COLOR="#RRGGBB">
```

Shading

Normally horizontal rules render with a three-dimensional image. Depending on background colors, such rules can be difficult to see, and for this reason there is a NOSHADE attribute. The syntax looks like this:

```
<HR NOSHADE>
<HTML><HEAD>
<TITLE>Example demonstrating horizontal rule
options.</TITLE>
</HEAD>
<BODY>
<P>This is a fifty-percent rule.</P>
<P><HR WIDTH=50%></P>
<P>This is a fifty-percent rule, RIGHT aligned.</P>
<P><HR WIDTH=50% ALIGN=RIGHT></P>
<P>This is a 10 pixel rule, default width.</P>
<P><HR SIZE=10></P>
<P>This rule is the same except for the NOSHADE.</P>
<P><HR SIZE=10 NOSHADE></P>
</BODY>
</HTML>
```

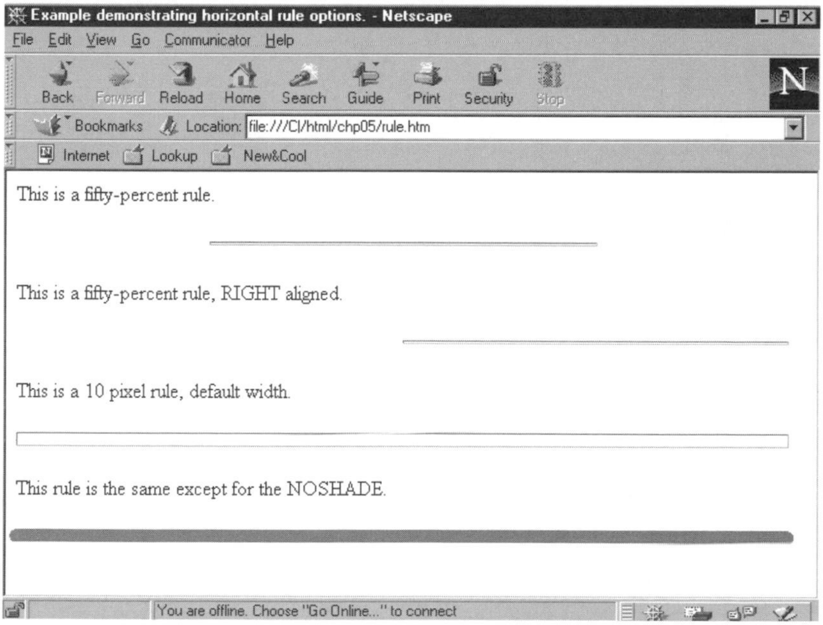

Figure 5–7: *Using the <HR> horizontal-rule element*

List Control

Structured lists allow you to quickly hit the high points of a subject, whether to show the hierarchy of information presented on a Web site's hotlinked pages or to describe your personal interests. There are three types of lists: (1) unordered or bulleted, (2) ordered, and (3) a special category for generating a list of defining terms.

Unordered

You use the <UL>, </UL> tag pair to delimit an unordered bulleted list. You use the <LI> and optional </LI> tags to define list items. When using the <UL>, </UL> tags for unordered, bulleted lists, you can select the type of bullet by using one of the following three attributes: CIRCLE, DISC, SQUARE, as rendered in Figure 5-8.

```
<HTML><HEAD>
<TITLE>Unordered List Bullet Options Example</TITLE>
</HEAD>
<BODY>
<LH>Unordered List Bullet Types.</LH>
<UL TYPE=DISC>
<LI>DISC bullet.
<UL TYPE=SQUARE>
<LI>SQUARE bullet.
<UL TYPE=CIRCLE>
<LI>CIRCLE bullet.
</UL>
</BODY>
</HTML>
```

Ordered

You use the <OL>, </OL> tag pair to delimit a numbered ordered list, along with <LI> and </LI> as above, with the addition of the attributes listed in Table 5-4.

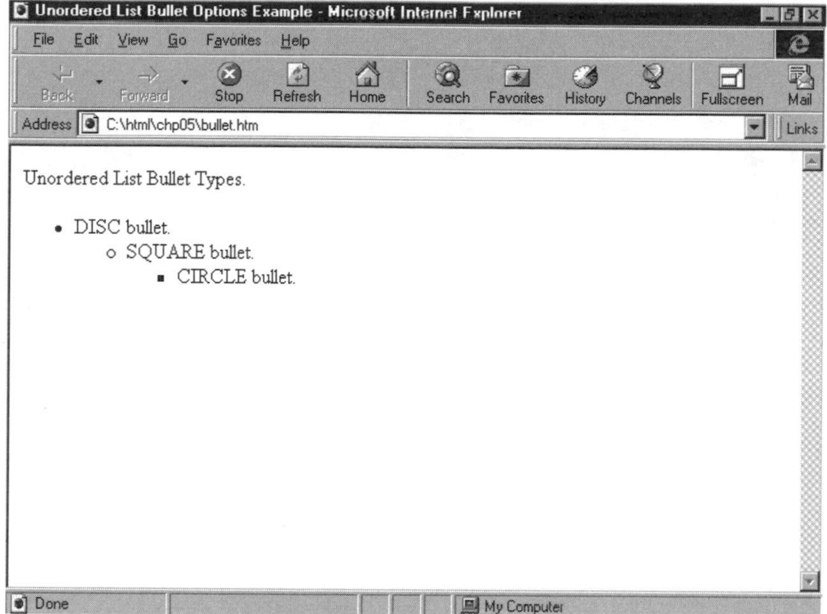

Figure 5–8: *Bulleted-list options*

Table 5–4: *Ordered-list attributes*

1	Arabic numerals–this is the default mode
A	All capital letters
a	All small letters
I	Large Roman numerals
i	Small Roman numerals

The following example demonstrates how you could use these options to generate a meaningful outline format. See Figure 5–9 for the rendered results.

```
<HTML><HEAD>
<TITLE>Ordered List Example</TITLE>
</HEAD>
<BODY>
<LH>Generating an Outline Format</LH>
<OL TYPE=I>
<LI>Large Roman Numeral Item
<OL TYPE=A>
<LI>Capital Letter Item
<OL TYPE=1>
<LI>Arabic Item
<OL TYPE=a>
<LI>Small Letter Item
<OL TYPE=i>
<LI>Small Roman Numeral Item
</OL>
</BODY>
</HTML>
```

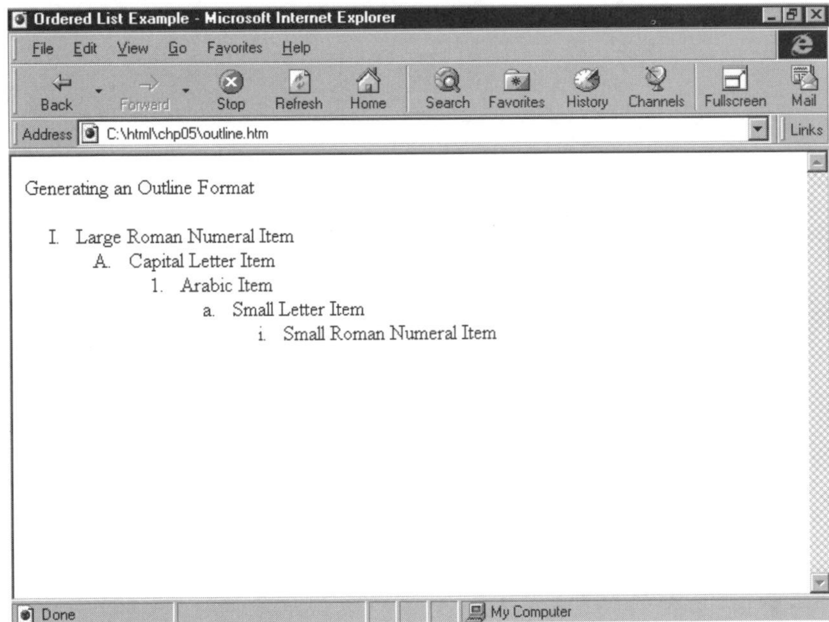

Figure 5–9: *Ordered list used to create an outline format*

Dictionary Tables

When you want to add a definition list with associated descriptions for each list item, use the <DL>, </DL> definition-list tag pair (see

Figure 5–10). Associated with the <DL>, </DL> pair are <DT> (used for the defining term) and <DD> (used for the defining description). These last two tags do *not* have end-tag counterparts.

```
<HTML><HEAD>
<TITLE>Definition List Example</TITLE>
</HEAD>
<BODY>
<DL>
<DT>TERM 1
<DD>TERM 1 definition here.
<DT>TERM 2
<DD>TERM 2 definition here.
<DT>TERM 3
<DD>TERM 3 definition here.
</BODY>
</HTML>
```

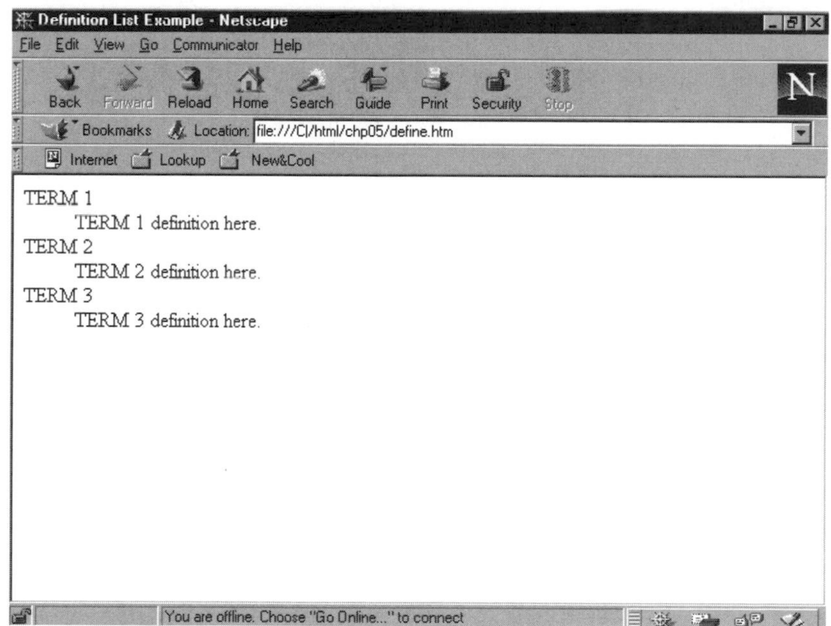

Figure 5–10: *Definition-list example*

Nested Lists

Lists can easily contain items that are in themselves lists, as in the following example (rendered in Figure 5–11):

```
<HTML><HEAD>
<TITLE>Nesting Lists Example</TITLE>
</HEAD>
<BODY>
<LH>Nested Lists Example.</LH>
<UL TYPE=DISC>
<LI>LEVEL 1 ITEM.
<UL TYPE=SQUARE>
<LI>Level 2 item.
<LI>Level 2 item.
<LI>Level 2 item.
</UL>
<LI>LEVEL 1 ITEM.
<LI>LEVEL 1 ITEM.
</UL>
</BODY>
</HTML>
```

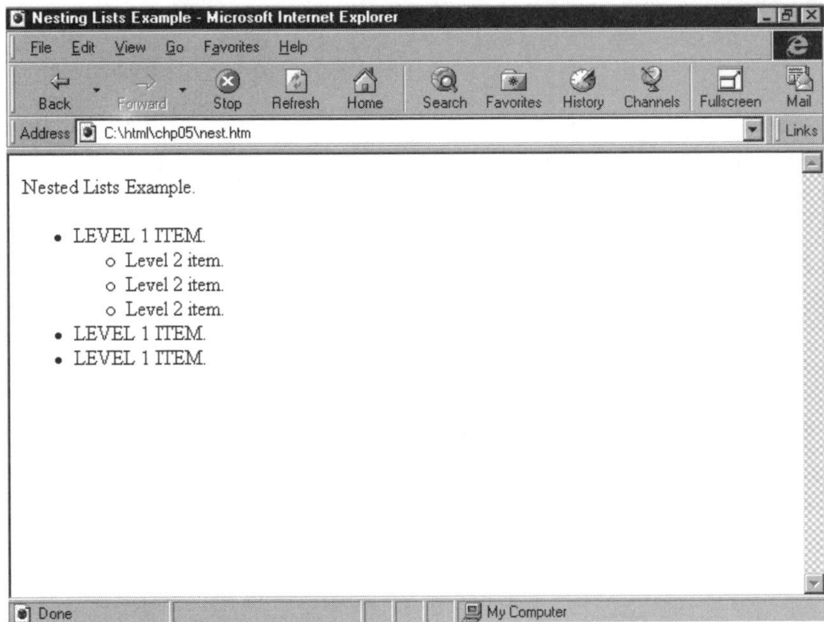

Figure 5–11: *Nested-list example*

<MARQUEE> (Internet Explorer)

Welcome to New York's Times Square and the Stock Exchange. With Microsoft's Internet Explorer <MARQUEE>, </MARQUEE> tags you can add a scrolling marquee to your own Web page! The attributes described below fine-tune <MARQUEE>'s behavior.

ALIGN

Marquees may be aligned with the TOP, MIDDLE, or BOTTOM of the surrounding text. The syntax looks like this:

```
ALIGN=TOP | MIDDLE | BOTTOM
```

BEHAVIOR

Movement within the marquee is defined by the BEHAVIOR type. Options include SCROLL, SLIDE, and ALTERNATE. The default BEHAVIOR is SCROLL, which begins with no marquee text visible, then scrolls the text across the screen and completely off. SLIDE also starts with no visible marquee text, begins to scroll onto the screen, stops when the message is still visibly displayed, and then begins the sequence over again. ALTERNATE is reminiscent of electronic pong, with the marquee text bouncing back and forth within the marquee area. The syntax looks like this:

```
BEHAVIOR=SCROLL | SLIDE | ALTERNATE
```

BGCOLOR

BGCOLOR uses the now familiar RGB color format to define the marquee's text background color, as in:

```
BGCOLOR="#RRGGBB"
```

DIRECTION

Marquee text can be scrolled to the LEFT or RIGHT with the DIRECTION attribute, as in:

```
DIRECTION=LEFT | RIGHT
```

HEIGHT

Setting the marquee's height is simple using the HEIGHT attribute and units in pixels. The syntax looks like this:

```
HEIGHT=number_of_pixels
```

HSPACE

HSPACE uses a number-of-pixels definition for the marquee's left and right margins. Identical values are used for both margins, as in:

```
HSPACE=number_of_pixels
```

LOOP

Boring, boring, boring–yes, a continuously scrolling marquee is like watching someone else's home birthday-party videos for the tenth time! The LOOP attribute sets a limit to how many times the end user is visually planed by the bouncing ribbon text. Note, however, that there is an unrecommended option of –1, which sets the LOOP to infinite (ugh). The syntax is straightforward:

```
LOOP=3
```

SCROLLAMOUNT

The SCROLLAMOUNT allows you to define the number of pixels used between each consecutive redraw of the marquee's text. The syntax is:

```
SCROLLAMOUNT=n
```

SCROLLDELAY

OK, OK! So you insist on a LOOP setting of –1. At least, then, use the SCROLLDELAY attribute to minimize *how often* the scrolling text is viewed within a certain time period. This avoids a hypnotizing windshield-wiper effect in favor of a more spontaneous time-delayed swipe. The syntax sets the number of milliseconds between each scroll:

```
SCROLLDELAY=number_of_milliseconds
```

VSPACE

Setting off marquee text from the marquee's border is easy with the VSPACE attribute. VSPACE specifies the number-of-pixels to apply to the marquee's top and bottom margins:

```
VSPACE=number_of_pixels
```

WIDTH

The last marquee attribute is WIDTH which defines the width of the marquee in pixels. One form of specification is a percentage, using the percent symbol (%). The syntax looks like this:

```
WIDTH=260
```

or

```
WIDTH=75%
```

The percentage option allows for a more self-adjusting placement on various display resolutions and is recommended when using marquee widths other than fullscreen. The following HTML document uses the Internet Explorer exclusive <MARQUEE> tag. (A static snapshot of this dynamic rendering is shown in Figure 5–12.)

```
<HTML><HEAD>
<TITLE>MARQUEE Example</TITLE>
</HEAD>
<BODY>
<H1>Internet Explorer MARQUEE Example.</H1>
<MARQUEE DIRECTION=LEFT BEHAVIOR=ALTERNATE
SCROLLAMOUNT=5 SCROLLDELAY=100>
Internet Explorer scrolling MARQUEE element.</MARQUEE>
</BODY>
</HTML>
```

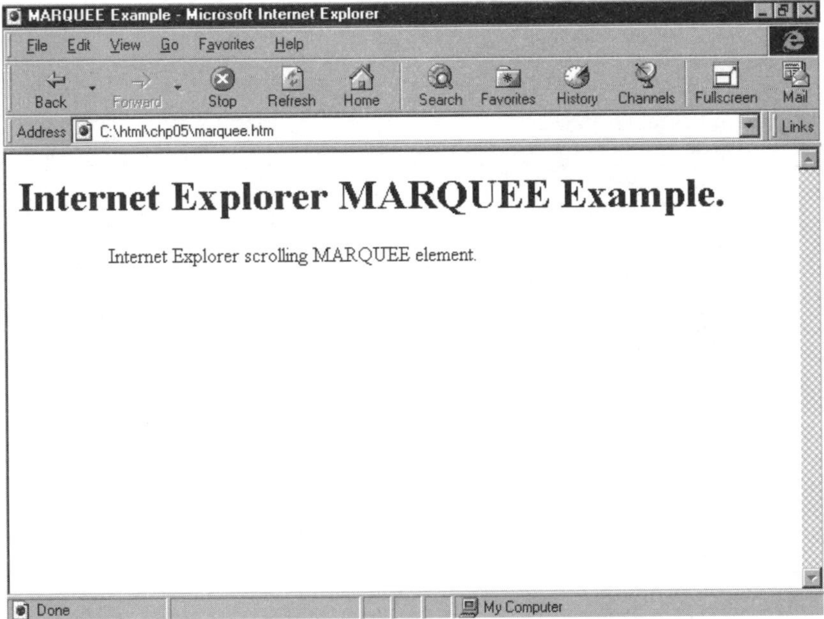

Figure 5–12: *Internet Explorer <MARQUEE> tag*

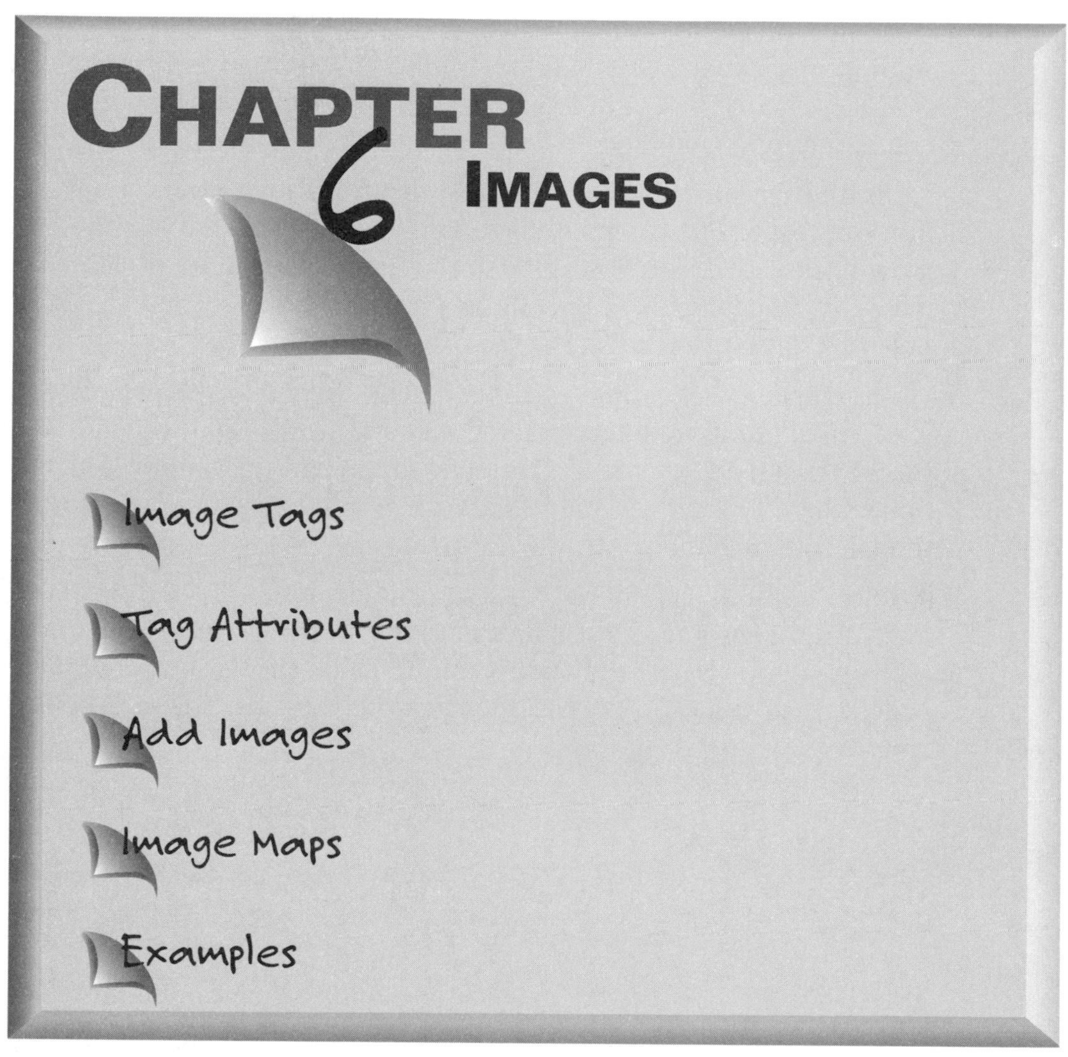

Introduction

HTML provides several techniques for rendering images on a Web page. Traditionally this has been the job of the <IMG> element, but HTML 4.0 allows images to be rendered with the use of the <OBJECT> container. In this chapter we'll concentrate on using the <IMG> element. In Chapter 15 you will learn how many of these same feats can be accomplished with the <OBJECT> container.

The <IMG> element has one major advantage over the <OBJECT> container–all popular browsers support its use.

Adding images to support a user's Web page is relatively easy. Adding images tastefully is quite another feat. Other considerations that accompany the use of images include download time, navigation, readability, and usability.

Multiple graphics images tend to slow up the navigation process in the Web page. For example, have you ever entered a Web site and grown frustrated when waiting for a large collection of graphics images to appear? Like many of us, you may have selected the alternate text option to navigate to the proper location.

For efficient navigation of a site, a well-designed Web page layout is essential. Have you ever entered a site to update file software and then had to read just about every paragraph of information to determine where to go to get the software? Poor Web page design is both time consuming and frustrating to the user.

In the sections that follow, we'll look at examples that will help you load, size, place, and use graphics images effectively. In the next chapter you'll learn how to introduce multimedia effects into your Web page design, building on the information you have gained in this chapter.

This Chapter's HTML Tags

The <IMG> element is the gateway for adding images of almost any type to your document (Table 6–1). In this chapter we'll investigate its versatility. You will learn many interesting techniques for manipulating images and some useful tips for using them effectively.

Table 6–1: *The <IMG> tag*

Tag	Description
<IMG>	A empty HTML element used to embed an image inline in a document at the location specified by the element's definition.

In the following sections of this chapter we'll investigate the versatility of the <IMG> element. You will learn many interesting techniques for manipulation images and some useful tips for using images effectively.

Image Fundamentals

First we'll investigate the syntax and parameters associated with the <IMG> element and how it may relate to the manipulation of images destined for Web pages.

The <IMG> Tag

The <IMG> tag is probably the most popular method available under HTML for adding images to a Web page. The new <OBJECT> container discussed in Chapter 15 offers another approach.

The <IMG> element uses a large number of attributes, which are listed and described in Table 6–2.

Table 6–2: *Attributes used by the <IMG> element*

Attribute	Description
align	Specifies the image's location in the viewing area. Use bottom to align the bottom of the element with the current baseline. Bottom is the default. Use middle to vertically align the center of the object with the current baseline. Use top to vertically align the object with the top of the current text line. Use left or right to align the image with the current left or right margin, respectively.
alt	Specifies text to be rendered when the image cannot be displayed.

Table 6–2: *Attributes used by the <IMG> element (continued)*

border	Specifies the border width placed around the image in pixels. When the image serves as a hyperlink, the border is drawn in the hyperlink color. Use a value of 0 for no border.
height	Specifies the height of an image in pixels. Specifying a value often speed up image loading by relieving the browser from determining layout size.
hspace	Specifies the amount of space to the left and right of an image. The amount of space is specified in pixels. No default is specified.
id	Specifies the image for the viewing area. It can also be used to locate other images or hyperlinks.
ismap	Specifies that an image map is a server side image map. (See also Chapter 10.)
lang	Specifies language information.
longdesc	Specifies a link to a long description
onclick	Specifies an action relating to a mouse click (push/release).
ondblclick	Specifies an action relating to a mouse double click (push/release).
onkeydown	Specifies an action relating to a key-down event.
onkeypress	Specifies an action relating to a key-press (down/release) event.
onkeyup	Specifies an action relating to a key-release event.
onmousedown	Specifies an action relating to a mouse-button push.
onmousemove	Specifies an action relating to the movement of the mouse.

Table 6–2: *Attributes used by the <IMG> element (continued)*

onmouseout	Specifies an action related to moving the mouse out of the area.
onmouseover	Specifies an action related to moving the mouse into the area.
onmouseup	Specifies an action relating to a mouse-button release.
src	Specifies the source of the image. This can be a file location or a full URL.
style	Specifies inline style information.
title	Specifies element titles.
usemap	Specifies a URL used with a client-side image map. (See also Chapter 10.)
vspace	Specifies the amount of space above and below an image. The amount of space is specified in pixels. No default is specified.
width	Specifies the width of an image in pixels. Specifying a value often speeds up image loading by relieving the browser from determining layout size.

Most common image types are rendered by built-in mechanisms provided by the browser. These image types may include–but are not limited to–gif, jpeg and png. When the data type isn't supported, the browser can use the alt attribute to specify a text alternative to the image. This attribute is useful in cases where images are not supported, a particular image format is not supported, or images cannot be displayed for a particular reason.

Browsers interpret an <IMG> element inline and attempt to render the image at the current element's definition.

Here is a simple example named Image1.html that will load a jpeg image to the viewing area from a WEB site:

```
<HTML>
<HEAD>
<TITLE>Viewing Flowers from Barbados</TITLE>
</HEAD>
<BODY>

<IMG src="http://www.mendesco.com/flower13.jpg">

</BODY>
</HTML>
```

Figure 6–1 shows how this image is rendered in the viewing area.

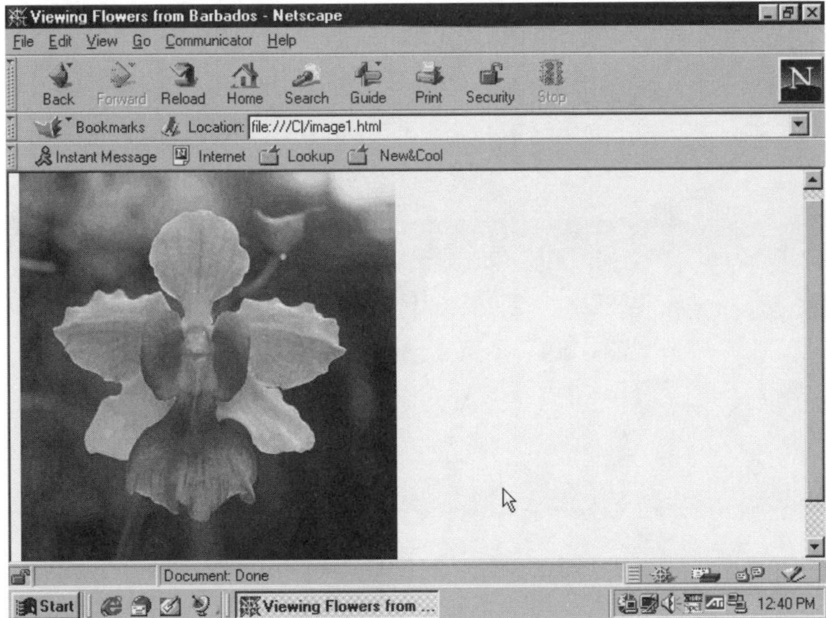

Figure 6–1: *The image of a flower is rendered in the viewing area*

The same image, if used frequently, could be saved and loaded from the hard disk. Here is the required modification to the previous example, named Image2.html:

```
<IMG src="flower19.jpg">
```

Images saved to a hard disk load more quickly. If you are working with multiple images or large image files, this might save you time under certain circumstances.

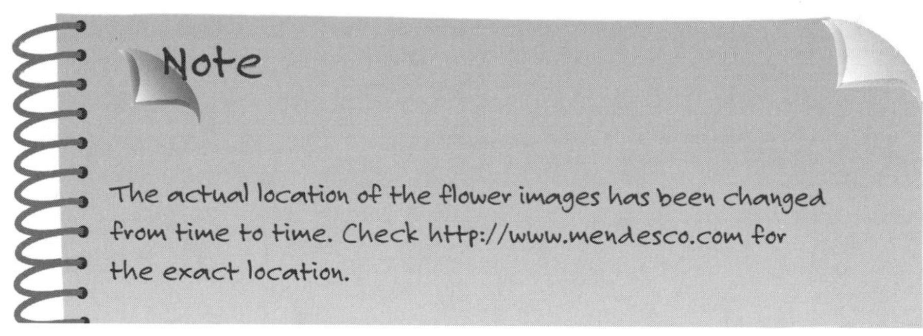

Note
The actual location of the flower images has been changed from time to time. Check http://www.mendesco.com for the exact location.

Using the Alt Attribute

The alt attribute allows you to specify alternative text that will be rendered if the image cannot be. Here is a simple example named Image3.html that will not load the image because it doesn't exist:

```
<HTML>
<HEAD>
<TITLE>Viewing Flowers from Barbados</TITLE>
</HEAD>
<BODY>

<IMG src="http://mendesco.com/flower300.jpg"
  alt="Attempted to load a Barbados flower">

</BODY>
</HTML>
```

Figure 6–2 shows the resulting screen message.

The alt attribute is useful when a browser cannot display images or cannot display a particular image format.

Using the Align Attribute

The align attribute is used for placing images in the viewing area. This attribute aligns images relative to text placed in the viewing area or against the left or right borders.

The Image4.html example aligns the image relative to the top of the line of text.

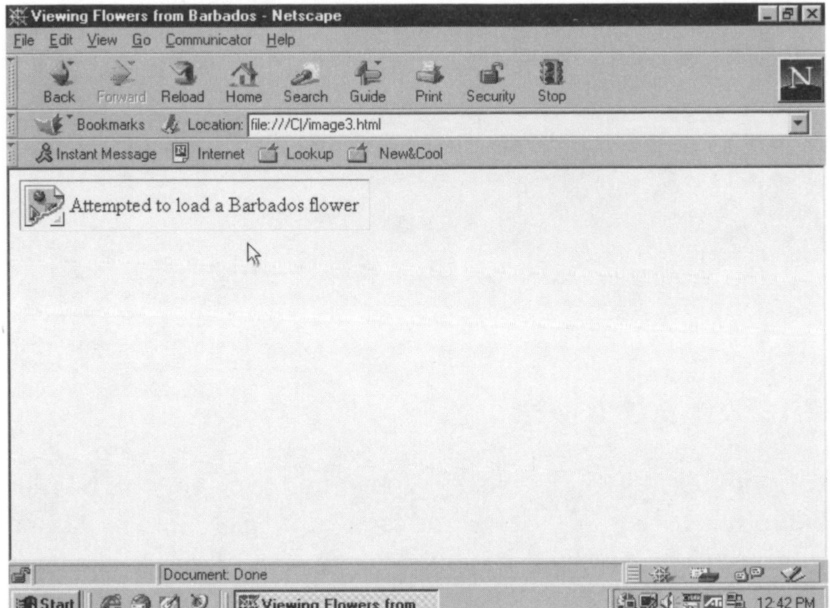

Figure 6–2: *Use the alt attribute when an image might not be rendered*

```
<HTML>
<HEAD>
<TITLE>Viewing Flowers from Barbados</TITLE>
</HEAD>
<BODY>

A flower from Barbados.
<IMG src="http://mendesco.com/flower19.jpg"
  align="top">

</BODY>
</HTML>
```

Examine Figure 6–3 and notice where the text and image are placed.

To align the same image with the align attribute set to "middle," use this variation in the previous example. This example is named Image5.html.

```
A flower from Barbados.
<IMG src="http://mendesco.com/flower19.jpg"
  align="middle">
```

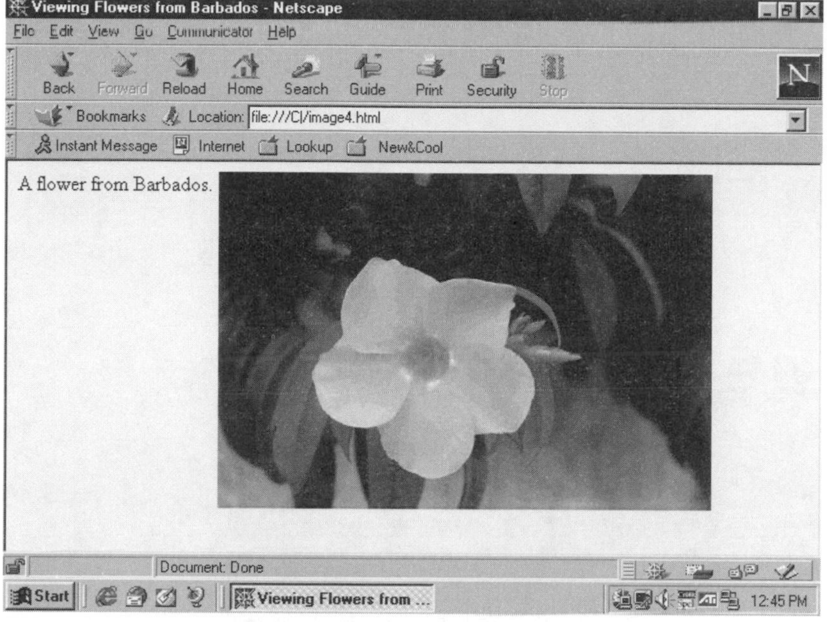

Figure 6–3: *Aligning images with the align attribute set to "top"*

Look at Figure 6–4 and notice where the text and image are placed.

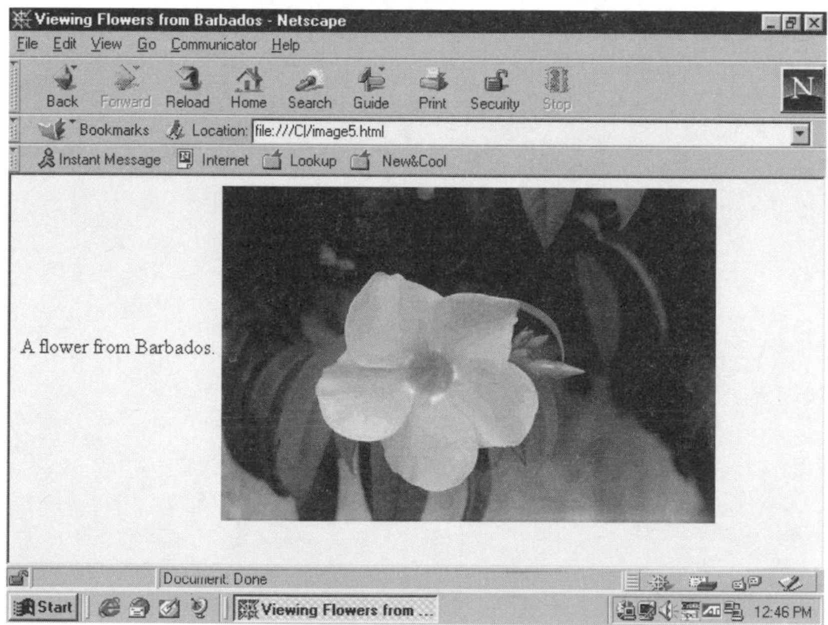

Figure 6–4: *Aligning images with the align attribute set to "middle"*

To align the same image with the align attribute set to "bottom,î use this variation. This example is named Image6.html.

```
A flower from Barbados.
<IMG src="http://mendesco.com/flower19.jpg"
  align="bottom">
```

When you examine Figure 6–5, you'll notice that the image is aligned with the bottom of the text line.

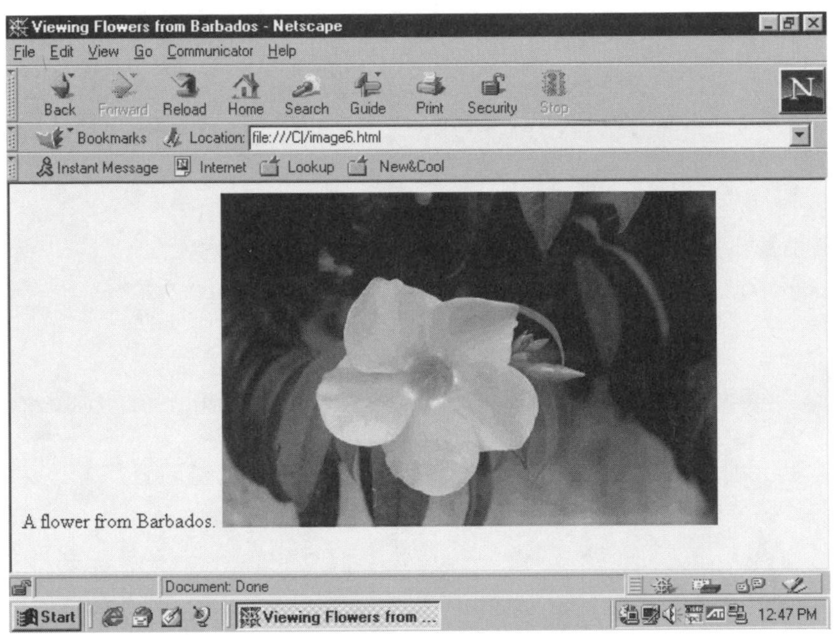

Figure 6–5: *Aligning images with the align attribute set to "bottom"*

The align attribute can be used to align the image relative to the left edge of the viewing area by setting it to "left." This example is named Image7.html.

```
A flower from Barbados.
<IMG src="http://mendesco.com/flower19.jpg"
  align="left">
```

Look at Figure 6–6. The image is placed along the left edge of the viewing area.

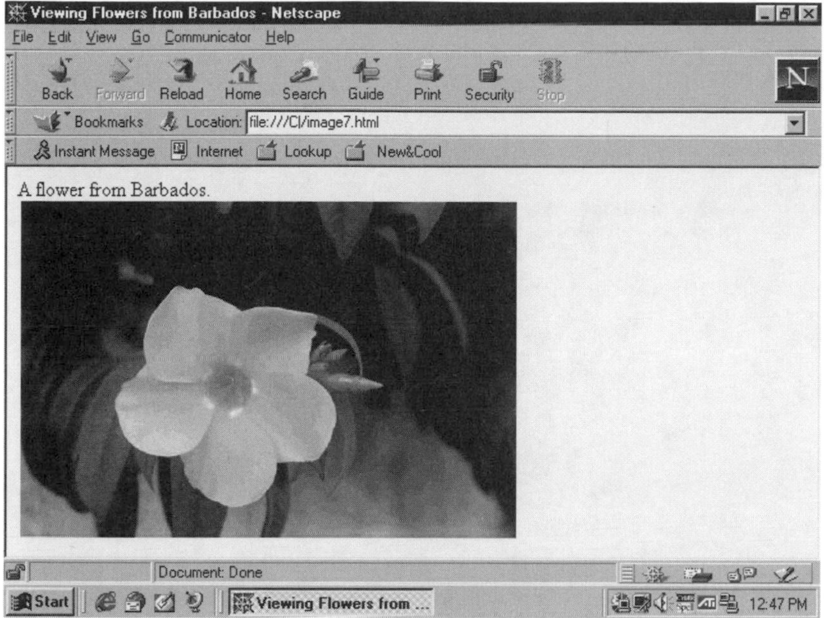

Figure 6–6: *Aligning images with the align attribute set to "left"*

Finally, the image can be rendered against the right edge by setting the align attribute to "right." This example is named Image8.html.

```
A flower from Barbados.
<IMG src="http://mendesco.com/flower19.jpg"
  align="right">
```

Notice, in Figure 6–7, that the image is placed along the right edge of the viewing area.

The align attribute is used to place the image in a relative position. Other attributes can determine the size of the image as you'll see next.

Using the Width and Height Attributes

Attributes such as width and height can be used to stretch or shrink the image. The value used is measured in pixels. In the following example, named Image9.html, the width of the image is forced to 400 pixels.

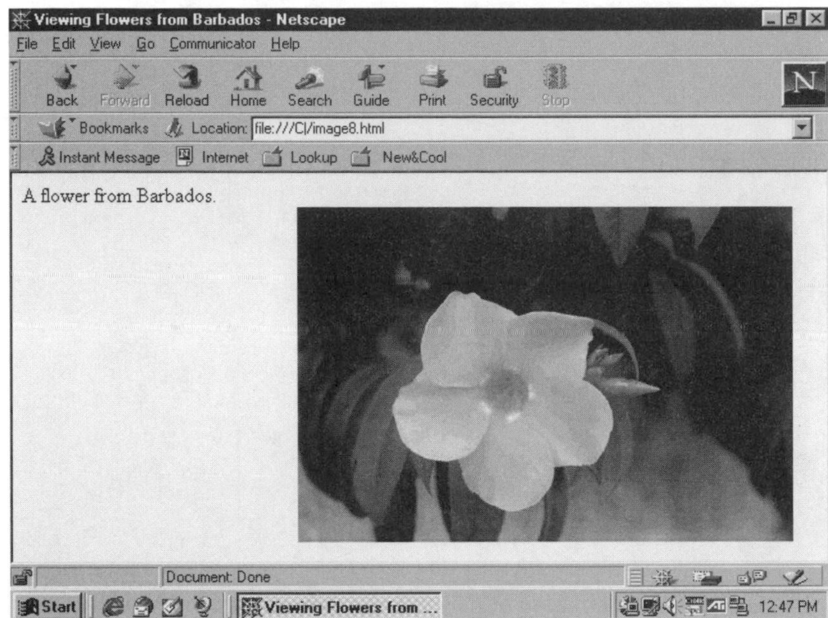

Figure 6–7: *Aligning images with the align attribute set to "right"*

```
<HTML>
<HEAD>
<TITLE>Viewing Flowers from Barbados</TITLE>
</HEAD>
<BODY>

A flower from Barbados.
<IMG src="http://mendesco.com/flower15.jpg"
  width=400>

</BODY>
</HTML>
```

Figure 6–8 shows the results of setting the image's width to 400 pixels.

The height attribute can be used to alter just the height of an image. In the example named Image10.html the height of an image is forced to 100 pixels.

```
A flower from Barbados.
<IMG src="http://mendesco.com/flower15.jpg"
  height=100>
```

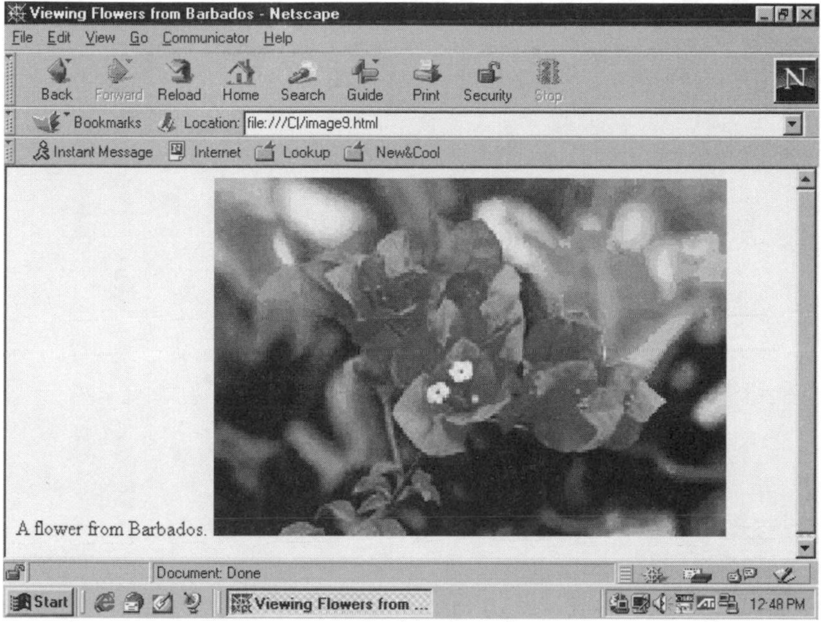

Figure 6–8: *Use the width attribute to set the width of the image in pixels*

Figure 6–9 shows the results of setting the image's height to 100 pixels. If only one attribute is set, such as height or width, the unspecified attribute will remain at the default value.

Both the height and width of an image can be altered simultaneously, as you can see in the example named Image11.html.

```
A flower from Barbados.
<IMG src="http://mendesco.com/flower15.jpg"
  width=400 height=200>
```

Figure 6–10 illustrates how the height and width of an image can be changed.

By using both the height and width attributes, you can expand or collapse an image to fit any viewing area.

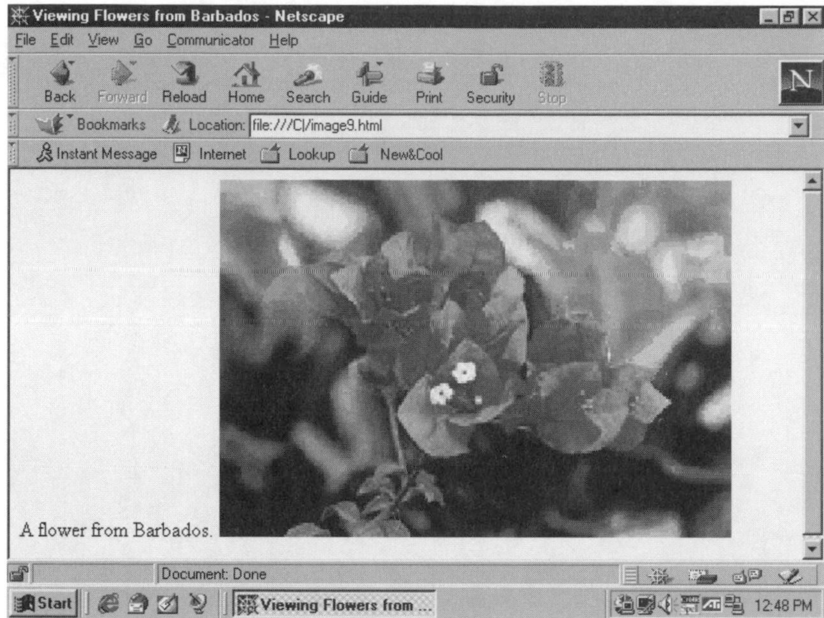

Figure 6–9: *Use the height attribute to set the height of the image in pixels*

Figure 6–10: *Use the height and width attributes to expand and collapse images*

Using the Border Attribute

The border attribute can be used to render a border around the image. The width of the border is specified in pixels. A default border is 1 pixel wide.

In the following example, named Image12.html, a border 10 pixels thick is drawn around an image whose width and height have been set to 200 pixels.

```
<HTML>
<HEAD>
<TITLE>Viewing Flowers from Barbados</TITLE>
</HEAD>
<BODY>

A flower from Barbados.
<IMG src="http://mendesco.com/flower22.jpg"
  border=10 width=200 height=200>

</BODY>
</HTML>
```

Figure 6–11 shows a bold border drawn around the image.

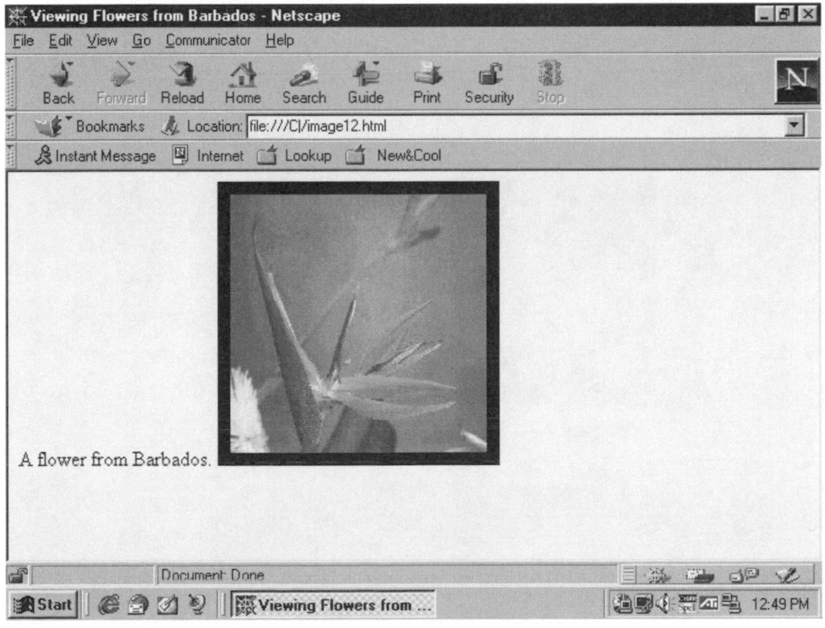

Figure 6–11: *Borders help emphasize images*

The border value can be set to zero to make the border invisible.

Using the hspace and vspace Attributes

The hspace and vspace attributes are used to set the white space that surrounds the image. In the following example, named Image13.html, the hspace and vspace attributes are set to 50 pixels each.

```
<HTML>
<HEAD>
<TITLE>Viewing Flowers from Barbados</TITLE>
</HEAD>
<BODY>

A flower from Barbados.
<IMG src="http://mendesco.com/flower24.jpg"
  hspace=50 vspace=50 border=2 width=300 height=200>

</BODY>
</HTML>
```

Examine Figure 6–12 and observe the white space surrounding the figure.

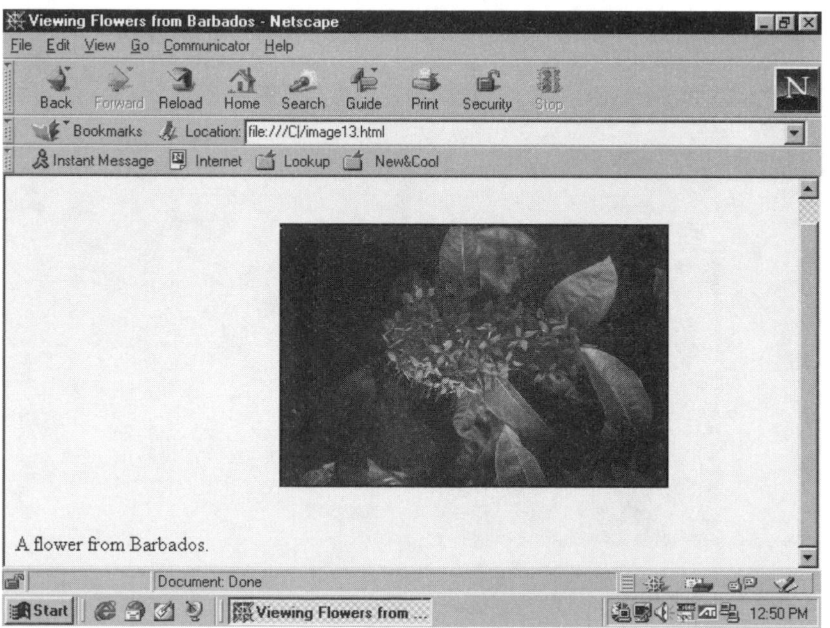

Figure 6–12: *The hspace and vspace attributes add white space to the area surrounding an image*

Notice, too, that this image is fixed at 300 (200 pixels and is surrounded by a border 2-pixels wide.

Images in the Background

Images can also serve as background wallpaper. Here one of the flowers from Barbados was saved to the hard disk and later used as a background wallpaper. This example is named Image14.html:

```
<HTML>
<HEAD>
<TITLE>Barbados Flowers</TITLE>
</HEAD>

<BODY background="flower19.jpg">
</BODY>

</HTML>
```

Examine Figure 6–13 and see how the background wallpaper is created from the original image.

Figure 6–13: *Images can be used as background wallpaper*

You might have concluded that this wallpaper is too busy to be used in a Web site. It would be difficult to read black text against this background. Perhaps a more subdued wallpaper would be more appropriate.

A Peek at Image Maps

In Chapter 10 you will learn how to build both client-side and server-side image maps. Image maps allow the user to click on an image and be linked to a specified location. The image is rendered with the <IMG> element that we have been working with in this chapter. The image map is identified with the <MAP> element, and each portion of the map is set using the <AREA> element. These tags will be discussed in Chapter 10.

Here is a portion of a client-side image map from Chapter 10. We present it to illustrate just how versatile the <IMG> element can be.

```
    .
    .
    .
<IMG src="ImgMap1.jpg" usemap="#firstmap">
<P>You want to go where today?<BR>
<MAP name="firstmap">
<AREA href="http://www.microsoft.com/office/"
  shape="rect"
  coords="0, 0, 210, 137">
<AREA href="http://www.microsoft.com/word/"
  shape="rect"
  coords="211, 0, 420, 137">
<AREA href="http://www.microsoft.com/excel/"
  shape="rect"
  coords="0, 138, 210, 275">
<AREA href="http://www.microsoft.com/access/"
  shape="rect"
  coords="211, 138, 420, 275">
</MAP>
    .
    .
    .
```

Figure 6–14 shows how this client-side image map is rendered in the viewing area.

We're sure client-side image maps have caught your attention. If you want, turn ahead to Chapter 10 for more details on using them in your documents.

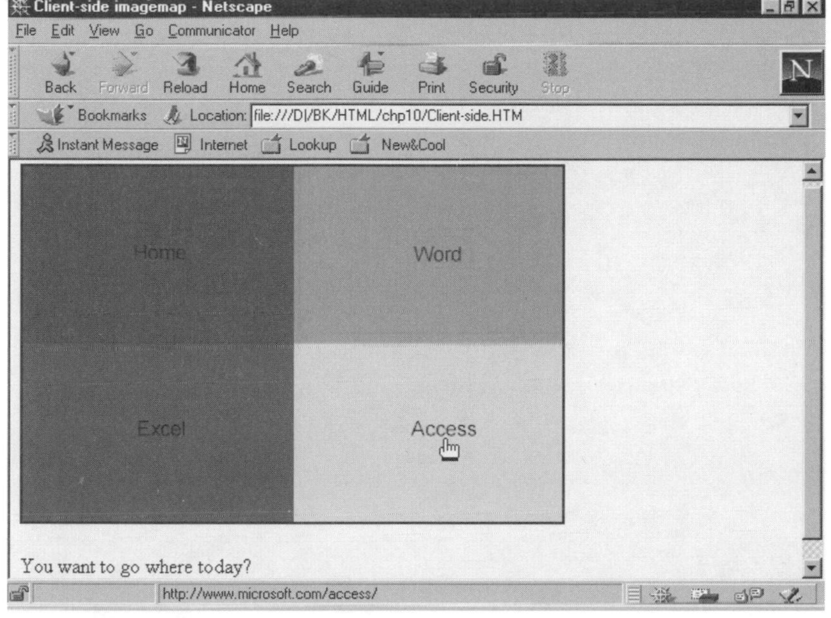

Figure 6–14: *The <IMG> element can be used to create client-side image maps*

Before You Leave

Images can certainly be used to enhance any Web site. A good rule of thumb, however, is to use them only when necessary and to keep them sizes as small as possible.

If you are using an image as background wallpaper, choose it carefully, and make sure any text that your are printing to the viewing area is clearly visible on top of the wallpaper design.

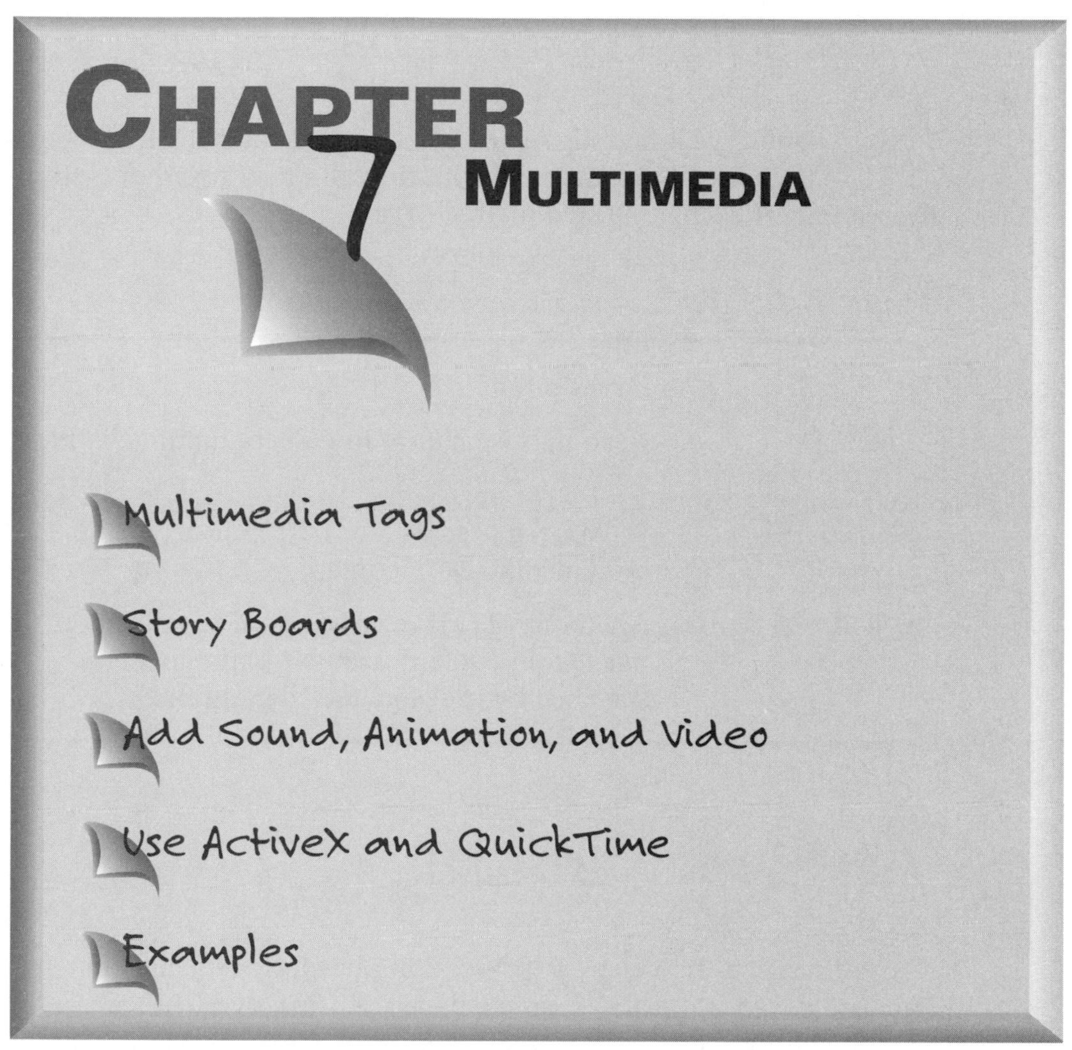

Introduction

"Lights, action, camera, JB!" Multimedia-enhanced Web pages have as much extra enticement over ordinary ones as television has over a magazine. This chapter shows you how to add sound and animation (via AVI and MOV files) to your design. But be careful: with today's average Web surfers riding no faster than 56K, a Web site flooded with too much multimedia content leaves them stranded out in the middle of the ocean, never quite making it to shore. Even worse, once having visited your crowded beach, they may *never return!*

This Chapter's HTML Tags

In this chapter we'll investigate the versatility of the <EMBED> and <IMG> elements. Tags discussed in this chapter, together with a description of each, are listed in Table 7–1.

Table 7–1: *HTML tags discussed in Chapter 7*

Tag	Description
<EMBED>	Used in this chapter to embed multimedia file content
<NOEMBED>	HTML tag used as alternate content for non-multimedia-aware content
<IMG>	An empty HTML element used to embed an image inline in a document at the location specified by the element's definition

The Story Board

The difference between a professionally designed multimedia-enhanced Web page and a time-delayed sensory-overload presentation is like that between a classic silent movie and the 3D version of Kong's Revenge–content. Many producers attempt to "entertain" the audience with new technology in place of a good story.

The simplest way to guarantee success is to make your site's content as clear, straightforward, and interesting as possible, *without any multimedia*. Then add multimedia as the icing on the cake.

To make certain a presentation's contents *flow*, follow the example of the most successful entertainment giant's–create a story board. A *story board* is a sequence of sketched images, laid out in a logical progression, hitting the highlights of a production's story sequence. It can help you make your Web page a logical and hopefully interesting narrative–about you, your club, or your company.

Internal and External Multimedia Content

There are two distinct sources for multimedia files.

- Internal or inline images appear directly on a Web page.
- External images are stored externally and are loaded only when a user chooses the appropriate hotlink on a Web page.

In general, external media include any file that cannot be automatically loaded, played, or displayed by a Web browser on a Web page.

Use of internal or inline multimedia files is limited to the types of files supported by most browsers: GIF and JPEG images. External files can include just about any kind you can create and store on a disk, including PostScript, zipped, MPEG video, and non-inline GIF files.

Since internal-file formats are supported directly by most browsers, let's look at what happens when you use external-file formats. Browsers handle an external file by first downloading it and then passing it to some other application on your system that is designed to read and handle the specific file format. Technically, the decision as to who handles the file is settled by one of two factors: the filename extension to the filename or the file's content-type.

When you access a file, the Web server may not actually send the filename. The data it sends back may be automatically generated and not have a filename at all. the server sends back a special code called the content-type, which tells the browser what kind of file it is sending: text/html, image/gif, video/mpeg, video/avi, and so on.

The browser and the Web server maintain lists in their configuration or preference files, enabling them to easily map file extensions to content-type. The server uses its list to decide which content-type to send to the browser with a given file extension. The browser uses its list to map this content-type to the appropriate plug-in on the user's system.

URLs and Multimedia Files

When a URL references a multimedia file on an external, remote location, this means that to load the file, the user's browser actually links to the remote location. This takes time. If the remote location is not online, the browser can't load the image at all. For this reason, having your graphic files on your own WWW server usually works better.

An exception occurs when you want to include an image from another location that changes over time (such as a digital clock or weather map) or a very large image. In the first case, the other site maintains the changing image and you see it directly from their site, but included in your Web page. In the second case, you save your server's disk space by pointing to the remote location for the multimedia image. Reusing the same graphic on a single Web page doesn't add significant time or disk-storage requirements when the user's browser activates caching (or the retrieval of previously accessed files).

Adding Sound

You can add audio to your HTML document in a number of ways, including:

- The anchor tag <A> and HREF attribute
- Plug-ins like RealAudio
- Intel processor-specific TrueSpeech
- Browser-specific tags like Microsoft's Internet Explorer <BGSOUND> tag

But, Is Anyone Listening?

Before we discuss *how* to add sound to an HTML document, consider these notes of caution:

- Some end users do not even own a sound card and therefore won't hear any sounds.
- Those who do own a sound card may turn their sound off!

Using the Anchor Tag <A>

The anchor tag <A> is undoubtedly the simplest way to add sound to your HTML document. You simply use the <A> and </A> tag pair to encapsulate the sound file's name, as in:

```
<A HREF="MyWelcome.au">Allow me to introduce myself."</A>
```

The anchor tag is used to insert hyperlinks into an HTML document. To include a link to an external sound on your Web page, you must have the sound file in the right format, just as you would for an image file. Presently, the only fully cross-platform sound-file format for the Web is Sun Microsystem's AU file format.

The AU audio format provides different types of sound sampling encryption, the most popular being the 8-bit format. However, AU files are not of the best audio quality. Other, better-quality sound formats include the Macintosh AIFF, the Windows WAV, or the more cross-platform MPEG audio.

Plug-ins such as RealAudio, with their associated proprietary file formats, have been developed specifically for playing audio files on the Internet and the World Wide Web. Whereas most audio files make you wait for the entire file to download before you can hear it, RealAudio uses a technique called streaming. *Streaming* allows a sound file to begin playing at the same time it is being downloaded—there is only a slight initial pause, as the file first arrives at your machine.

Unfortunately, like all plug-ins, RealAudio files require a special server to deliver them, and linking to them involves a slightly different process than linking to regular audio files. For these reasons we defer discussion of this subject until later on in the chapter.

Common sound-file formats and their extensions recognized by today's browsers are listed in Table 7–2.

Table 7-2: *Sound file formats and their file extensions*

Sound File Format	Sound File Extension
AIFF/AIFC	.aiff, or .aif (for 8.3 file formats)
AU	.au
MIDI	.mid
MPEG	.mp2 (video and sound)
Wave	.wav

Using Microsoft's <BGSOUND> Tag

The background sound tag, <BGSOUND>, allows you to link to any WAV file using the SRC attribute, and set a repeat-play count, as in the following example:

```
<BGSOUND SRC=http://www.mysite.com/elevatormusic.wav
   LOOP=INFINITE>
```

The LOOP attribute repeats indefinitely if set to a value of -1 or INFINITE; otherwise the number of plays is limited to the value specified (for example, 4 iterations).

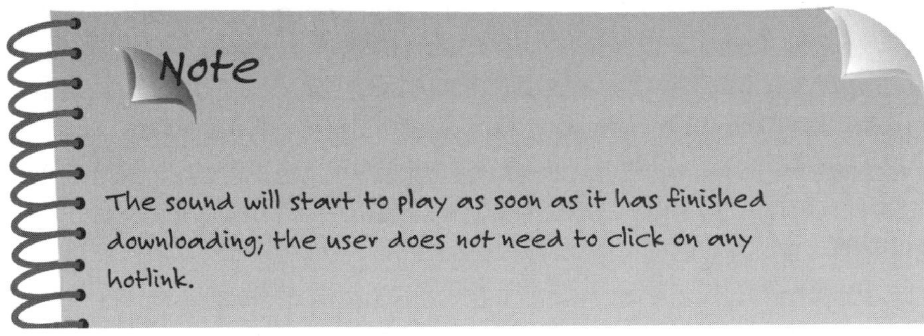

Note
The sound will start to play as soon as it has finished downloading; the user does not need to click on any hotlink.

Be careful when using sound in your documents. A constantly repeating sound can be even more annoying than constantly blinking text. It is better to have one short sound that grabs your reader's attention than a 30-minute WAV file that irritates. In general, the only reason for using sound is for a *special* effect–so the sound should be brief.

Image-File Size

Before launching into the world of visual imagery, you need to know a little about how to control image-file size. One way is to limit the number of bits stored per pixel. Although this reduces the resolution of the image as rendered by the browser, try storing your image with 7 or 5 bits per pixel if you really need to show a large image as quickly as possible. Another approach is to reduce the number of colors in the picture to lower its overall image size.

Various graphics programs allow you to import an image in one resolution, change its parameters, and save a streamlined rendition. Standard GIF images require an 8-bit-per-pixel format, providing 256 colors. Reducing the ratio to 7 bits per pixel limits reproductions to 128 colors, while a 5 bit version contains only 32 color variations.

Applications like Corel7 even allow you to set the number of colors (for example, 43) with the software selecting the appropriate number of pixels (in this example, 7 bits-per-pixel). There is an advantage to this approach, as the 85 unused color definitions are set to all zeros, resulting in a smaller image, with faster rendering, than one set explicitly to a 7-bits-per-pixel standard format.

Adding Animated GIFs

Many people are surprised to discover that the a GIF file format is not just for single-frame images but also for multiple images, stored in a single file, which can be rendered into an animation sequence. Incorporating animated images into your Web page is straightforward when using the <IMG> image tag and its associated SRC attribute, as in:

```
<IMG SRC=http://www.mysite.com/animate.gif>
```

The following HTML document launches the Norton Utilities tutorial-genie animated GIF file:

```
<HTML>
<HEAD>
<TITLE>Adding Animated GIFs to a Web Page</TITLE>
</HEAD>
<BODY>
<P>An Animated Norton Utilities Genie!"</P>
<IMG src="c:/UT/Norton/HTML/nsgmain.gif">

</BODY>
</HTML>
```

Figure 7–1 displays the magical guide.

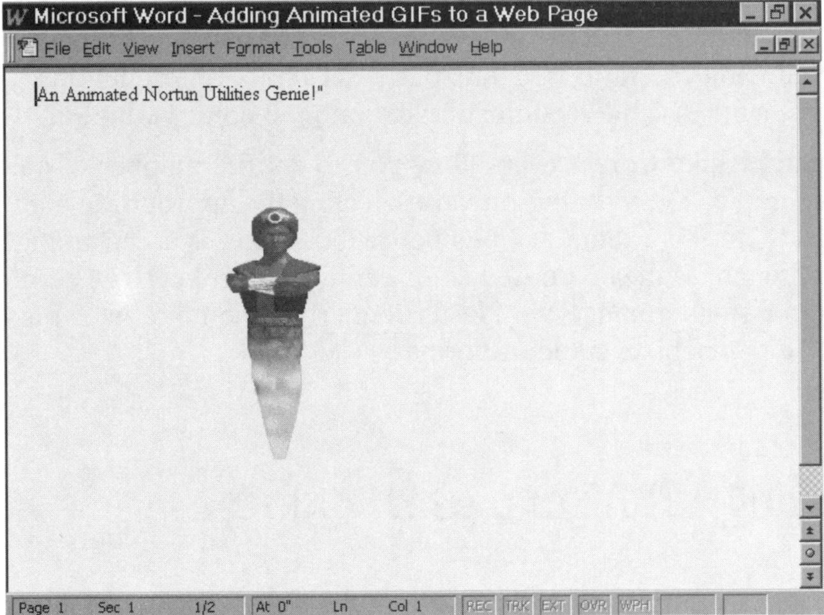

Figure 7–1: *Adding an animated GIF to a Web page*

The good news is that an animated GIF is treated the same way as any other image file on your Web page.

Adding Different Types of Media with <EMBED>

Created originally by Netscape, the <EMBED> tag allows you to add different types of multimedia to your HTML document. File formats currently supported include:

- QuickTime multimedia movies in MOV file format
- LiveAudio MIDI, AIFF, AU, and WAV file formats
- LiveVideo AVI (Audio Video Interleave) file format

The <EMBED> tag has three attributes:

- SRC
- HEIGHT
- WIDTH

The <EMBED> tag also works with special downloaded plug-ins and may contain additional plug-in-specific attributes, such as Netscape's PLAY_LOOP repetition parameter or Microsoft's PALETTE selector. (*Note:* Netscape's PARAMETER_NAME attribute is equivalent in function to Microsoft's OPTIONAL_PARAMETER.)

SRC Attribute

The SRC attribute allows you to define the URL multimedia file source.

HEIGHT and WIDTH Attributes

The HEIGHT and WIDTH attributes define in number of pixels the height and width of the embedded multimedia file.

Adding an AVI File

The following HTML document shows how to add an insert disk animated AVI file to your Web page:

```
<HTML>
<HEAD>
<TITLE>Adding AVI Files to a Web Page</TITLE>
</HEAD>
<BODY>
<P>Adding a Simple Downloading AVI File Image.</P>
<EMBED SRC="D:/BK/HTML/CHP07/setup.avi"WIDTH=40
HEIGHT=30


PLAY_LOOP=3>

</BODY>
</HTML>
```

Figure 7-2 shows the resulting image and the AVI player frame including the play, stop-play, and file image slider-selector controls.

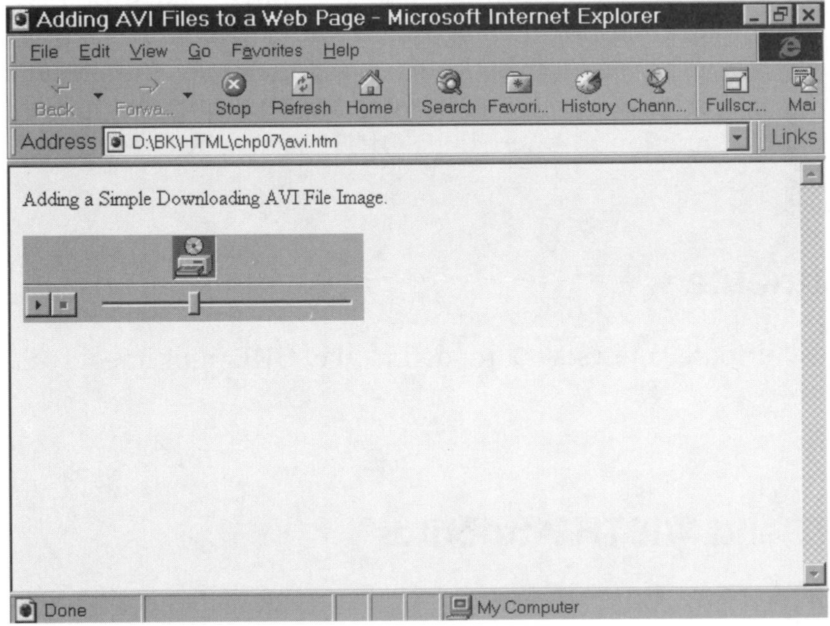

Figure 7-2: *Using <EMBED> with Microsoft's Internet Explorer and an AVI file*

A properly designed Web page using the <EMBED> tag should always include a <NOEMBED> counterpart for those Web surfers whose browsers do not support AVI playback.

<NOEMBED> for Non-Multimedia-Aware Browsers

It's a good habit always to include a <NOEMBED> for every <EMBED> tag you use in an HTML document. This practice politely prompts end-uses with a message alerting them to an unrecognized multimedia file format.

An example of <NOEMBED> for the previous HTML document would look like this:

```
<HTML>
<HEAD>
<TITLE>Adding AVI Files to a Web Page</TITLE>
</HEAD>
<BODY>
<P>Adding a Simple Downloading AVI File Image.</P>
<EMBED SRC="D:/BK/HTML/CHP07/setup.avi"WIDTH=40
HEIGHT=30

PLAY_LOOP=3>

<NOEMBED>

Unfortunately, your browser does not support AVI file
Playback--you will not see the animated download file
Image.

</NOEMBED>

</BODY>
</HTML>
```

Adding Video Using Internet Explorer's DYNSRC Attribute

Starting with Microsoft's Internet Explorer 2.0 browser, HTML programmers have been able to use the <IMG> proprietary attribute DYNSRC (Dynamic Source). This attribute must be used as part of the standard <IMG> HTML tag. It is designed to allow you to embed inline video clips in an AVI file format. DYNSRC is also extended to allow you to embed VRML elements! The syntax for an image looks like this:

```
<IMG SRC=http://www.mysite.com/staticlogo.jpg
   DYNSRC="animlogo.avi">
```

If the browser does not support the DYNSRC attribute, it simply ignores it and instead uses the alternate image specified by the SRG attribute.

Microsoft added several parameters to the DYNSRC attribute that allow you to control the playback:

- CONTROLS–The CONTROLS parameter allows you to add VCR-type buttons below the video frame, providing play and stop capabilities.
- START–The START parameter selects one of two start-play modes. The first is FILEOPEN, which automatically plays the AVI file video as soon as the entire HTML page and AVI file are downloaded. The alternate START mode is called MOUSEOVER. MOUSEOVER prevents the video from starting until the user passes the mouse over the top of the video frame. Both values can be set, but they must be separated with a comma. You would use both values together if you wanted the video to play as soon as the Web page opened, and then again whenever the user moved the mouse over it.
- LOOP–Like the standard HTML LOOP attribute, LOOP defines the number of video playback repetitions. The value can be set explicitly, as in LOOP = 4, or given a value of –1 or INFINITE to generate nonstop playback-rewind-playback cycles

A complete example would look like this:


```
<IMG DYNSRC="myvideo.avi" SRC="staticvideo.jpg"
   WIDTH=160 HEIGHT=120 START="FILEOPEN,MOUSEOVER"
   CONTROLS>
```

Notice that DYNSRC also supports the WIDTH and HEIGHT attributes. Also, when selecting MOUSEOVER, it does not make any sense to implement the LOOP = INFINITE attribute. MOUSEOVER will be ignored, because you have set the video to loop indefinitely.

Using ActiveX Controls

ActiveX is yet another way in which Web page designers can deliver specialized content to the user. ActiveX controls are objects that can be inserted into Web pages or other applications. The ActiveX standard, developed by Microsoft, is a bit of a cross between Java and plug-ins. Like Java, it is loaded automatically when it encounters the browser. Like a plug-in, after it is downloaded onto the user's system, it remains there for the future and doesn't have to be reloaded. If you are a Visual Basic developer, you will be very familiar with ActiveX controls, as they were formerly known as OLE controls or OCXs.

ActiveX controls also offer a wide variety of content options, including Windows-type controls, spreadsheets, and Shockwave. There are even several ActiveX controls included with Internet Explorer that enable you to bring your Web page alive with special formatting features, animation, video, and much more.

ActiveX controls have a broad range–from simply controlling the label displayed inside a standard control, to letting you see another desktop across the Internet. If you can think of a particular control that you need for some specialized purpose, chances are that someone has already created it.

To include an ActiveX control, you simply use the <OBJECT> tag as in:

```
<OBJECT CLASSID="classID" DATA="data.fil" HEIGHT=140
   WIDTH=120> </OBJECT>
```

The classIDs are supplied by the software vendor who developed the ActiveX control, and the data.fil identifies the file containing the ActiveX content–for example, a DCR file for a Shockwave Director movie. The following additional attributes are available:

- ALIGN–Like the <IMG> tag ALIGN attribute, ALIGN sets the alignment of an ActiveX control's spacing in relation to surrounding text. Options include BOTTOM (the default, MIDDLE, TOP, LEFT, or RIGHT.
- CODEBASE–CODEBASE is a URL specifying the source for the ActiveX control. Windows maintains an internal registry containing virtually every bit of information about a particular machine's hardware and software configuration. When your browser loads the ActiveX's classID, it automatically scans the Windows registry for a match. If a match is found, the local version is used; if not, the browser automatically uses the CODEBASE URL to find the missing ActiveX control and download it.
- CODETYPE–The <OBJECT> tag supports the CODETYPE attribute, allowing you an alternate approach to letting your browser decide whether it can handle the specified ActiveX object. ActiveX controls have a CODETYPE of *application/x-oleobject*.
- PARAM and VALUE–This ActiveX control specific attribute allows you to uniquely communicate with a third-party vendor's ActiveX control. As each custom control needs to communicate with your Web page, the vendor supplies the list of parameters used for the interface. You pass parameters to the control using the PARAM and VALUE attributes. To do this you simply use the <PARAM> tag between the <OBJECT>, </OBJECT> tag pair. (Consult the documentation supplied by the vendor for specific details on the use of PARAM and VALUE.) A generic example would have the following form:

```
<PARAM name="param" VALUE="value">
```

Two Free Useful Utilities

While not intended to be a product endorsement, the following section describes two very useful utilities, Microsoft's ActiveX Control Pad and Apple's QuickTime Video, that you can download for *free*. Both tools allow you to easily incorporate custom multimedia content into your Web page.

Microsoft ActiveX Control Pad

At the time of this writing, Microsoft is providing–*free*–the ActiveX Control Pad, to anyone willing to log on to their site, *www.microsoft.com,* surf over to the ActiveX Developers section, and download it. This easy-to-use application allows you to embed ActiveX controls into your HTML document with mouse point-and-click precision. Figure 7–3 displays the initial ActiveX Control Pad main window set to create a new Web page.

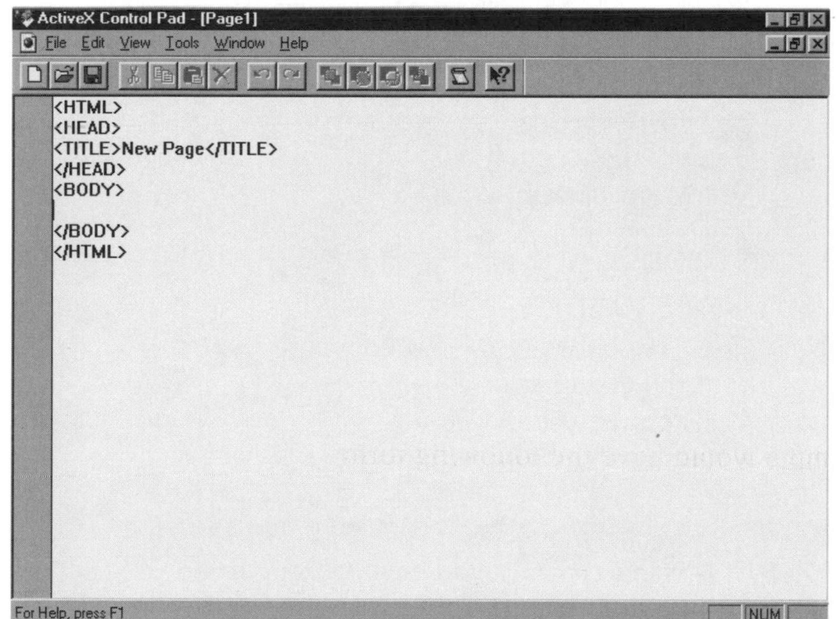

Figure 7–3: *Initial Microsoft ActiveX Control Pad window*

Inserting an Activex control is as straightforward as clicking on the Edit|Insert ActiveX Control... menu option seen in Figure 7–4 and then choosing one of the downloaded ActiveX controls or any other registered ActiveX controls you may have on your system. Figure 7–5 displays a sample list of registered ActiveX Controls.

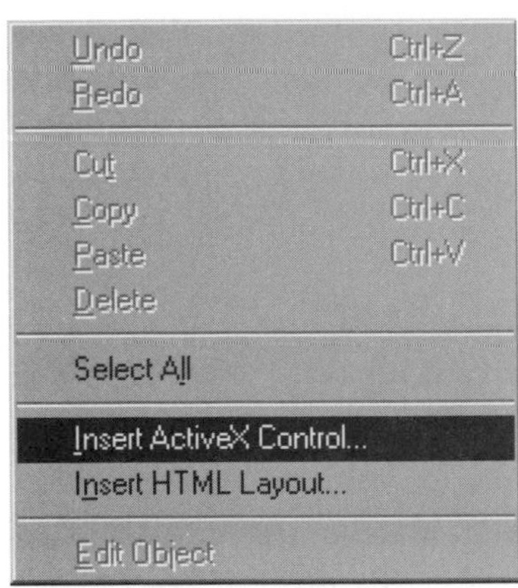

Figure 7–4: *Choosing the Edit/ActiveX Control... option*

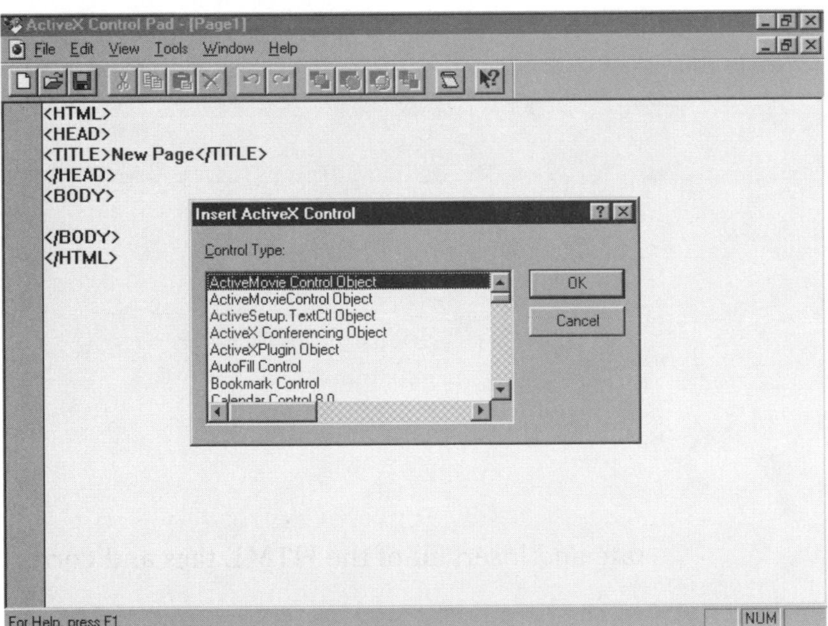

Figure 7–5: *ActiveX Control Pad's list of registered ActiveX controls*

Once you have inserted the control, the ActiveX Control Pad displays the control and a Properties dialog box as seen in Figure 7–6.

The figure shows the *FileName* property selected, with a sample file name ready to be applied with a click on the Apply button.

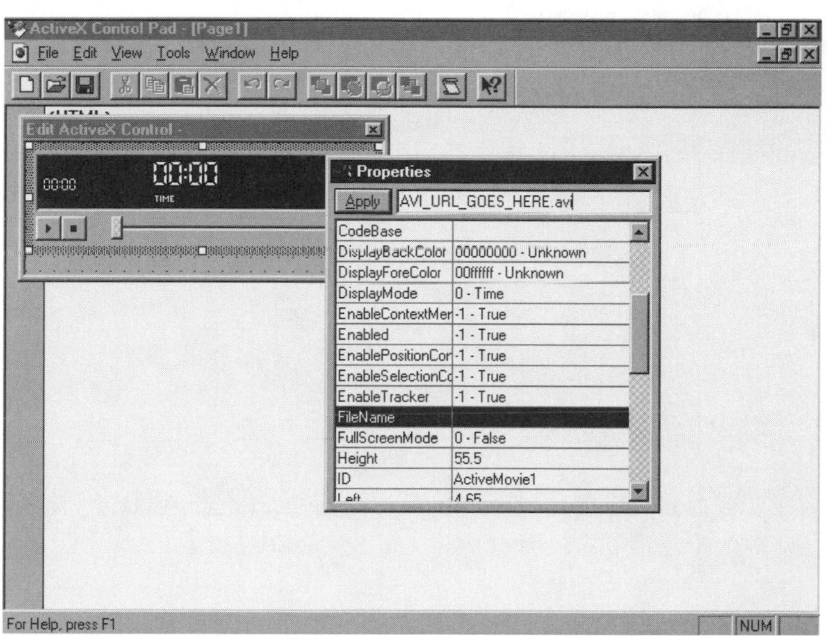

Figure 7–6: *Control Pad displaying a selected control and associated properties dialog box*

Some properties, as seen in Figure 7–7, have a predefined set of parameters. Figure 7–7 displays the BorderStyle options None or Fixed Single.

Having selected and set the parameters for an ActiveX control, you are ready to save and test the HTML document as seen in Figures 7–8 and 7–9.

Figure 7–9 shows another image of the now almost completed AVI file playback.

The best part about the Microsoft ActiveX Control Pad is its ability to automatically generate and insert all of the HTML tags and correct attributes. Figure 7–10 shows all of the automatically generated HTML code necessary to create and use the ActiveX ActiveMovie control.

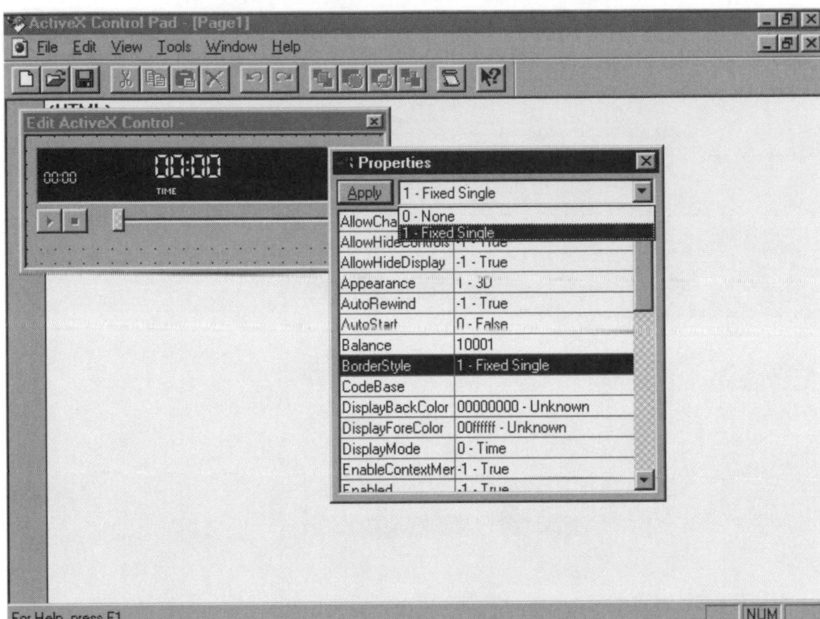

Figure 7–7: *Predefined properties drop-down list for BorderStyle*

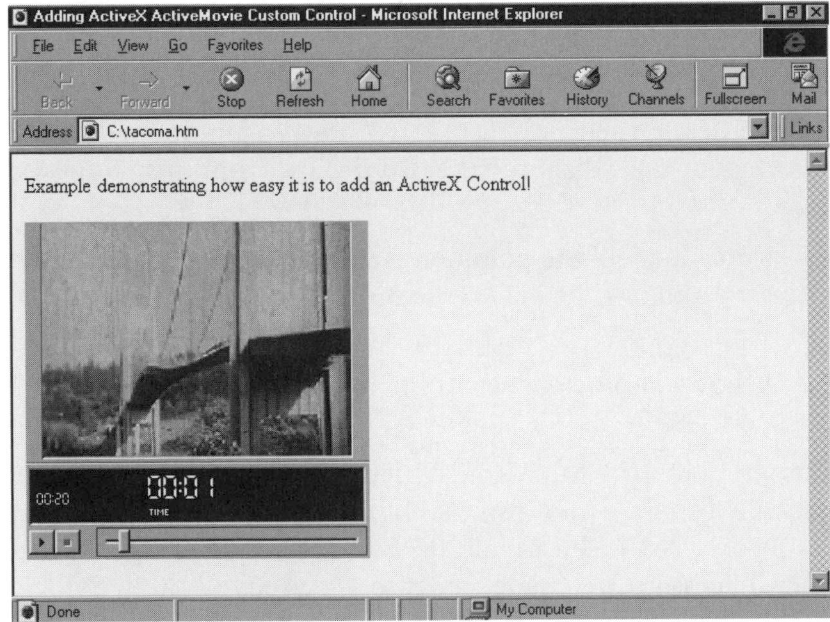

Figure 7–8: *Beginning playback of the ActiveMovie AVI file*

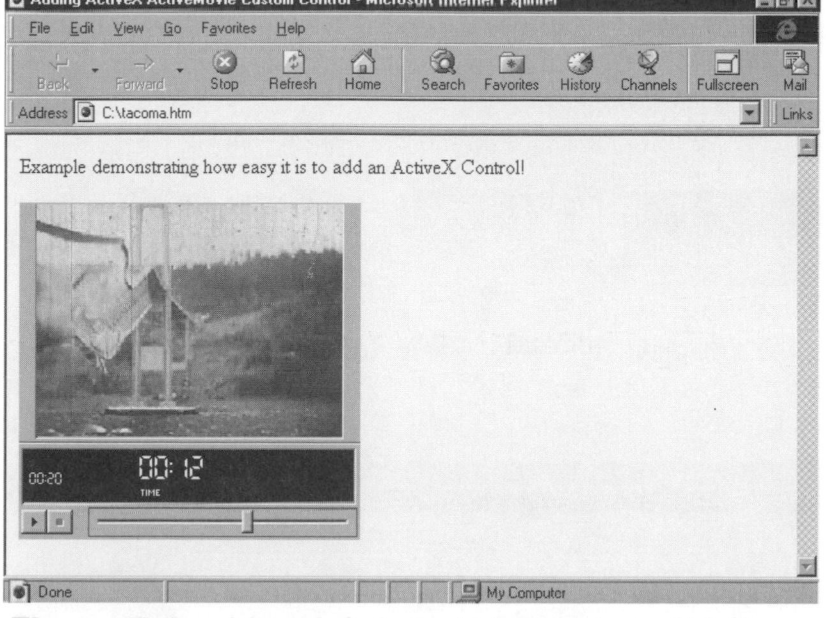
Adding ActiveX ActiveMovie Custom Control - Microsoft Internet Explorer
File Edit View Go Favorites Help
Back Forward Stop Refresh Home Search Favorites History Channels Fullscreen Mail
Address C:\tacoma.htm
Links
Example demonstrating how easy it is to add an ActiveX Control!
00:20
00: 12
TIME
Done
My Computer

Figure 7–9: *Microsoft ActiveX ActiveMovie AVI file playback almost completed*

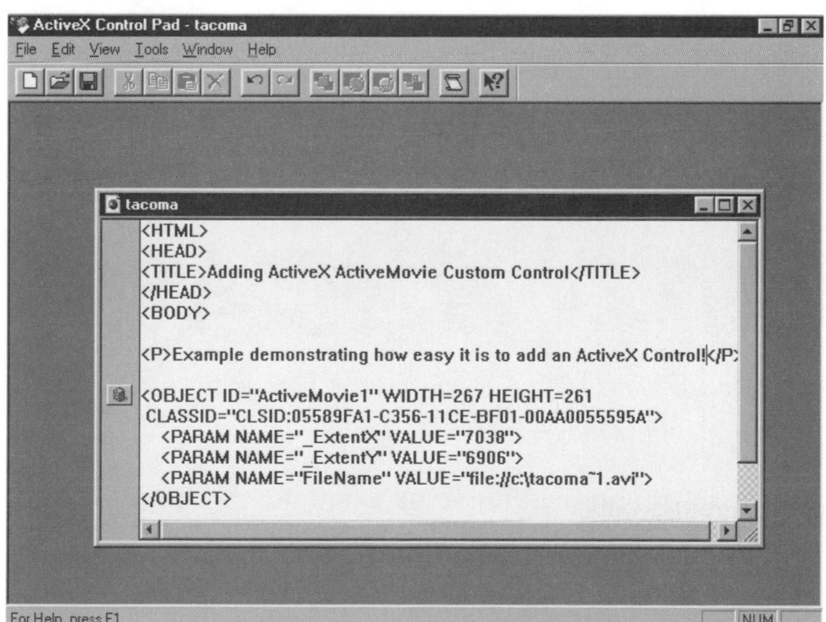
ActiveX Control Pad - tacoma
File Edit View Tools Window Help
tacoma
<HTML>
<HEAD>
<TITLE>Adding ActiveX ActiveMovie Custom Control</TITLE>
</HEAD>
<BODY>
<P>Example demonstrating how easy it is to add an ActiveX Control!</P>
<OBJECT ID="ActiveMovie1" WIDTH=267 HEIGHT=261
CLASSID="CLSID:05589FA1-C356-11CE-BF01-00AA0055595A">
<PARAM NAME="_ExtentX" VALUE="7038">
<PARAM NAME="_ExtentY" VALUE="6906">
<PARAM NAME="FileName" VALUE="file://c:\tacoma~1.avi">
</OBJECT>
For Help, press F1
NUM

Figure 7–10: *ActiveX Control Pad's autogenerated ActiveX HTML document*

The ActiveX Control Pad goes one step further in its use of ActiveX controls by launching and then embedding a Visual Basic Script file. Clicking on the Tools main menu displays the Script Wizard... option seen in Figure 7–11.

Figure 7–11: *Launching the Visual Basic Script editor from within the ActiveX Control Pad*

Figure 7–12 displays the Visual Basic Script Wizard with the main Event and Actions windows.

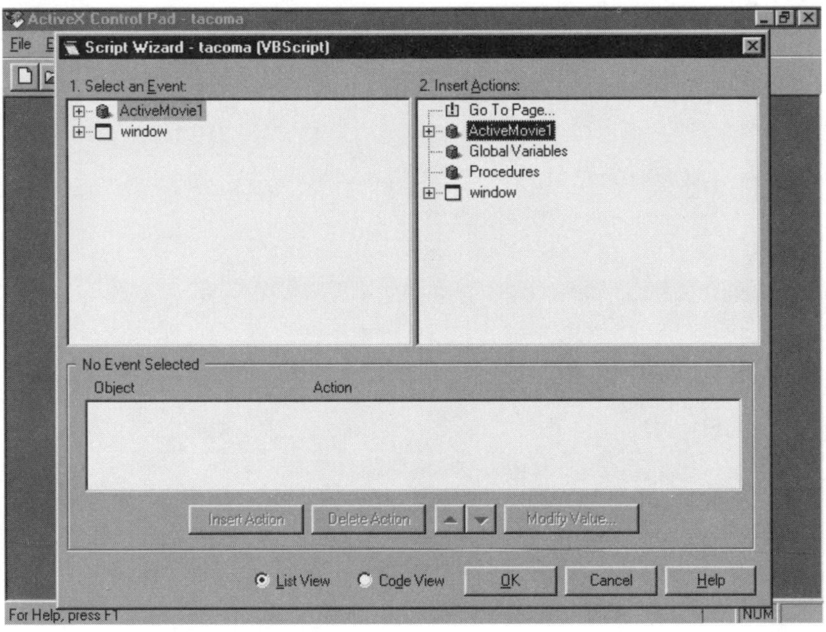

Figure 7–12: *Editing Visual Basic Script files with the ActiveX Control Pad*

See Chapter 13, “Scripting,” for some examples of how you might use this integrated ActiveX Control Pad feature.

QuickTime

Another popular multimedia file format is Apple's QuickTime MOVie. Once again, with a quick surf over to *www.apple.com* you can download a system-specific QuickTime Vidco Player. Like Microsoft's ActiveX Control Pad installation, the qt32.exe self-extracting Windows95/NT program performs all of the necessary unzip and install options necessary to make your default browser QuickTime-aware.

The QuickTime plug-in can play many kinds of QuickTime movies. It currently supports all QuickTime 2.5 track types, including text tracks, MIDI tracks, and so on. Using these kinds of movies, you can add compelling features to your pages without significantly affecting the time they take to download. Some examples:

- Background music–Import a standard MIDI file into QuickTime using Movie Player and save it as a QuickTime movie. (Make sure you select the "Make movie self contained" and "Playable on non-Apple computers" options.) The resulting file will be very small and can be used with the looping and autoplay settings to act as background music for your page.
- Animation–You can use any of the numerous QuickTime movie-editing applications, or use Movie Player for simple editing. Many animation tools such as Cinemation 1.1 allow you to you to create animations and save them as QuickTime movies.
- QuickTime VR–QuickTime VR Objects and Panaromas can be relatively small and highly compelling.

Once you have installed the QuickTime Player, embedding and using a MOV file is easy. Figure 7–13 shows the minimal HTML tags and attributes necessary to play the Apple Sample QuickTime MOVie. Figure 7–14 displays the resulting Web page as viewed from within Microsoft's Internet Explorer 4. Figure 7–15 shows the Sample QuickTime MOVie as it is about to finish.

Creating QuickTime Content for the Internet

This section explains some of the differences and some tips and tricks you can use to optimize your QuickTime movies for playback over the Internet. As you will soon discover, there is a big difference between QuickTimc movies that work well over the Internet and the QuickTime movies you may be used to seeing on CD-ROMs

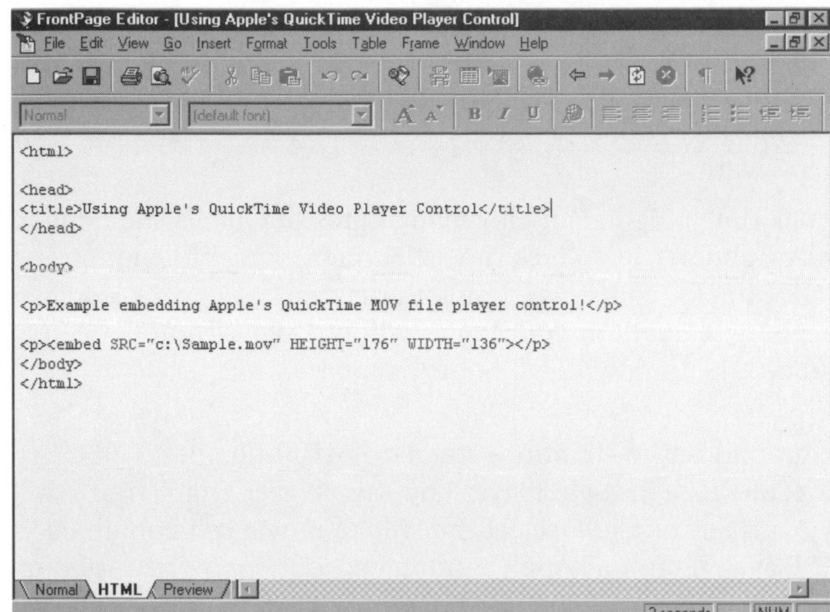

Figure 7–13: *Minimal HTML tags and attributes needed to view QuickTime MOVies*

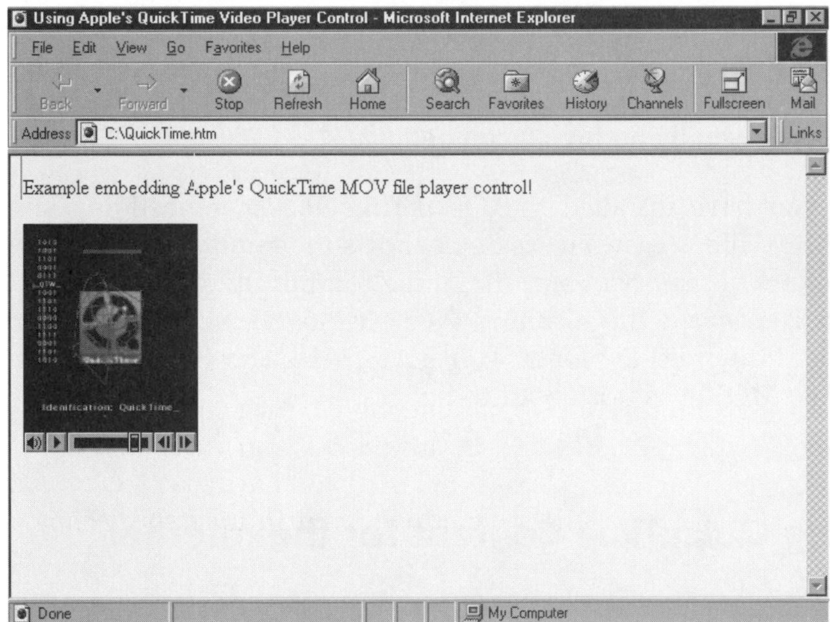

Figure 7–14: *Viewing the Apple Sample QuickTime MOVie*

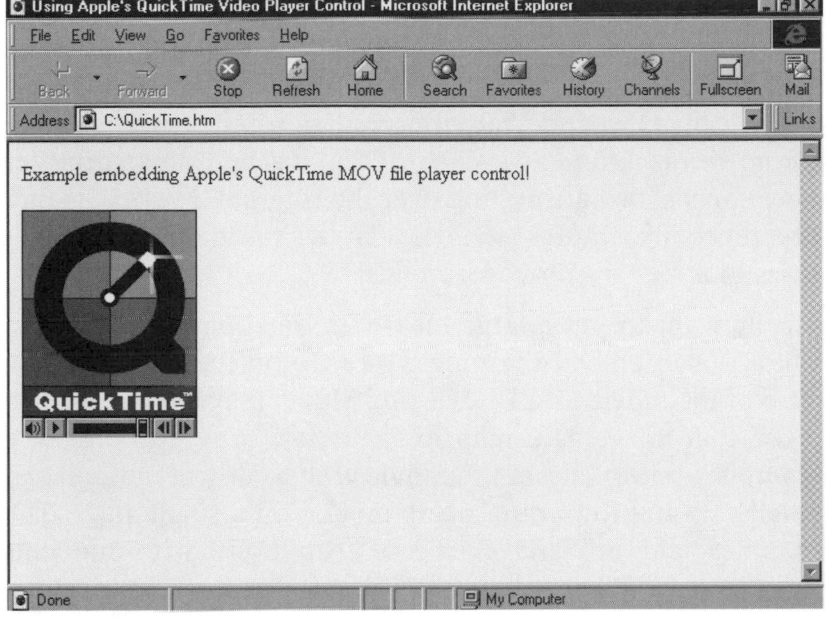

Figure 7–15: *The almost-finished Apple Sample QuickTime MOVie*

First, don't forget that many people still have 14.4- or 28.8-kBps modem links to the Internet. A 28.8-kBps modem can download a movie at about 2.5 kBps maximum, so a 10 second, 500 kB movie can take several minutes to download. Even if you are creating content for an intranet-only T1 or T3 connection, you will find yourself limited by bandwidth. (A T1 line can transfer about 100 kBps, so under the best conditions a 500 kB movie may appear almost instantly–but in practice anything more than 50 kBps is tremendously unlikely, and 10 kBps is much more realistic.)

Unfortunately, digital video movies tend to be large. A typical 30-second sound and video QuickTime movie designed for CD-ROM delivery can amount to several megabytes and can take minutes to download even over a fast connection. So if you have existing content prepared for CD-ROM delivery, you will want to take short clips of the movie and probably recompress them at a smaller size and lower data rate.

Video Compression Utilities

There are two excellent products on the market for video compression: Movie Cleaner Pro and WebMotion plug-in for Movie Cleaner, available from Terran Interactive. WebMotion has built-in settings for compressing movies for transmitting over the Internet. Movie Cleaner Pro has preprocessing features (such as adaptive noise reduction) that make movies look better at low data rates.

If you really want to put a large movie up on your site for down load, it's best not to embed the movie directly on the page. Rather, save a frame of the movie as a PICT using Movie Player, convert it to GIF, and use that image as a map to the actual movie. Or make a postage-stamp-size short clip of the movie with a "download fullsize" option. Finally, try not to put too many movies on a single page. The download times add up, and this can keep users with modems waiting.

Multimedia Reminders

In this chapter you have learned just how easy it is to add multimedia content to an HTML document. But remember that some end users have no sound capabilities or have the sound turned off. Others may resent the increased download time generated by an image that is too large or has too high a resolution image–to the point where they will not return to your site. And finally, multimedia splash is never a substitute for quality content.

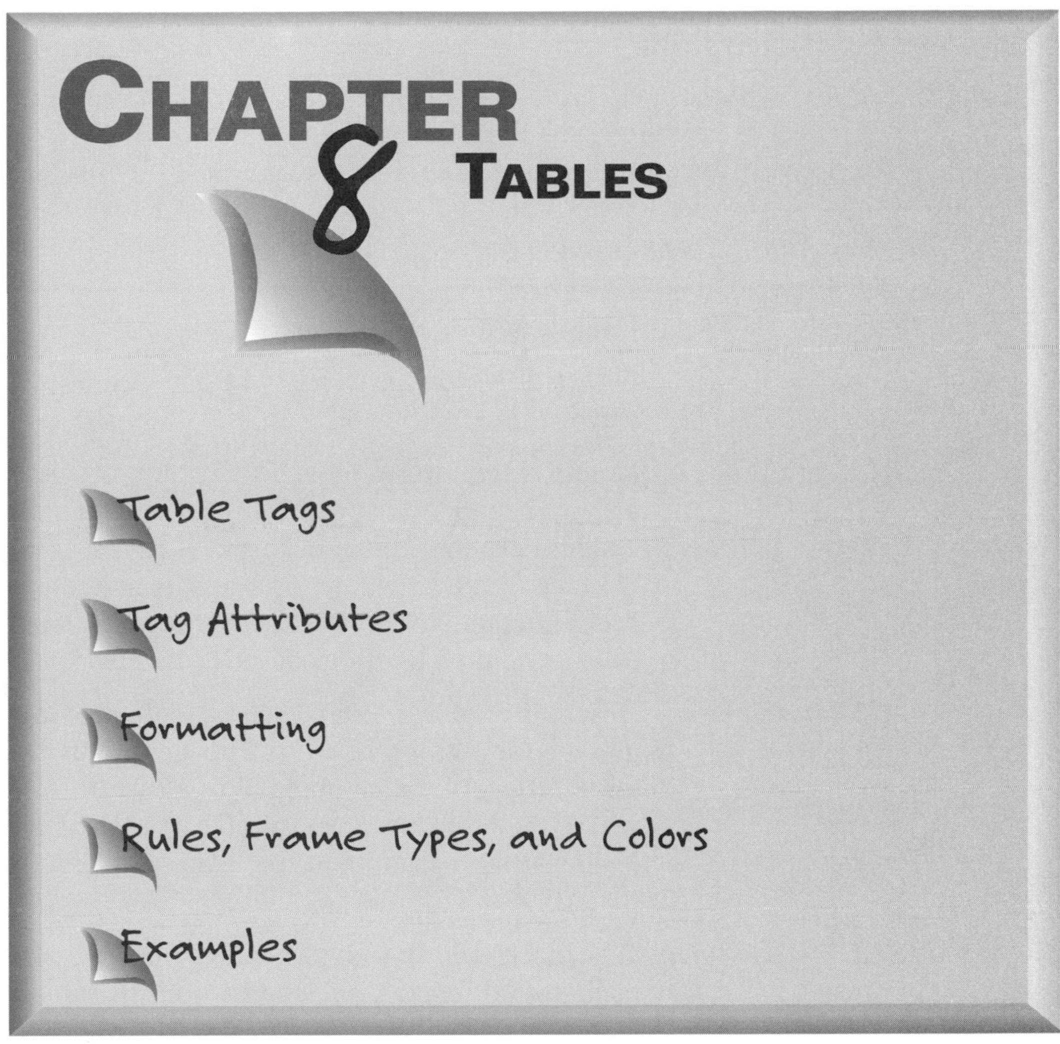

Introduction

The HTML table model allows you to arrange all types of data into rows and columns of cells. These cells may include text, preformatted text, images, links, forms, form fields, other tables, and so on Table cells may contain either header information using the <TH> tag or data using the <TD> tag. Cells may span multiple rows and columns.

You can use tables for many different purposes. The obvious use is for structuring information–for example, international exchange rates and technical data. Tables can also be used to improve the layout of your HTML document by allowing you to place text in columns like a newspaper, or even to align images.

This Chapter's HTML Tags

Tags discussed in this chapter, together with a description of each, are listed in Table 8–1.

Table 8–1: *Table-creation tags list*

Tag	Description
<ALIGN>	Directs the browser to align a table in the viewing area.
AXES (attribute)	(Internet Explorer only) This attribute provides a space-separated list of ID values referencing header cells that relate to this cell. In the absence of this attribute, user agents may make other attempts to identify the pertinent header cells using the algorithm described below.
AXIS (attribute)	(Internet Explorer only) This attribute provides a name for a group of related headers. This allows the table to be mapped to a hierarchy, where the branches correspond to choosing a header from a group and the leaf nodes are data cells.
<BACKGROUND>	(Internet Explorer only) Specifies the URL of a background image displayed behind the table text.
<BGCOLOR>	(Internet Explorer only) Sets the background color of each cell in the table.
<BORDER>	Defines the width of the table border, in pixels.
<BORDERCOLOR>	(Internet Explorer only) Defines the color of a table's border.
<BORDERCOLORDARK>	(Internet Explorer only) Defines the color of the shaded edge of a 3D table border. Colors can be defined using color names, Hex values, or RGB values.

Table 8–1: *Table-creation tags list (continued)*

Tag	Description
<BORDERCOLORLIGHT>	(Internet Explorer only) Defines the color of the side of a 3D border that is not shaded. Colors can be defined using color names, Hex values, or RGB values.
<CAPTION>	Displays the table caption.
CELLPADDING (attribute)	Defined in pixels, this attribute sets the spacing within each cell.
CELLSPACING (attribute)	Defined in pixels, this attribute defines the amount of space between table cells.
<COL>	Groups columns within column groups in order to share attribute values.
<COLGROUP>	Defines a column group.
<FRAME>	Specifies how a frame appears around the table. Options include ABOVE, BELOW, BOX, HSIDES, LHS, RHS, VOID, and VSIDES.
<RULES>	Defines how horizontal rules are used as borders within the interior of a table. Options include ALL, BASIC, CALLS, NONE, and ROWS.
SUMMARY (attribute)	This attribute is used to provide a summary of the table's purpose and structure in order to allow the browser to output to nonvisual media such as speech and Braille.
<TABLE>	Defines the table.
<TBODY>	Defines the table body.
<TD>	Defines a cell's contents.
<TFOOT>	Defines the table footer.
<TH>	Defines the cell contents of the table header.
<THEAD>	Defines the table header.
<TR>	Defines a row of table cells.

In the sections of this chapter that follow we'll investigate the versatility of table elements for rendering text in columnar formats. To create tables in HTML, you define the parts of your table and which bits of HTML go where; then you add HTML table code around those parts. You refine the table's appearance with alignments, borders, and colored cells.

Before you launch into your first table example, though, a word of caution. Creating tables by hand in HTML is no fun. The code for tables was designed to be easy to generate by programs, not to be written by hand, and it can be a bit confusing. Initially, you will do a lot of experimenting, testing, and going back and forth between your browser and your code to get a table to look and work the way you would like.

<TABLE> Creation

To create a table in HTML, you use the <TABLE>, </TABLE> tags surrounding the text for the table's caption and then the contents of the table itself, as in:

```
<TABLE>
…Caption and table contents go here…
</TABLE>
```

Defining Rows and Columns with <TR> and <TD>

You define a table's contents row by row by nesting the associated text between a <TR> and </TR> tag pair. Each table row in turn has a number of columns or table cells, which are surrounded with the <TH> and </TH> tag pair for column headings, or <TD> and </TD> tags for cellular data items, as in:

```
<HTML>
<HEAD>
<TITLE>Table Row and Column Elements</TITLE>
</HEAD>
<BODY>
<TABLE>
```

```
<TR>
    <TH>Column I</TH> <TH>Column II</TH> <TH>Column III</TH>
</TR>
<TR>
    <TD>Data 1-1</TD> <TD>Data 1-2</TD> <TD>Data 1-3</TD>
</TR>
<TR>
    <TD>Data 2-1</TD> <TD>Data 2-2</TD> <TD>Data 2-3</TD>
</TR>
</TABLE>
</BODY>
</HTML>
```

Figure 8–1 displays the resulting page. Compare this with Figure 8–2, which adds the BORDER = 5 attribute.

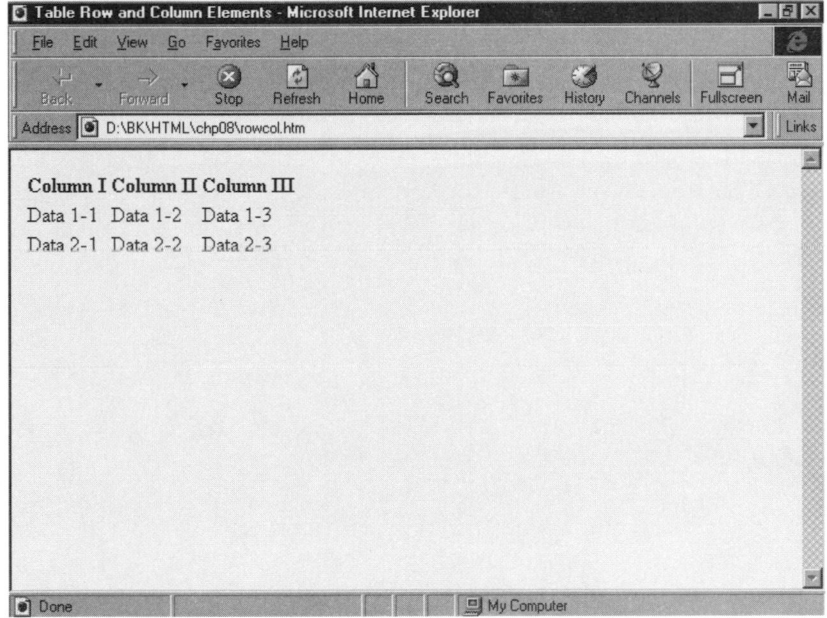

Figure 8–1: *Using the <TABLE>, <TH>, and <TD> elements*

Other Ways to Define Columns

There are several ways to define the number of columns:

1. Specify the number of columns with the COL and COLGROUP tags. (*Note:* These tags can occur only at the start of the table,

immediately after the optional CAPTION attribute.)

2. Scan each row in turn to compute the number of columns needed, taking into account cells that span multiple rows and/or columns. Set the number of columns for the table to be the maximum number of columns needed by any row. For any row that has fewer columns, pad the end of that row with empty cells. Where the "end" of a row is depends on the table's directionality (see the description of the DIR attribute later in this chapter.)
3. Use the use the COLS attribute in the <TABLE>, </TABLE> tag pair. This is the weakest method, since it doesn't provide any additional information about column widths. This may not matter, however, if the author uses style sheets to specify widths.

The following examples demonstrate the various options for defining table columns. Each example renders a table with three columns:

```
<TABLE>
  <COL><COL><COL>
…Table contents go here…
</TABLE>
```

or

```
<TABLE>
  <COL span="3">
…Table contents go here…
</TABLE>
```

or

```
<TABLE>
<TR>
  <TD><TD><TD>
</TR>
</TABLE>
```

or

```
<TABLE cols="3">
…Table contents go here…
</TABLE>
```

Setting Up Column Groups with COLGROUP

You use the <COLGROUP> tag to create an explicit column group. Each group may contain zero or more <COL> elements. The width attribute of the <COLGROUP> defines a default width for each column. The special value "0*" tells the browser to set every column in a group to its minimum width. This behavior may be overridden by the presence of a <COL> element. The table in the following example contains two column groups. The first has 7 columns and the second 5 columns. The default width for each column in the first group is 40 pixels. The width of each column in the second group will be the minimum for the column.

```
<TABLE>
<COLGROUP span="7" width="40">
<COLGROUP span="5" width="0*">
<THEAD>
<TR> ...
</TABLE>
```

In the next example the table is defined to have two column groups. The first contains four columns; the second, two columns. The available horizontal space will be allotted as follows: First the browser will render 40 pixels to the first column, allotting 20 to the second group. Then, the minimal space required for the second column will be allotted to it. The remaining horizontal space will be divided into six equal portions. Column three will receive two of these portions; column four, one; and column five, three.

```
<TABLE>
<COLGROUP>
  <COL width="40">
  <COL width="30">
  <COL width="0*">
  <COL width="2*">
<COLGROUP align="right">
  <COL width="1*">
  <COL width="3*" align="char" char=".">
<THEAD>
<TR> ...
</TABLE>
```

We have set the value of the ALIGN attribute in the second column group to *right*. All cells in every column in this group will inherit this value, but may override it. In fact, the final <COL> does just that, by specifying that every cell in the column it governs will be aligned along the period (.) symbol.

COLSPAN, ROWSPAN, NOWRAP

You may also use the <TD> COLSPAN attribute to define the number of table columns that a cell spans. COLSPAN allows you to combine cells, just as you can in a spreadsheet application. If you need to include the same data in more than one adjacent cell in a row, use COLSPAN. The syntax is straightforward:

```
<TD COLSPAN=number_of_adjacent cells>
```

ROWSPAN is similar in that it defines the number of table rows that a cell spans. ROWSPAN also allows you to join adjacent cells so that you can render one set of data across multiple rows. The syntax looks like this:

```
<TD ROWSPAN=number_of_adjacent_rows>
```

Finally, NOWRAP prevents cell contents from wrapping within a cell. You use this attribute when you are formatting data. Be careful, though: using this attribute can generate extremely wide cells. The syntax for NOWRAP looks like this:

```
<TD NOWRAP>
```

Adding a <BORDER>

One of the first enhancements you can add to the table's appearance is a border. The BORDER element is defined in number of pixels. BORDER has a default value of 1 pixel when left undefined.

```
<HTML>
<HEAD>
<TITLE>Table Row and Column Elements with Border</TITLE>
</HEAD>
<BODY>
```

```
<TABLE BORDER="5">
<TR>
    <TH>Column I</TH> <TH>Column II</TH> <TH>Column III</TH>
</TR>
<TR>
    <TD>Data 1-1</TD> <TD>Data 1-2</TD> <TD>Data 1-3</TD>
</TR>
<TR>
    <TD>Data 2-1</TD> <TD>Data 2-2</TD> <TD>Data 2-3</TD>
</TR>
</TABLE>
</BODY>
</HTML>
```

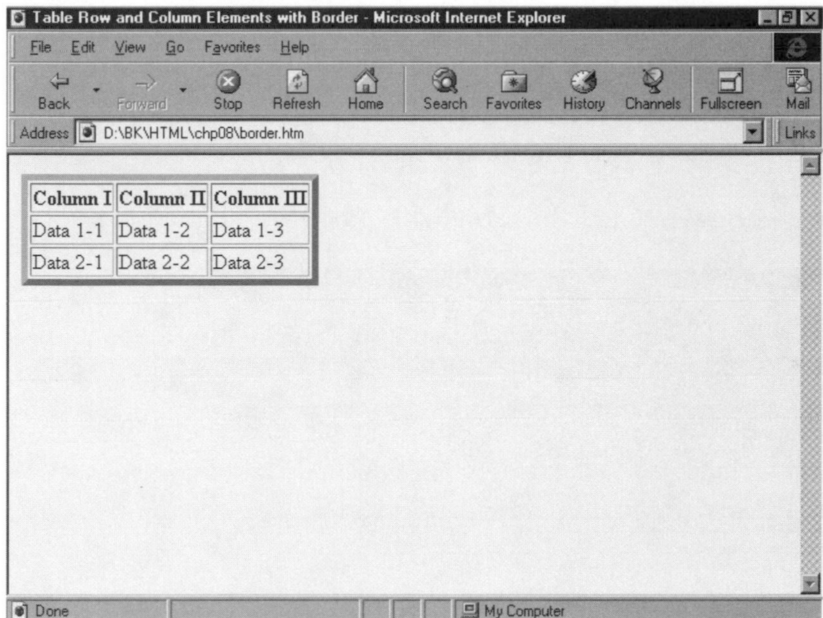

Figure 8–2: *Original table redefined with a rendered border attribute*

Adding Table <CAPTION>s

To add a brief table description for your table, add a <CAPTION>, </CAPTION> tag pair right after the <TABLE> tag. You can think of the <CAPTION> tag for tables as being equivalent to the <HEAD> tag for the <BODY> of your HTML document. <CAPTION> has a placement option of TOP or BOTTOM. The following example places the caption in the more common BOTTOM position:

```
<HTML>
<HEAD>
<TITLE>Table Row and Column Elements with Border and
    Caption</TITLE>
</HEAD>
<BODY>
<TABLE BORDER="5">
<CAPTION ALIGN=BOTTOM>Completed Example Table with
    caption.</CAPTION>
<TR>
    <TH>Column I</TH> <TH>Column II</TH> <TH>Column III</TH>
</TR>
<TR>
    <TD>Data 1-1</TD> <TD>Data 1-2</TD> <TD>Data 1-3</TD>
</TR>
<TR>
    <TD>Data 2-1</TD> <TD>Data 2-2</TD> <TD>Data 2-3</TD>
</TR>
</TABLE>
</BODY>
</HTML>
```

Figure 8–3 now renders the table with a bottom-aligned caption.

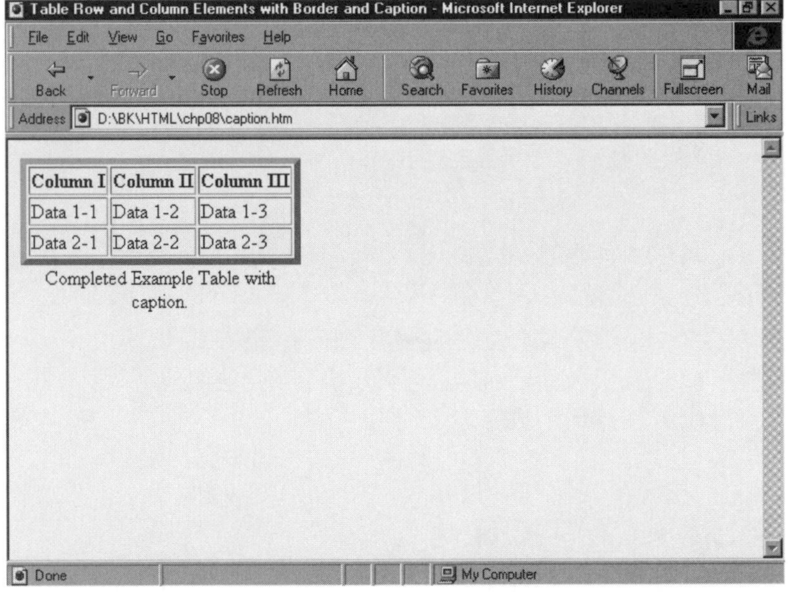

Figure 8–3: *Original table rendered with a CAPTION*

Selecting Table Position with ALIGN

Depending on your table's contents, you may generate a more easily viewed rendering by instructing the browser to align the table either to the LEFT (the default mode), CENTER, or RIGHT on your Web page. The following HTML document adds CENTER table alignment to the previous example.

```
<HTML>
<HEAD>
<TITLE>Table Rendered with CENTER Alignment</TITLE>
</HEAD>
<BODY>
<TABLE ALIGN=CENTER BORDER>
<TR>
    <TH>Column I</TH> <TH>Column II</TH> <TH>Column III</TH>
</TR>
<TR>
    <TD>Data 1-1</TD> <TD>Data 1-2</TD> <TD>Data 1-3</TD>
</TR>
<TR>
    <TD>Data 2-1</TD> <TD>Data 2-2</TD> <TD>Data 2-3</TD>
</TR>
</TABLE>
</BODY>
</HTML>
```

Figure 8–4 displays the modified table alignment.

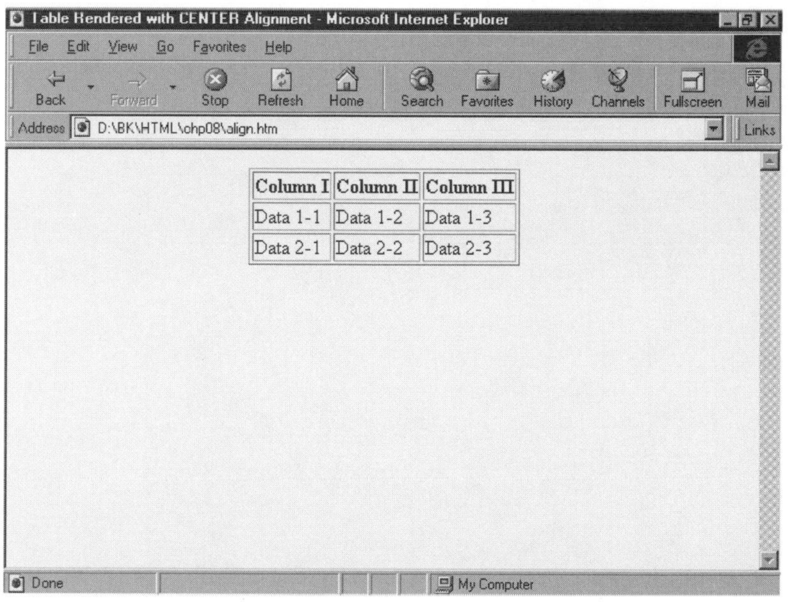

Figure 8–4: *Table centering using ALIGN=CENTER attribute*

The next example demonstrates how to align cell contents. Once again, data elements have LEFT, CENTER, and RIGHT alignment options only.

```
<HTML>
<HEAD>
<TITLE>Table Rendered with Varying Cell Content
    Alignment</TITLE>
</HEAD>
<BODY>
<TABLE ALIGN=CENTER BORDER>
<TR>
    <TH>Column I</TH> <TH>Column II</TH> <TH>Column III</TH>
</TR>
<TR ALIGN=CENTER>
    <TD>Center 1-1</TD> <TD>Center 1-2</TD> <TD>Center 1-3</TD>
</TR>
<TR ALIGN=RIGHT>
    <TD>Right 2-1</TD> <TD>Right 2-2</TD> <TD>Right 2-3</TD>
</TR>
</TABLE>
</BODY>
</HTML>
```

Figure 8–5 renders the modified cell contents. Row one aligns each cell using the CENTER attribute and row two uses RIGHT alignment. The default is LEFT.

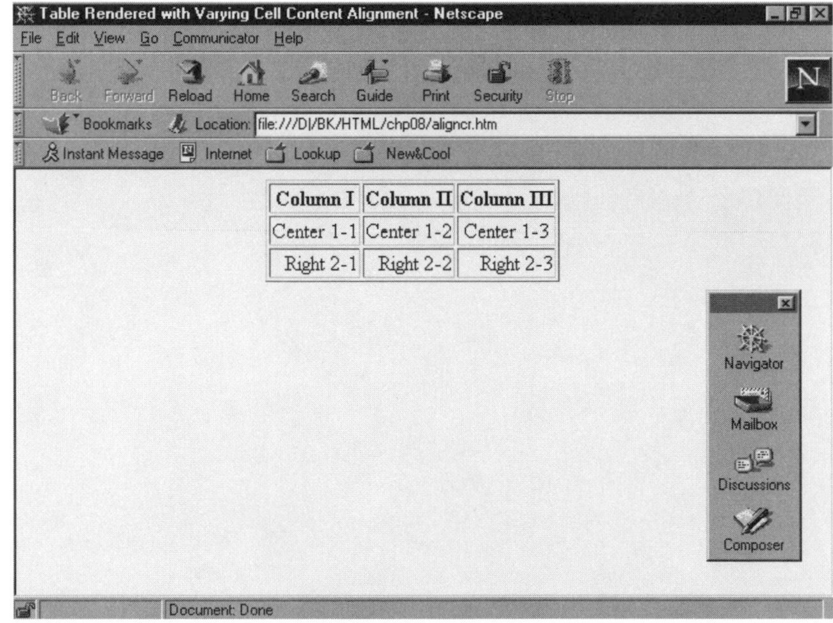

Figure 8–5: *Modifying cell ALIGNment with CENTER and RIGHT*

VALIGN, CHAR, and CHAROFF

The VALIGN attribute is similar to ALIGN only it defines the vertical alignment of text in the cells in the row. The syntax is:

```
<TR VALIGN="TYPE">
```

where TYPE is either TOP, MIDDLE, BOTTOM, or BASELINE. Table 8–2 describes each option.

Table 8–2: *VALIGN types and descriptions*

Type	Description
TOP	Cell contents are aligned with the top of each cell space
MIDDLE	Cell contents are aligned with the middle of each cell space. Cell data is centered vertically within the cell. This is the default value
BOTTOM	Cell contents are aligned with the bottom of each cell space
BASELINE	Cell contents are aligned along a common baseline

The <TR> CHAR attribute allows you to align cell contents with a specific character. The default character is the decimal point. The syntax looks like this:

```
<TR CHAR="single_character">
```

CHAR and CHAROFF attributes usually appear in pairs. CHAROFF defines the offset to the first alignment character. The offset is usually from the left margin for Latin-based cell text contents. If a line doesn't include the alignment character, browsers usually shift the cell contents so that they end at the alignment position. The syntax for CHAROFF looks like this:

```
<TR CHAROFF="25%">
```

Setting Internal Cell Dimensions with CELLPADDING

As you will soon discover, just about every aspect of a table's appearance has an author-definable setting. You can even determine the amount of spacing above, below, and around each cell's contents by applying a number-of-pixels value to the CELLPADDING attribute. The following HTML sets this value to 30:

```
<HTML>
<HEAD>
<TITLE>Table Rendered with 30-Pixel Cell Widths</TITLE>
</HEAD>
<BODY>
<TABLE CELLPADDING=30>
<CAPTION>"Example Changing Cell Wall Dimensions."</CAPTION>
<TR>
    <TH>Column I</TH> <TH>Column II</TH> <TH>Column III</TH>
</TR>
<TR>
    <TD>Center 1-1</TD> <TD>Center 1-2</TD> <TD>Center 1-3</TD>
</TR>
<TR>
    <TD>Right 2-1</TD> <TD>Right 2-2</TD> <TD>Right 2-3</TD>
</TR>
</TABLE>
</BODY>
</HTML>
```

Figure 8–6 renders the newly padded cell's dimensions.

Figure 8–6 also demonstrates the visual impact of a borderless table, which takes on the appearance of columnar data lists.

CELLSPACING, FRAME, RULES, and WIDTH Attributes

Another approach to table data spacing is to use the CELLSPACING attribute. Unlike CELLPADDING, which defines the number of pixels surrounding the cell's contents, CELLPADDING defines the number of pixels *between* each cell wall, as in:

```
<TABLE CELLSPACING=5>
```

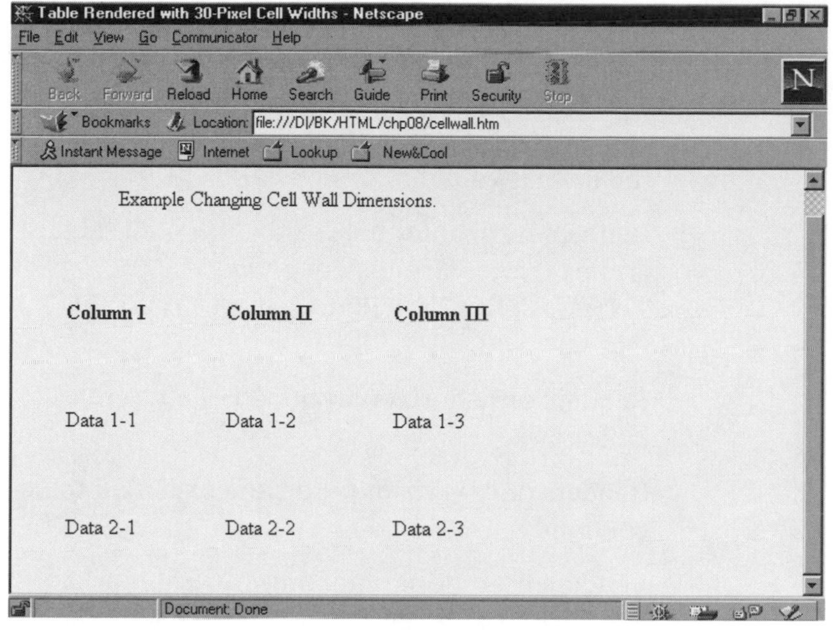

Figure 8–6: *Using the CELLPADDING attribute to change cell-content spacing*

The table WIDTH attribute allows you to set the width of the entire table, defined in number-of-pixels or as a percentage of the window's dimensions, as in:

```
<TABLE WIDTH="50%">
```

The RULES attribute defines which inner borders of the table to render. The syntax is:

```
<TABLE RULES="TYPES"
```

Table 8–3 lists the legal available RULE types.

Like RULES, the FRAME attribute describes how the outer border of the table is rendered. The FRAME attribute is more diverse than the BORDER attribute. The syntax looks like this:

```
<TABLE FRAME="TYPE">
```

Table 8–4 lists the available FRAME TYPEs.

Table 8–3: *RULES types and descriptions*

Type	Description
NONE	Does not render any internal borders This is the default value.
GROUPS	Renders horizontal borders between all table groups (Note: Groups are defined by the THEAD, TBODY, TFOOT, and COLGROUP tags.)
ROWS	Renders only horizontal borders between all table rows
COLS	Renders only vertical borders between all table columns
ALL	Renders both horizontal and vertical borders between all table cells

Table 8–4: *FRAME types and descriptions*

Type	Description
VOID	Does not render any outer border This is the default value.
ABOVE	Renders only the top outer border
BELOW	Renders only the bottom outer border
HSIDES	Renders only the top and bottom outer borders
LHS	Renders only the left-hand-side outer border
RHS	Renders only the right-hand-side outer border
VSIDES	Renders only the left and right outer borders
BOX	Renders an outer border on all sides of the table frame.
BORDER	Same as BOX

Adding Color and Image with Internet Explorer's BORDERCOLOR, BGCOLOR, BACKGROUND, Using <COLGROUP>

Just as you would rather view a color television image than a black-and-white one, your Internet Explorer Web page visitors will prefer viewing tables rendered in color. But first note the cardinal rule on color selection, recognized by all professional graphics: limit the *number* of colors in a graphic display to **three!** Using more than three creates visual confusion and reduces the intended impact.

One of the best uses for color is within a table. When a table contains many columns and numerous rows of data, and one is scanning extreme right-and-bottom cells, far from their row and column headings, it becomes difficult to know what data goes with which label. Simply highlighting alternate rows or columns in a different color eliminates this grid confusion.

Using <COLGROUP> and BGCOLOR

In order to effect a row-by-row attribute change, you first need to define column groups. Each column group you define can contain its own unique set of attributesóin this case, background color. The <COLGROUP> tag has the following attributes: ALIGN, CHAR, CHAROFF, VALIGN, SPAN, and WIDTH. The following HTML example combines <COLGROUP> and BGCOLOR:

```
<HTML>
<HEAD>
<TITLE>Candy-Striped Column Highlighting</TITLE>
</HEAD>
<BODY>
<TABLE BORDER=15>
<COLGROUP ALIGN=CENTER>
```

(continued)

```
<COLGROUP SPAN=3 ALIGN=LEFT>
<COLGROUP SPAN=2 ALIGN=RIGHT BGCOLOR="GRAY">
<CAPTION ALIGN=TOP>Visually Separating Columns with
    Color</CAPTION>
<TR><TH><TH COLSPAN=3>Internal<TH COLSPAN=2>External
<TR><TH><TH>Modems<TH>28K<TH>36K<TH>36K<TH>56K
<TR><TH>Card<TD><TD>2<TD>1<TD>0<TD >2
<TR><TH>Board<TD>1<TD>1<TD>0<TD>1<TD>0
<TD><TH>Sales<TD>0<TD>0<TD>0<TD>1<TD>1
<TR><TH>Quantity<BR>On Order<TD>0<TD>2<TD>0<TD>0<TD>0
</TABLE>
</BODY>
</HTML>
```

Figure 8–7 demonstrates how column highlighting helps separate rows and columns of information.

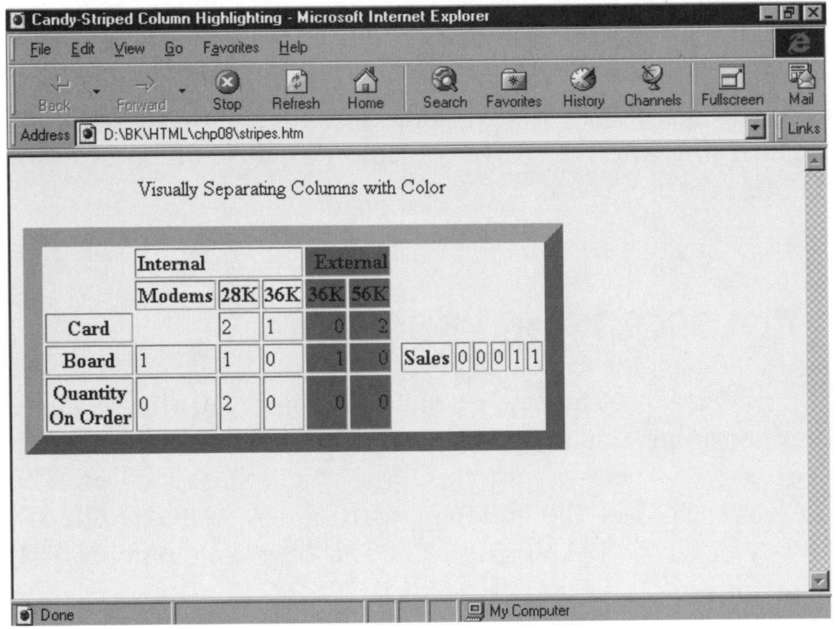

Figure 8–7: *Separating columns of information with color highlighting*

Of course, on a color display, changing the BORDERCOLOR can help attract the end-user's eye to thc entire table. The following HTML change demonstrates how easy this is:

```
<TABLE BORDER="15" BORDERCOLOR="BLUE">
```

Changing a Table's BACKGROUND

Cell-background enhancements aren't limited just to colors. Using the BACKGROUND attribute inside a <TABLE> </TABLE> definition allows you to paint each cell with a graphics image.

```
<HTML>
<HEAD>
<TITLE>Candy-Striped Column Highlighting</TITLE>
</HEAD>
<BODY  TEXT="WHITE">
<TABLE BORDER="15"
BACKGROUND="d:\bk\html\chp08\Firework.jpg">
<COLGROUP ALIGN=CENTER>
<COLGROUP SPAN=3 ALIGN=LEFT>
<COLGROUP SPAN=2 ALIGN=RIGHT BGCOLOR="GRAY">
<TR><TH><TH COLSPAN=3>Internal<TH COLSPAN=2>External
<TR><TH><TH>Modems<TH>28K<TH>36K<TH>36K<TH>56K
<TR><TH>Card<TD><TD>2<TD>1<TD>0<TD >2
<TR><TH>Board<TD>1<TD>1<TD>0<TD>1<TD>0
<TD><TH>Sales<TD>0<TD>0<TD>0<TD>1<TD>1
<TR><TH>Quantity<BR>On Order<TD>0<TD>2<TD>0<TD>0<TD>0
</TABLE>
</BODY>
</HTML>
```

Figure 8–8 renders the table with a slightly more explosive background.

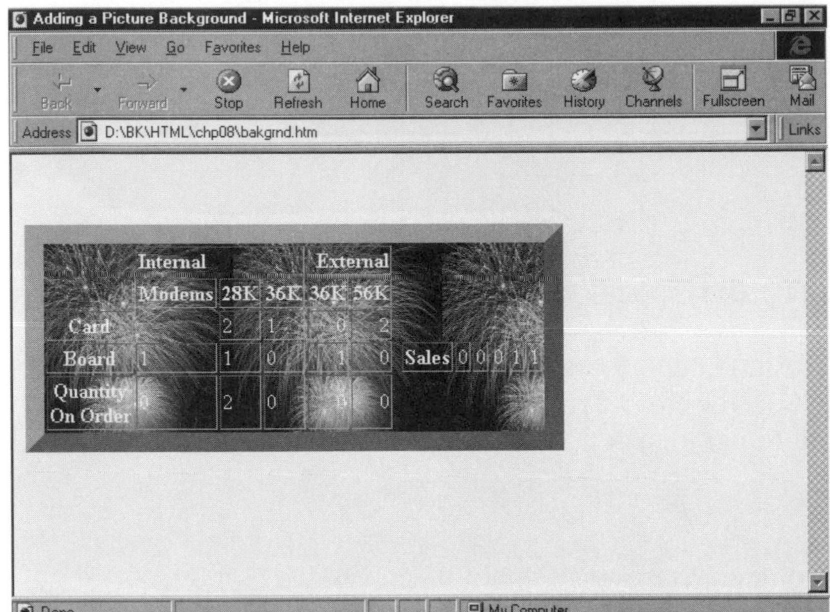

Figure 8–8: *Adding visual impact with a table BACKGROUND image*

Loading Tables from Right to Left with <DIR>

The direction in which a table's contents are rendered is specified by the DIR attribute for the <TABLE>/ </TABLE> tag pair. For a left-to-right table (the default), column one is at the left side of the table and row one is at the top. For a right-to-left table, column one is at the right side and row one is at the top.

Similarly, for left-to-right tables (the default), extra row cells are added to the right of the table, and for right-to-left tables, extra cells are added to the left side. When set for the <TABLE> tag, the DIR attribute also affects the direction of text within table cells. To specify a right-to-left table, set the DIR attribute as follows:

```
<TABLE DIR="RTL">
…Table contents go here…
</TABLE>
```

Should you need to change the direction of text within an individual cell, use the DIR attribute within the tag that defines the cell itself.

Table Footers

The HTML table tags <THEAD>, <TFOOT>, and <TBODY> allow you to group table rows into a head, foot, and one or more body sections. This allows browsers to scroll through table contents separately from their head and foot sections. When long tables are printed, the head and foot information may be repeated on each page that contains table data.

In order for the browser to display the footer before receiving all of the rows of data, the <TFOOT> tag must always appear before the <TBODY> tag and be nested inside the <TABLE>, </TABLE> tag pair. The list below summarizes which tags are required and which may be omitted:

- The TBODY start tag is always required except when the table contains only one body and no head or foot sections. The TBODY end tag may always be safely omitted.
- The start tags for THEAD and TFOOT are required when the head and foot sections, respectively, are present, but the corresponding end tags may always be safely omitted.

The following example demonstrates how to break your HTML table into a header, footer, and body sections:

```
<TABLE>
   <THEAD>
      …header information goes here…
   </THEAD>
   <TFOOT>
      …footer information here…
   </TFOOT>
   <TBODY>
      …finally the table body here…
   </TBODY>
</TABLE>
```

Spoken Tables with AXIS and AXES

The HTML attributes AXIS and AXES allow you to enhance a table's visual presentation by adding an auditory component. If you know that your Web page might be viewed by the visually impaired, you can have the tables rendered using the latest in speech- and Braille-based technologies. In the following example table, the value of the AXES attribute is set to reference the corresponding header cell for that column:

```
<TABLE BORDER="10" SUMMARY="Manufacturer, Number in
   stock, product, is backordered.">
<CAPTION>Quantity of Instock-Items.</CAPTION>
<TR>
   <TH ID="t1">Manufacturer</TH>
   <TH ID="t2">Instock</TH>
   <TH ID="t3" ABBR="Product">Type of Product</TH>
   <TH ID="t4">Backordered?</TH>
<TR>
   <TD AXES="t1">USRobotics</TD>
   <TD AXES="t2">11</TD>
   <TD AXES="t3">56K Modems</TD>
   <TD AXES="t4">Yes</TD>
<TR>
   <TD AXES="t1">Toshiba Am.</TD>
   <TD AXES="t2">15</TD>
   <TD AXES="t3">Techra</TD>
   <TD AXES="t4">Yes</TD>
</TABLE>
```

This mark-up could be rendered to speech as:

```
Caption: Quantity of Instock-Items

Summary: Manufacturer, Number, product, is backordered.

Name: US Robotics, Instock: 11, Product: Modems,
Backordered?: Yes

Name: Toshiba Am., Instock: 15, Product: Techra,
Backordered?: Yes
```

Note how the header *Type of Product* is abbreviated to *Product* using the ABBR attribute. In the absence of the AXES attribute, a browser may choose to search for an ordered list of headers using one of the following methods:

- A left-to-right cell-position scan is used order to detect header cells (the search is canceled whenever the table extent is reached or a data cell is found after a header cell).
- An upward column search is used for header-cell information (the search is canceled whenever the table extent is reached or a data cell is found after a header cell).
- Row headers are inserted into the table in the order they appear: for example, the leftmost headers are inserted before the header to the right, or column headers are inserted after corresponding row headers in the order they appear in the table, and the topmost header is inserted before the header below it.
- When a header cell contains the AXES attribute, the header is referenced by this attribute and is inserted into the listóstopping the directional search.
- When a cell contains both the <TD> tag and AXIS attribute, the cell is treated as acting as a <TH> tagged cell.

HTML Table Example

The following example HTML renders a portion of Appendix D using grouped rows and columns. It is an excellent example from which to clone or on which to base your own meaningful tables:

```
<HTML>
<HEAD>
<TITLE>Attribute Name</TITLE>
</HEAD>
<BODY>

<TABLE BORDER CELLSPACING=1 CELLPADDING=7 WIDTH=583>
<CAPTION>Portion of Appendix D</CAPTION>

<TH BGCOLOR="GRAY"><FONT FACE="Arial,Times New Roman"
   SIZE=4><P>Attribute Name</FONT>
```

(continued)

```
<TH BGCOLOR="GRAY"><FONT FACE="Arial,Times New Roman"
   SIZE=4><P>Related Elements</FONT>
<TH BGCOLOR="GRAY"><FONT FACE="Arial,Times New Roman"
   SIZE=4><P>Note</FONT>

<TR><TD WIDTH="27%" VALIGN="TOP">
<FONT FACE="Arial,Times New Roman"
   SIZE=3><P><B>abbr</B></FONT></TD>
<TD WIDTH="29%" VALIGN="TOP">
<FONT FACE="Times,Times New Roman" SIZE=2><P>TD</P>
<P>TH</FONT></TD>
<TD WIDTH="44%" VALIGN="TOP">
<FONT FACE="Times,Times New Roman"
   SIZE=2><P>Abbreviation used for header.</FONT></TD>
</TR>

<TR BGCOLOR="GRAY"><TD WIDTH="27%" VALIGN="TOP">
<FONT FACE="Arial,Times New Roman"
   SIZE=3><P><B>accept-charset</B></FONT></TD>
<TD WIDTH="29%" VALIGN="TOP">
<FONT FACE="Times,Times New Roman"
   SIZE=2><P>FORM</FONT></TD>
<TD WIDTH="44%" VALIGN="TOP">
<FONT FACE="Times,Times New Roman"
   SIZE=2><P>Character sets that are
   supported.</FONT></TD>
</TR>

<TR><TD WIDTH="27%" VALIGN="TOP">
<FONT FACE="Arial,Times New Roman"
   SIZE=3><P><B>accept</B></FONT></TD>
<TD WIDTH="29%" VALIGN="TOP">
<FONT FACE="Times,Times New Roman"
   SIZE=2><P>INPUT</FONT></TD>
<TD WIDTH="44%" VALIGN="TOP">
<FONT FACE="Times,Times New Roman" SIZE=2><P>MIME
   types available for file uploading.</FONT></TD>
</TR>

<TR BGCOLOR="GRAY"><TD WIDTH="27%" VALIGN="TOP">
<FONT FACE="Arial,Times New Roman"
   SIZE=3><P><B>accesskey</B></FONT></TD>
<TD WIDTH="29%" VALIGN="TOP">
<FONT FACE="Times,Times New Roman" SIZE=2><P>A</P>
<P>AREA</P>
<P>BUTTON</P>
<P>INPUT</P>
<P>LABEL</P>
<P>LEGEND</FONT></TD>
<TD WIDTH="44%" VALIGN="TOP">
<FONT FACE="Times,Times New Roman" SIZE=2><P>Key
```

```
   character accessibility.</FONT></TD>
</TR>

<TR><TD WIDTH="27%" VALIGN="TOP">
<FONT FACE="Arial,Times New Roman"
   SIZE=3><P><B>action</B></FONT></TD>
<TD WIDTH="29%" VALIGN="TOP">
<FONT FACE="Times,Times New Roman"
   SIZE=2><P>FORM</FONT></TD>
<TD WIDTH="44%" VALIGN="TOP">
<FONT FACE="Times,Times New Roman" SIZE=2><P>Provides
   information for the server-side form
   handler.</FONT></TD>
</TR>

</TABLE>

</BODY>
</HTML>
```

Figure 8–9 shows the resulting table using many of the common table elements discussed in this chapter. You will notice from the HTML document that creation of a lengthy table is a painstaking endeavor, as you manually enter detailed HTML and data elements for each row and column.

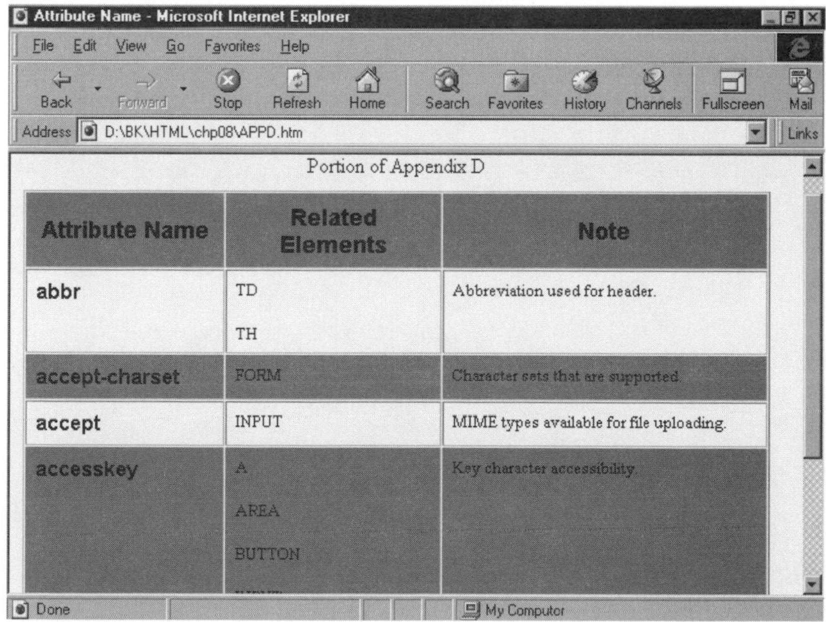

Figure 8–9: *Portion of Appendix D*

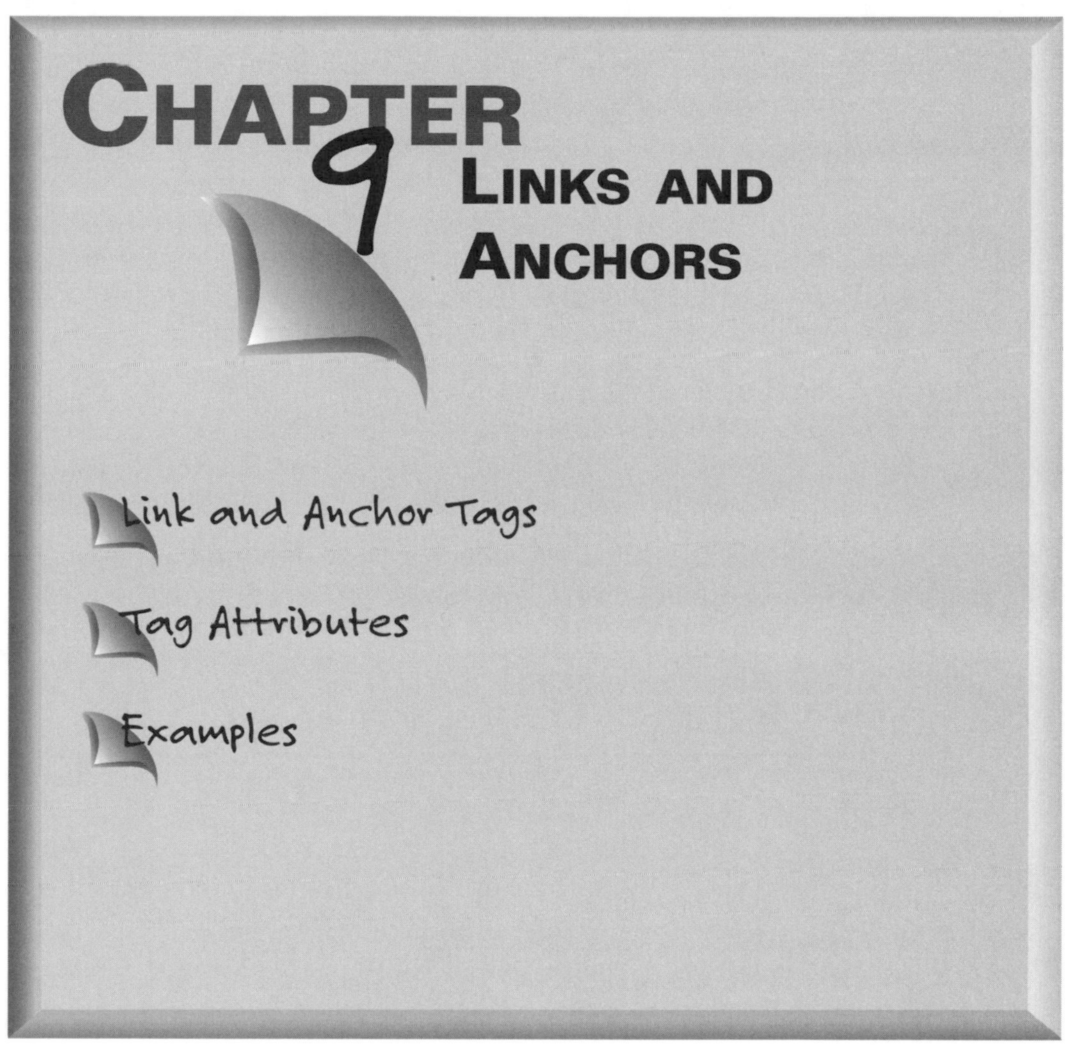

Introduction

HTML offers a unique advantage over other markup languages: its ability to incorporate hypertext and interactive documents. This chapter looks deeper into the link or hyperlink, the basic hypertext construct. A *link* is a connection from one Web resource to another. This end-user-friendly feature underlies much of the popularity of Web surfing.

Technically speaking, a link has two ends or anchors, along with an associated direction. The source anchor is located on the originating

HTML document and points to the destination anchor. The destination anchor can include any type of browser-aware resource such as a text document, graphic image, sound bite, video stream, or even a program.

This Chapter's HTML Tags

The <A>nchor element is the gateway for adding hyperlinks to almost any document type. Hyperlinks are not limited just to text. You can also use an image as a hyperlink by placing the image between the <A> and </A> anchor tags in the same way you would place text.

Table 9–1 describes the <A>nchor and <LINK> tag elements. In the section that follow we'll investigate the versatility of the anchor element.

Table 9–1: *Elements for defining and using links*

Tag	Description
<A>	The <A>nchor element is used to define both the source and destination of a hypertext link. Frequently used attributes include HREF, NAME, REL, REV, COORDS, SHAPE and TITLE.
<LINK>	The <LINK> element specifies the current document's relationship with other documents. It is rarely used, however, because it requires properly defined values that, as yet, haven't been fully determined (see Chapter 4).

Using the ANCHOR Element

HTML provides two elements for defining and using links, the <LINK> and <A> elements, along with the HREF, NAME, REV, REL, COORDS, SHAPE, and TITLE attributes. Each has its own syntax. For example, <LINK> can appear only in the head of an HTML document, while <A> can be placed anywhere in the <BODY>. (*Note:* <LINK> is discussed in detail in Chapter 4.)

Browsers process the referenced link in different ways, depending on the resource type. In some instances the browser opens a new document window; in others it may actually launch a separate program to handle the resource. However, most browsers render an <A>nchor flagged element by underlining the reference, indicating the presence of the link. If the <A>nchor reference uses the NAME attribute, the reference defines an anchor that is probably accessed by other links. HTML allows the <A>nchor reference to use both the HREF and NAME attributes at the same time.

Correct <A>nchor Names

HTML <A>nchor names have a set of rules all their own. First, they must be unique within the defining document. Since they are case-insensitive, the following example is illegal with respect to uniqueness (the two names being the same except for case):

```
<A NAME="Section1">...>/A>
<A NAME="SECTION1">...>/A>
```

Second, <A>nchor-name comparisons between fragment URL IDentifiers and <A>anchor names must be executed to generate an identical pair. For example, the following example is correct, using the rules of string matching:

```
<A HREF="#Section1">...>/A>
...additional document goes here...
<A HREF="Section1">...>/A>
```

The next example highlights some of the peculiarities in various browsers, as some will consider the example HTML a match, others will not. Note, however, that the example is technically legal HTML:

```
<A NAME="#Section1">...>/A>
...additional document goes here...
<A HREF="Section1">...>/A>
```

While on the subject of <A>nchor rules, here's one more: <A>nchors may not be nested. The following example demonstrates an illegal attempt at putting an <A>nchor within another <A>nchor reference:

```
<A NAME="GG1 Locator" HREF="gg1usasl">First Anchor
<A NAME="GG1 East Coast" HREF="gg1ec.html">Nested Anchor
</A></A>
```

Using <A>nchor with the HREF Attribute

The most frequent use for an HTML link is to access another resource on the Internet. The following HTML example contains three links. The first accesses a fellow hobbyist's Web site, the second references a hobby-related sales brochure, and the third attaches to a JPG image file:

```
<HTML>
<HEAD>
<TITLE>Using HyperText Links</TITLE>
</HEAD>
<BODY>
<H1>Using HyperText Links</H1>
A Friend's Web-site
   <A HREF="www.myhome.com/jim/index.html"></A>.<BR>
For Catalog Info see
   <A HREF="www.myhome.com/jim/catalog.html"></A>.<BR>
My Favorite GG1 image
   <A HREF="www.myhome.com/jim/gg1.gif"></A><BR>.<BR>
</BODY>
</HTML>
```

By clicking with the mouse, using keyboard input, or nowadays using voice commands, users activate the link allowing them to visit such resources (see Figure 9–1). Note that an attribute in each source anchor specifies the address of the destination anchor with a URL. Sometimes the destination anchor of a link is an element within the source HTML document. In this case the destination anchor is given an anchor name, and any URL addressing this anchor must include the name as its fragment identifier.

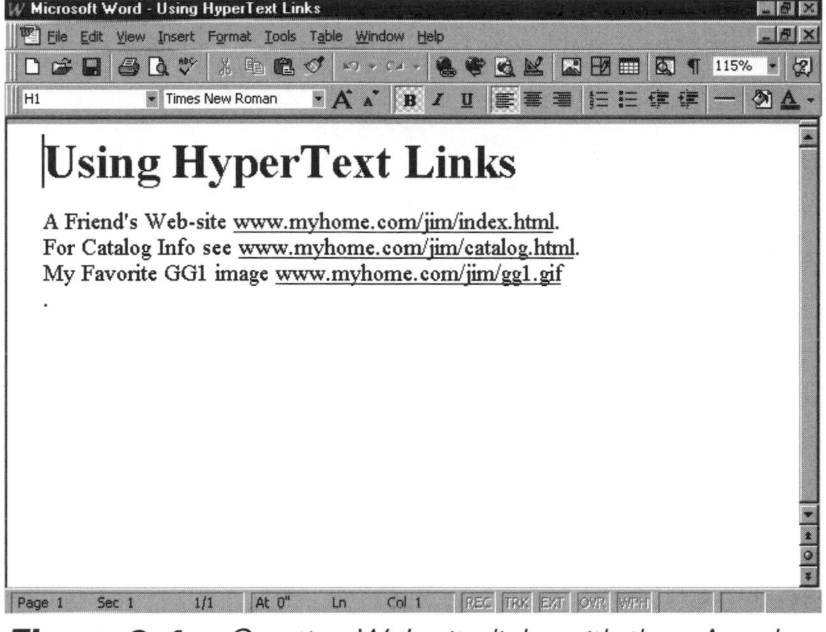

Figure 9–1: *Creating Web-site links with the <A>nchor HREF attribute*

A destination anchor must include either an <A>nchor element (naming it with the ID attribute) or any other element (naming with the ID attribute). For example, an HTML author could easily create a catalog whose entries link to header elements within the document, as in:

```
<BODY>
<H1>GG1's Past and Present</H1>
<A HREF="#Past">GG1s of Yesteryear</A><BR>
<A HREF="#Present">Where are GG1s Today?</A><BR>
<A HREF="#Present.1">An Original Pensy GG1</A><BR>
…and so on with detailed catalog information here…
…remainder of body goes here…
<H2><A name="Past">GG1 Conductor Tells All</A></H2>
…confessions of train conductor…
<H2><A name="Present">Across the US</A></H2>
…Nation-wide info goes here…
<H3><A name="Present.1">East Coast Locations</A></H2>
…East Coast info goes here…
```

However HTML anchor elements also allow the author to actually make the header elements the anchors. Many HTML authors prefer the more streamlined version seen next:

```
<BODY>
<H1>GG1s Past and Present</H1>
<A HREF="#Past">GG1s of Yesteryear</A><BR>
<A HREF="#Present">Where are GG1s Today?</A><BR>
<A HREF="#Present.1">An Original Pensy GG1</A><BR>
…and so on with detailed catalog information here…
…remainder of body goes here…
<H2 id="Past">GG1 Conductor Tells All</H2>
…confessions of train conductor…
<H2 id="Present">Across the US</H2>
…nation-wide info goes here…
<H3 id="Present">East Coast Locations</H3>
…East Coast info goes here…
```

Using <A>nchors with TITLE Attributes

You use the <A>nchor element to specify a relationship between the current, or source, document and another resource. Although the link referenced has no content, the relationships it defines may be recognized and rendered by the browser. <A>nchor is frequently used in conjunction with the TITLE attribute to add information about the nature of a link. How the browser interprets the resource depends on its content type. The reference might be rendered as a tool tip. It may play a background theme or even speak the information out loud. The following example demonstrates the syntax for using the TITLE attribute:

```
<BODY>
…the main body goes here…
For further information see
<A HREF="../GG1Begin.html" TITLE="GG1 Background">History</A>.
To see your first GG1<A HREF="../gg1jpgs/gg1-1.jpg"
  TITLE="JPEG image of the original GG1">Pensy GG1</A>
</BODY>
```

Using the <A>nchor ID Attribute

Another way to create an anchor is to use the ID attribute within the start tag of any element. The following HTML example begins by attaching an ID to an H2 element:

```
<BODY>
If you are interested in GG1 use today see GG1s Today
<A HREF="#GG1Today">GG1s Today</A>.
...defined elsewhere within the document...
<H2 ID="GG1Today">GG1s Today</H2>
...or generate a backwards reference with...
If you think the past was interesting see GG1s Today
<A HREF="#GG1Today">GG1s Today</A> for an update.
</BODY>
```

The GG1Today anchor is linked via the `<A HREF="#GG1Today">` element. The ID name attributes share the same name space, so once again the rule of uniqueness applies. This means that the following HTML document is illegal:

```
<BODY>
<A HREF="#GG1Today">...</A>
...some document goes here...
<H1 ID="GG1Today">
...more HTML text...
<A NAME="GG1Today"></A>
</BODY>
```

HTML specifies that the NAME attribute may contain entities–for example, numeric character references in either decimal or hexadecimal, or named character references. For these reasons the following are legal NAME attributes:

```
D&#253;rst
```

and

```
D&yacute;rst
```

Note, however, that the ID attribute cannot contain entities.

A Word about URL Paths

You always want to set up your HTML document so that your links work properly. In HTML, path information is always defined with a URL. Relative URLs are resolved according to a base URL, which may come from a variety of sources. By simply including a BASE element you define the starting point for all further relative URL references (*Note:* The OBJECT and APPLET elements define attributes that take precedence over the value set by the BASE element.) Remember that the BASE tag must be present within the <HEAD> section of an HTML document–for example:

```
<HTML>
 <HEAD>
   <TITLE>GG1 Catalog</TITLE>
   <BASE HREF="http://www.myservice.com/GG1/cover.html">
 </HEAD>

 <BODY>
   Take a look at this powerful electric train engine
    <A HREF="../GG1jpgs/GG1.jpg">The Original</A>!
 </BODY>
</HTML>
```

The relative address ../GG1jpgs/GG1.jpg is actually parsed as:

```
http://www.myservice.com/GG1jpgs/GG1.jpg
```

Forward and Backward Links

While linking within an HTML document makes for easy table and index creation, the most frequent use for a link is to reference another Web source. However, you can also use links to create forward or backward link relationships by including a link type. For example, examine the following HTML text:

```
<HEAD>
…header HTML goes here…
<TITLE>GG1s in the 1950s</TITLE>
<LINK REL="PREV" HREF="GG11940.html">
<LINK REL="NEXT" HREF="GG11960.html">
</HEAD>
```

Notice the use of the REL link type attribute for the first HREF of PREV and the second one of NEXT. Links defined with a LINK element are not rendered with the document's contents, although some browsers may render them in other ways using navigation tools.

This next example uses GIF images to make the link selection a little more visual:

```
<HTML>
<HEAD>
<TITLE>Using GIF Images with Links</TITLE>
</HEAD>
<BODY>
<P>Simply click <BRE>
on the appropriate button<BR>
to move forward or backwards<BR>
through the links.</P>
<A HREF="page1.html">
<IMG SRC="c:\html\chp09\Back_up.gif">
</A>
<A HREF="page3.html">
<IMG SRC="c:\html\chp09\Forw_up.gif">
</A>
</BODY>
</HTML>
```

Notice that the HREF values are set to logically relate to each arrow's image (as seen in Figure 9–2). Figure 9–2's solution to activating an HTML's links is preferred whenever the end user does not need to know the details of a link address.

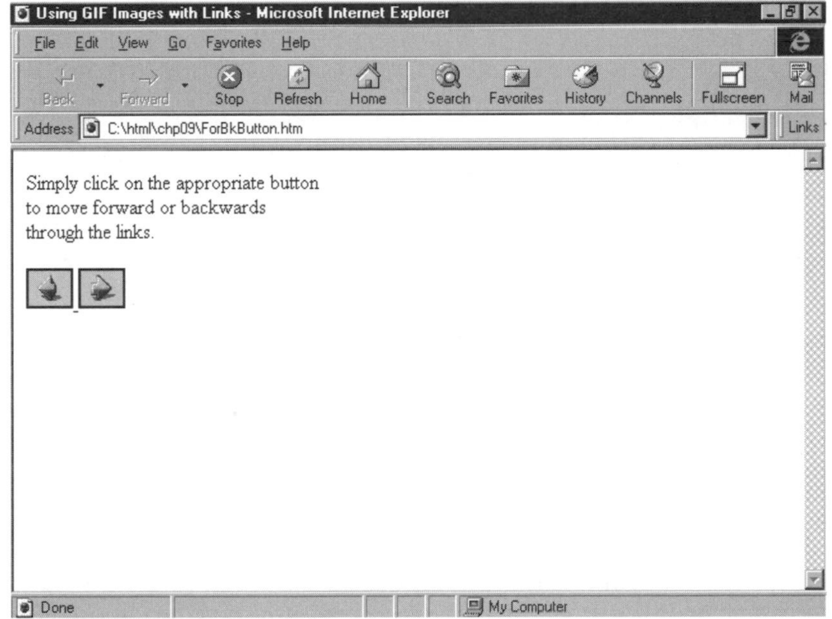

Figure 9–2: *Associating GIF images with links*

Link Types

Link types are defined by the values you supply to the REL and REV attributes (*Note:* link types may not contain any white space and are case-insensitive) and are interpreted by browsers and search engines in a variety of ways. Both attributes may be specified in the same element start tag. Authors may use the recognized link types listed in Table 9–2 together with their conventional interpretations.

Table 9–2: *Link types used with LINK REL and REV attributes*

Alternate	The alternate link type defines alternate versions for the HTML document containing the link. You can use the ALTERNATE and LANG attributes to infer multilanguage translations of the source document, or in conjunction with the MEDIA attribute to provide access to alternate multimedia formats.
Appendix	Indicates that the link is to an appendix for the source HTML document.
Bookmark	Indicates that the link is to a referencing bookmark. Bookmarks are frequently used as entry gateways into larger compositions, with the source document containing multiple bookmarks streamlining content access. Bookmarks can be labeled with a TITLE attribute.
Chapter	Defines the referenced text as being a chapter of the source document.
Contents or ToC	Defines the referenced text as containing a table of contents.
Copyright	Defines the referenced text as containing copyright information.
Glossary	Defines the referenced text as containing a glossary of terms pertaining to the current document.
Help	Defines the referenced text in a help format frequently containing more LINKs to additional resource materials.

Table 9–2: *Link types used with LINK REL and REV attributes (continued)*

Index	Defines the referenced text as a resource containing an index for the source document.
Next	Indicates that the referenced text follows some logical progression of the main topic. Some browsers may choose to preload the next document, thereby streamlining download time.
Prev or Previous	Defines the referenced text as logically preceding the current HTML resource.
Section	Defines the referenced text as a file containing a section of a larger work.
Start	Defines the referenced text as being the initial HTML resource in a series of documents and directs search engines as to which document is considered by the author to be the starting point for the complete work.
Stylesheet	Defines the referenced text as an HTML an external style sheet and is used in conjunction with the ALTERNATE LINK type when multiple style sheet options are needed.
Subsection	Defines the referenced text as being a subsection of a larger work.

e-Mail Links Using the MAILTO Attribute

The next time you want to generate a Web page that allows surfers to easily e-mail the author, try using the <A>nchor tag along with the MAILTO attribute. MAILTO references are not typical links in that they do not lead to another document. Instead, they send e-mail to the defined e-mail address. When a browser receives this type of request, it frequently launches a mail program that opens a blank e-mail form with the destination e-mail address automatically entered into the To: field.

The syntax for MAILTO is straightforward: simply define the HTREF attribute with a legal MAILTO address to cause e-mail to be sent when a link is activated. This next example demonstrates the syntax:

```
<BODY>
…more document goes here…
To order any GG1 material seen here click on the link
<A HREF="MAILTO:GG1Expert@mysubscription.com">GG1 Expert</A>.
</BODY>
```

Multilanguage Links

If you have done any Web surfing at all, you already know that many sites contain multilanguage versions for their international surfers. Since both the <A>nchor and <LINK> tags may point to documents written in different languages and using different character sets, the two tags support the CHARSET and LANG attributes. These attributes detail how the browser is to interpret the information at the destination link.

When used properly, both CHARSET and LANG allow browsers to avoid rendering garbage. Instead, they may locate resources necessary for the correct rendering of the document. If, if they cannot locate the resources, they should at least warn the user that the document will be unreadable and explain the cause (see Chapter 4 for a discussion of these attributes).

The following HTML example demonstrates a straightforward use of the <LINK> tag and LANG attribute to set up a multilingual presentation:

```
<HEAD>
<LINK LANG="EN" TITLE="English Format"
      REL="alternate"
      HREF="http://USsite.com/page1/index.html">
<LINK LANG="I-CHEROKEE" TITLE="Cherokee Format "
      REL="alternate"
      HREF="http://cherokee.com/page1/index.html">
<LINK LANG="X-PIG-LATIN" TITLE="Fun format"
      REL="alternate"
      HREF="http://kido.com/page1/indexs.html">
</HEAD>
```

Of course the multidestination format is not strictly limited to text media. The <LINK> tag can also provide a variety of information to search engines, including links to alternate versions of a document, designed for different media–for instance, a version especially suited for printing or access to the starting pages of a collection of documents.

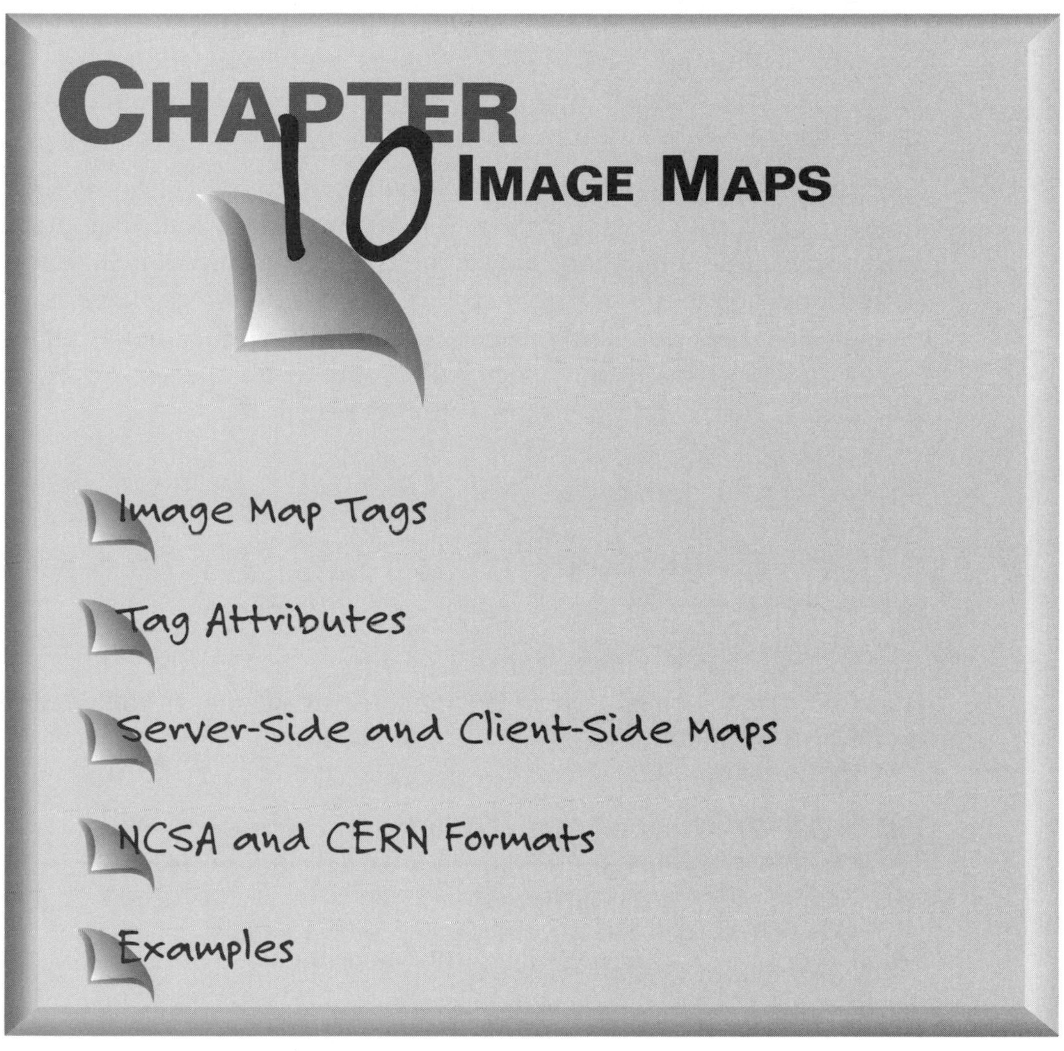

Introduction

Image maps are found frequently in HTML documents. They allow the user to click the mouse on a portion of a graphics image in order to access information pertaining to that portion of the graphics. The information accessed in this manner can be a simple document or image stored as a file on the computer or a specific URL location.

Imagine a HTML document that contains the graphics image of the building layout on a college campus. The user could click the mouse on any building to bring up previously saved file information on any particular building. Likewise, imagine a medical office that uses an image of the human body. Health workers could click the mouse on a nose, ear, foot or hand to be connected, via a URL, to the specialist in that field.

Image maps are divided into two broad techniques. (1) *Server-side image maps* work on all browsers. Their downside is that they place more of the communications burden on the server, since it is the server that implements the image map. (2) *Client-side image maps* have gained increased popularity because the HTML document implements the image map, thus placing less burden on the server. Their downside is that not all browsers support their use.

This Chapter's HTML Tags

Two new tags are encountered in this chapter: <MAP> and <AREA>. Traditionally they been used with client-side image maps. You'll learn about each of these tags and how to use them.

Table 10–1: *New tags used with image maps*

Tag	Description
<MAP>	Used to identify a map name
<AREA>	Used to define the area that responds to a mouse click within an image

Server-Side Image Maps

Server-side image maps, like cash, are accepted everywhere. This fact would generally make them the preferred technique. However, they place an additional burden on the server. When the user clicks the mouse on a portion of an image, the browser sends the coordinates of the mouse and the image's name to the server. The server examines the image map file and returns the URL information to the browser.

As a final step, the browser sends its request for the URL location back to the server.

Just in case the user's browser is text based, it is always advisable to include text-based hyperlinks in addition to the URLs supplied by the image map. This can be done as a final step in the creation of this portion of the HTML document, after the image map has been completely tested.

In addition to the image map's specifications in the HTML document, server-side image maps require an image, a file specifying the regions where the mouse can be clicked, and a CGI script to process the image map information.

Image File

Images used in image maps can be created with applications such as Microsoft Paint, Microsoft Image Composer, and CorelDraw. It is also possible to use digitized photographs produced by scanners or digital cameras. The main requirement for the image editor is that it can return coordinate information as the mouse is passed over the various image areas and that it can return the file in an acceptable format. The most popular graphics file formats include JPG and GIF.

Figure 10-1 shows the first of four rectangular regions used to create an image in Microsoft Image Composer.

Notice the coordinate information that is being returned in the lower-right portion of the image editor shown in Figure 10–1. This information will be required in order to identify the various regions in the image where the mouse can be clicked.

Figure 10–2 shows the completed image that will be saved as a file named ImgMap1.jpg. As each of the four rectangular areas is placed in the image, the coordinate information for the upper-left and lower-right coordinates is written down for future use.

Figure 10–3 is an example of a digitized photograph brought into the image editor. If this image is to be used as an image-map image, you might want to record coordinate information regarding the position of the bird's wings, feet, tail, eyes and so on.

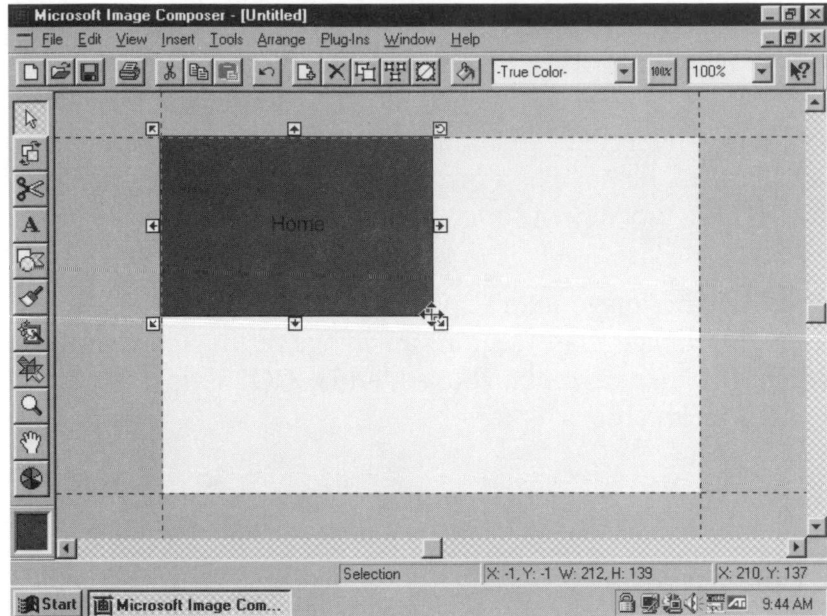

Figure 10–1: *A rectangular area is drawn in the Microsoft Image Composer*

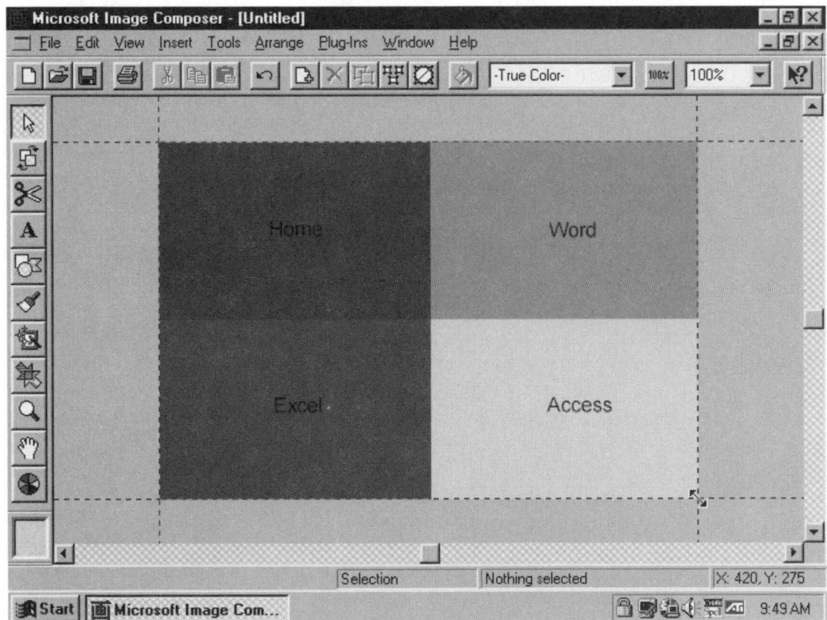

Figure 10–2: *A completed image-map image with four rectangular areas*

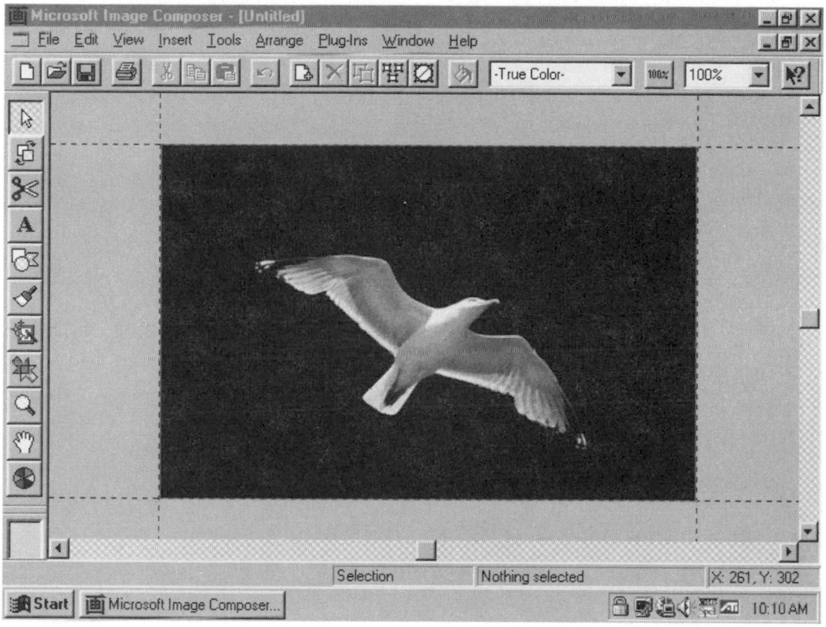

Figure 10–3: *A digitized photograph is loaded into the Microsoft Image Composer*

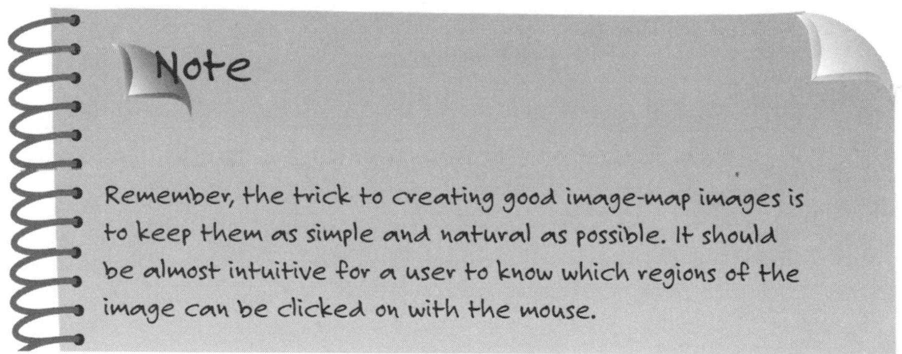

Note
Remember, the trick to creating good image-map images is to keep them as simple and natural as possible. It should be almost intuitive for a user to know which regions of the image can be clicked on with the mouse.

Image-Map Files

The image map MAP file is used to identify the regions where the mouse can be clicked in the image. This is why you wrote down the coordinate information when you created your image in the image editor. Two slightly different formats are used for recording this information: NCSA (America) and CERN (Switzerland).

NCSA File Format

NCSA (National Center for Supercomputing Applications) image-map file formatting is the de facto file-format standard for most American servers. If you are programming only for this geographic area, the NCSA file format is the one you will use. If you anticipate worldwide acceptance, you'll want to consider the CERN format also.

When developing NCSA image-map files, five shapes are acceptable. *Rectangles* use the rect keyword. *Circles* use the circle keyword. *Polygons* use the poly keyword. *Points* use the point keyword. *Defaults* (usually areas not covered by a specific region) use the default keyword. The syntax for each shape is straightforward.

rect	UniqueURL upperleft-x, upperleft-y, lowerright-x, lowerright-y
circle	UniqueURL center-x, center-y, radius
poly	UniqueURL x1, y1, x2, y2, ... xn, yn
point	UniqueURL x, y
default	UniqueURL

In a particular application where each area was a rectangle, the actual code for the NCSA image map might look like the following:

```
rect http://www.microsoft.com/office/ 0, 0, 210, 137
rect http://www.microsoft.com/word/ 211, 0, 420, 137
rect http://www.microsoft.com/excel/ 0, 138, 210, 275
rect http://www.microsoft.com/access/ 211, 138, 420, 275
```

In this example, four rectangular areas are identified in the image. The coordinates are given in pixel units with *X* increasing as you move from left to right and *Y* increasing as you move from top to bottom. Remember, these are the numbers returned by the graphics editor. Each area is approximately the same size, and each references a unique URL location. In this example, the URL locations reference Microsoft product locations.

CERN File Format

CERN (Conseil European pour la Recherche Nucleaire) image-map file formatting is the de facto file-format standard for most European servers. If you are programming only for this geographic area, the CERN file format is the one you will use. If you anticipate worldwide acceptance, you'll want to consider the NCSA format, too.

When developing CERN image-map files, four shapes are acceptable. *Rectangles* use the rectangle keyword. *Circles* use the circle keyword. *Polygons* use the polygon keyword. *Defaults* (areas not covered by a specific region) use the default keyword. The syntax for each shape is straightforward.

rectangle	(upperleft-x, upperleft-y) (lowerright-x, lowerright-y) UniqueURL
circle	(center-x, center-y) radius UniqueURL
polygon	(x1, y1) (x2, y2) .... (xn, yn) UniqueURL
default	UniqueURL

Note: The abbreviations rect, circ, poly and def are also acceptable.

In a particular application where each area was a rectangle, the actual code for the CERN image map might look like the following:

```
rectangle (0, 0) (210, 137) http://www.microsoft.com/office/
rectangle (211, 0) (420, 137) http://www.microsoft.com/word/
rectangle (0, 138) (210, 275) http://www.microsoft.com/excel/
rectangle (211, 138) (420, 275) http://www.microsoft.com/access/
```

In this example, four rectangular areas are identified in the image. The coordinates used are those returned by an image editor. The coordinates are given in pixel units with *X* increasing as you move from left to right and *Y* increasing as you move from top to bottom. Each area is approximately the same size, and each references a unique URL location. In this case, the URL locations reference the same Microsoft product locations as in the NCSA example.

CGI Script

In most cases it is possible to use the default CGI script provided by the server. The CGI script is responsible for reporting the area of the image that was clicked with the mouse and then taking the appropriate action. NCSA servers use the imagemap keyword while CERN servers use the htimage keyword.

The HTML Document

HTML documents can include image maps with relatively simple syntax. Here is an example that is used with a NCSA server.

```
<A href="/locationURL/imagemapURL">
<IMG src="imagemap.jpg" ismap>
</A>
```

Here *locationURL* points to the CGI script location used to process the mouse-click information. The *imagemapURL* references the location of the MAP file holding the coordinate information for the image's various areas. The <A> tag indicates that href points to a MAP file rather than to a URL location.

You are familiar with <IMG> tags from Chapter 6, but this might be the first time you have seen the ismap attribute used. The ismap attribute is used to notify the browser that the image is an image map.

A practical portion of HTML code identifying our image map might take on the following appearance:

```
<A href="/cgi-bin/imagemap">
<IMG src="ImgMap1.jpg" ismap>
</A>
```

Features Unique to Server-Side Image Maps

Server-side image maps do not work offline as their client-side counterparts do. This, of course, is because of the interaction required between the browser and the server.

As you slide the mouse over a server-side image map, only the *X*, *Y* coordinate information for the image is returned to the user. With client-side image maps, the actual URL is shown.

You must gain permission from the server to identify your MAP location in its file system. Our example might be entered as follows:

```
ImgMap1 : /images/ImgMap1.MAP.
```

Client-Side Image Maps

Client-side image maps are more like credit cards. Unlike cash transactions, credit cards are not accepted at all locations doing business, but they are frequently more convenient to use. Client-side image maps, while not as universally supported as server-side image maps, are supported by a very large number of browsers. This fact, coupled with their increased speed and their ability to reduce server traffic, makes them ideal candidates for most image-map work.

Client-side image maps, unlike their server-side counterparts, do not place an additional burden on the server, since the browser coordinates all interactions between the image area clicked on with the mouse and any associated file or URL.

As with server-side image maps, it is always advisable to include text-based hyperlinks in addition to the URLs supplied by the image map, just in case the user's browser is text based. Do this as a final step in the creation of the HTML document, after the image map has been completely tested.

Client-side image maps require an image and the image map's specifications in the HTML document.

Image File

The images used in client-side image maps are identical to the types of images that can be used in server-side image maps. Images can be created with applications such as Microsoft Paint, Microsoft Image Composer, and CorelDraw. It is also possible to use digitized photographs produced by scanners or digital cameras. Remember that the main requirements for image editors is that they can return coordinate information as the mouse is passed over the various image areas and that they can return the file in an acceptable format. The most popular graphics file formats include JPG and GIF.

Keep your image maps as clean and free of "clutter" as possible. Use simple drawing shapes or photographs with intuitive areas for user interaction

The HTML Document

All of the code for processing an image map is contained in the HTML document. Two tags help handle this code: <MAP> and <AREA>.

The <MAP> Tag

The <MAP> tag identifies the map with a unique name. It uses the following syntax:

```
<MAP name="mapname">
.
.
.
</MAP>
```

The <AREA> Tag

The <AREA> tag identifies the areas or hotspots of an image that are associated with a mouse click. It makes use of several attributes, including shape, coords, nohref and href.

Shape

The shape attribute can be set equal to rect (default), circle, or polygon. You can also use the default attribute for cases where the mouse is clicked outside of any specified areas in the image.

Coord

The coord attribute is used to provide the coordinates of the particular area of the image. The syntax is:

For a rectangle: coords=upperleft-x, upperleft-y, lowerright-x, lowerright-y

For a circle: coords=center-x, center-y, radius

For a polygon: coords=x1, y1, x2, y2, ... xn, yn

In the case of overlapping shapes, the browser resolves the problem by using the first shape listed after the <AREA> tag.

Nohref

The nohref attribute is used to indicate that there is no hyperlink associated with a mouse click in the specified area.

Href

The href attribute is used to specify the URL when the mouse is clicked in the corresponding area of the image.

For example, we created a simple image earlier in this chapter named ImgMap1.jpg. Figure 10–2, presented earlier, shows that this image contains four rectangular areas of approximately the same size. This image information could be included in an HTML document with the use of the <AREA> tag in the following manner:

```
<AREA shape="rect" coords="0, 0, 210, 137"
 href="http://www.microsoft.com/office/">
<AREA shape="rect" coords="211, 0, 420, 137"
 href="http://www.microsoft.com/word/">
<AREA shape="rect" coords="0, 138, 210, 275"
 href="http://www.microsoft.com/excel/">
<AREA shape="rect" coords="211, 138, 420, 275"
 href="http://www.microsoft.com/access/">
```

Recall that the image editor returned the coordinates shown here for the hotspots to us when the image was created.

A Complete Client-Side Image Map

If we use the ImgMap1.jpg image file created earlier in this chapter and the code developed in the previous section, it is a fairly easy task to complete a client-side image-map application. Examine the following listing:

```
<HTML>
<HEAD>
<TITLE>Client-side imagemap</TITLE>
</HEAD>
<BODY>
<IMG src="ImgMap1.jpg" usemap="#firstmap">
<P>You want to go where today?<BR>
<MAP name="firstmap">
<AREA shape="rect" coords="0, 0, 210, 137"
 href="http://www.microsoft.com/office/">
<AREA shape="rect" coords="211, 0, 420, 137"
 href="http://www.microsoft.com/word/">
<AREA shape="rect" coords="0, 138, 210, 275"
 href="http://www.microsoft.com/excel/">
<AREA shape="rect" coords="211, 138, 420, 275"
 href="http://www.microsoft.com/access/">
</MAP>
</BODY>
</HTML>
```

Figure 10–4 shows this HTML document using the Netscape browser. As you examine this figure, notice that the mouse pointer is resting over the "Access" portion of the image. Now notice that the URL for Access is shown on the bottom-left of the browser.

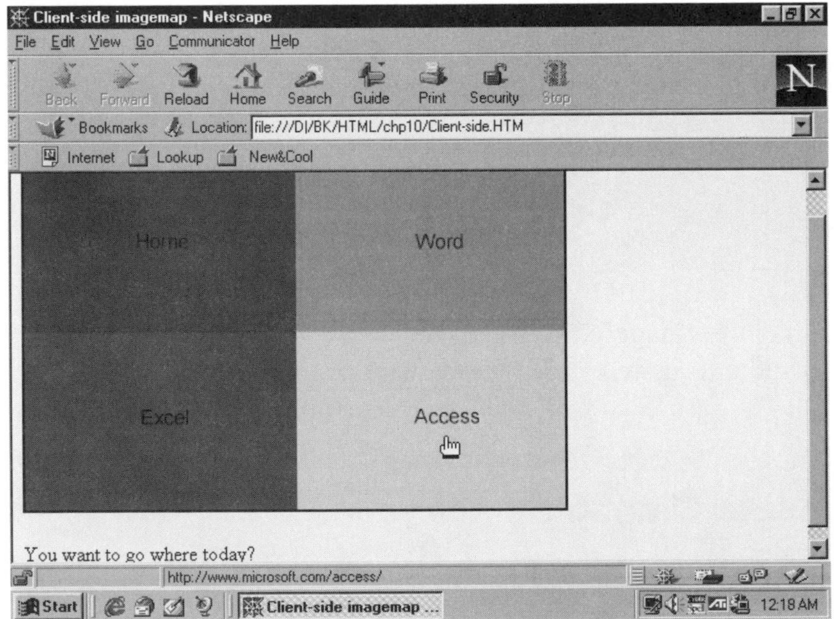

Figure 10–4: *The Netscape browser illustrates our simple client-side image-map example*

All that remains for this simple application (you didn't forget, did you?) is to add the text-based hyperlinks in addition to the URLs supplied by the image map.

Features Unique to Client-Side Image Maps

Client-side image maps, unlike their server-side counterparts, work offline. This, of course, is because the browser handles all the interactions between images areas that are clicked with the mouse and the information that is to be returned.

As you slide the mouse over a client-side image map, the actual URL is shown. Recall that for server-side image maps only the *X*, *Y* coordinate information for the image is returned to the user.

If you are concerned about nonsupport issues revolving around client-side image maps, you can provide both client-side and server-side options.

```
<A href="/cgi-bin/images/ImgMap1.map">
<IMG src="/images/ImgMap1.jpg" usemap="#ImgMap1" ismap>
</A>
```

In this example, if client-side image maps are not supported, a server-side map will be used.

Before You Leave

Before leaving this topic you may want to experiment with your own server-side or client-side image maps. Perhaps you'll want to use a favorite photograph of your family that you've digitized. Wouldn't everyone in your family like to contact your Web site to find out how to locate Uncle Ed and Aunt Bertha?

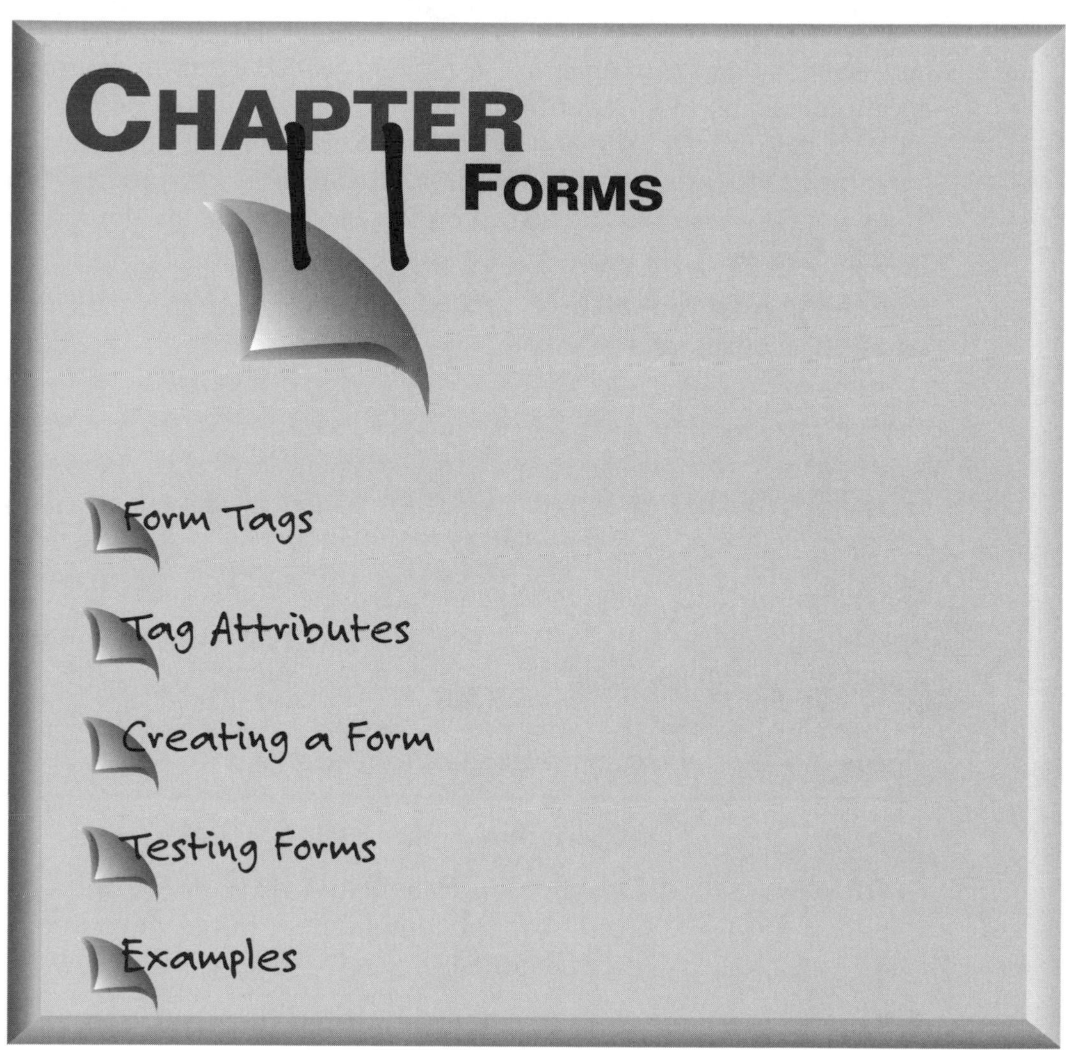

Introduction

Many Web sites are not interactive–that is, they cannot retrieve information from a user. Personal Web sites hosted by many Internet providers allow no interactive capability at all. If you or your company are interested only in disseminating information, then the techniques you have learned to this point are sufficient for your purposes. If your Web site requires interactive capabilities, you'll want to study this chapter dealing with forms.

HTML forms are defined as documents that contain normal content, mark-up and combinations of elements called *controls*. Controls accept and respond to input from the user. This input may be as simple as a button click or menu selection. User input can also include paragraphs of text entered at the keyboard. In order to process this input, a CGI script must be placed on the server to handle the form's specific features. CGI scripting is discussed in Appendix C.

In this chapter you will learn how to create forms with buttons, text areas, checkboxes, and so on.

This Chapter's HTML Tags

Nine tags are used when working with forms. The <FORM> tag serves as the entry point for form description and can use any combination of the remaining eight tags described in Table 11–1.

Table 11–1: *New tags relating to forms*

Tag	Description
<FORM>	Establishes a form in an HTML document. Forms cannot contain other forms, nor can they be nested.
<INPUT>	This element defines which input controls a form uses. Controls include radio, checkbox, submit, and so on.
<BUTTON>	The <BUTTON> element allows you to expand the available button types.
<SELECT>	This element, used with <OPTION>, creates a menu or drop down list control.
<OPTGROUP>	This element allows the developer to group choices in hierarchical form. It is useful for long lists and so on.
<OPTION>	This element, used with <SELECT>, specifies the items in a menu or drop-down list control.

<TEXTAREA>	This element is used to specify a large area used for text entry on a form.
<LABEL>	This element is used to attach information to other control elements, such as tables and so on.
<FIELDSET>	This element, used in conjunction with <LEGEND>, groups related controls together.
<LEGEND>	This element, used in conjunction with <FIELDSET>, uses the align attribute to specify the position of the legend with respect to the <FIELDSET>.

In the sections that follow you'll learn about each of these tags and the role that they play in form development.

Form Components

Forms are created with an opening <FORM> tag and closed with a </FORM> tag. From that point on, forms will be as varied as the purposes that they were designed for. Forms may include combinations of controls, including; text entry boxes, push buttons, checkboxes ,and so on. The scope of the form's name attribute for any control within a <FORM> is the <FORM> itself.

The <FORM> Tag

The <FORM> element allows several attributes. Table 11–2 lists and describes these attributes.

The most frequently used syntax for sending a form to a program using the HTTP post method is the following:

```
<FORM action="http://testsite.com/cgi-bin/script.cgi" method="post">
.
.
.
</FORM>
```

Table 11–2: *<FORM> element attributes*

Attribute	Description
accept	A comma-separated list of MIME types that the server will handle.
accept-charset	Specifies a list of character encodings, for input data, that are accepted by the server.
accesskey	Specifies direct keyboard access to form fields.
action	Specifies a required server-side form handler. Can be an HTTP URL or a mailto URL.
disabled	Specifies that a form control is initially insensitive.
enctype	Used to specify the MIME type encoding for submitting forms. The default value is x-www-form-URLencoded.
method	HTTP method used to submit the form. Here get is the default and it appends name/value pairs to the URL given by action, then sends the new URL to the server. The post method is preferred because it includes name/value pair in the body of the form rather than in the URL itself.
onchange	Allows the form provider to verify user-entered data.
onsubmit	Indicates that the form was submitted.
onreset	Indicates that the form was reset.
readonly	Specifies that a form field cannot be changed.
target	Specifies where the returned data should be sent. This is optional; it is used by Netscape and the Microsoft Internet Explorer to specify a frame or window.

Likewise, the form can be submitted to an e-mail address using the following syntax:

```
<FORM action="mailto:Tango_Tia@SUNYBroome.edu" method="post">
.
.
.
</FORM>
```

The post method should be used in most cases. The get method is the default and is included for backward compatibility with older systems. The get method passes the information directly to the URL. Information sent in this manner is usually limited to a total of 255 characters. The post method, on the other hand, sends data as a separate stream to the script. This technique bypasses the limitations of the get method and allows unlimited amounts of information to be received.

A form can contain a wide variety of controls, but it cannot contain another form. Likewise, forms cannot be nested.

The <INPUT> Tag

The <INPUT> element serves as the starting point for adding buttons, checkboxes, passwords, and so on to a form. The syntax for the <INPUT> element is:

```
<INPUT type="element_type" name="ref_name">
```

Each type of input is entered as a CGI name/value pair. The element_type defines the field's screen appearance, while ref_name represents a keyword referenced by the server's CGI script. The server's CGI script is used to process the form's data.

Table 11–3 lists and describes various <INPUT> types.

An attribute name is required for all controls except submit and reset. Table 11–4 lists a variety of new attributes encountered with these <INPUT> types.

Table 11–3: *<INPUT> element types*

Input Type	Description
button	A type of push button with no default behavior.
checkbox	An on/off type switch. Active when "on." Multiple checkboxes within a group can be checked.
file	Prompts the user for a file name.
hidden	This input type is not rendered by the user agent. The element's name and value are submitted with the form.
image	A type of submission push button using a graphical image as the button.
password	A single-line text-entry box that allows text to be entered but hides characters from view with a series of asterisks.
radio	An on/off type switch. Active when "on." Only one radio button in a group can be set active. Multiple groups are permitted, however.
reset	A type of push button which when activated resets all of the form's controls back to the initial values.
submit	A type of push button which when activated submits the form's contents.
text	Single-line text-entry box.

Table 11–4: *Input type element attributes*

Attribute	Description
type	Type of control needed.
name	Submit as part of the form.
value	Required for radio and checkboxes.
checked	Used by radio and checkboxes to indicate selection.
disable	Control is not available in this context.
readonly	Used for text and passwords.
size	Specific to each type of field. For example, size gives the width, in characters, of a text control.
maxlength	Maximum number of characters for a field.
src	For fields using images.
alt	A short description.
usemap	Use a client-side image map.
align	Use for vertical or horizontal alignment.
tabindex	Position in tabbing order.
accesskey	Accessibility key character.
onfocus	The element receiving the focus.
onblur	The element losing the focus.
onselect	The selected text.
onchange	The element value was changed.
accept	List of MIME types for file upload.

In this section we'll examine each of the input-type elements in more detail.

The Button Type

This type creates a push button with no default behavior. The button's behavior is specified by associating the button with client-side scripts (see Chapter 10). These are activated when events pertaining to the button take place, such as a button push. The name of the value attribute is the button's label. In the following portion of code the function named "confirm" will be executed when the button is pushed.

```
<INPUT type="button" value="Push Here" onclick="confirm()">
```

The script must be defined by a SCRIPT element.

The Checkbox Type

This type behaves like an on/off switch. This action can represent on/off, true/false, yes/no, and so on. The checkbox is "active" when the switch is on and "inactive" when the switch is off. The checkbox value is submitted with the form when the checkbox is active.

A form may contain multiple checkboxes with the same name attribute. These are considered a group. On submission, each active checkbox in a group sends its name/value pair. This action allows multiple checkboxes to be selected by the user.

Checkboxes are usually small rectangular areas that can contain a check mark or "x" when selected. Checkboxes can use the value and checked attributes.

```
<INPUT type="checkbox" name="Additional_Information"
value="Yes, please" checked>
```

The File Type

This type prompts the user for a file name. When the form is submitted, the contents of the file as well as any user input are submitted to the server.

Multiple files should send files in a MIME multipart document.

The Hidden Type

This type is not visible. However, the element's name and value are submitted with the form rendered by the user agent. This unique text field is frequently used to send information to a CGI script. For example:

```
<INPUT type="hidden" name="Additional_Information"
   value=""New_Input.html">
```

The Image Type

This type creates a graphical image that is used to represent a submit type button. The value of the src attribute is used to specify the URL of the image. Since the image may not be viewable by all users, a text alternative should also be specified with the alt attribute.

When the image is clicked, the form is submitted, and the *X*, *Y* coordinates of the mouse are passed to the server. The *X* coordinate increases from left to right and is measured in pixels. The *Y* coordinate increases from top to bottom and is also measured in pixels. Submitted data is passed as name.x = X coordinate and name.y = Y coordinate using the name attribute.

A possible future extension to image is to add the usemap attribute to <INPUT> for use as a client-side image map when type=image. In this manner the area element corresponding to the mouse location when the image is clicked would be passed to the server.

The Password Type

This type behaves like a single-line text element. However, as each character is entered, it is replaced on the screen with an asterisk. The actual text is submitted by the password control. No actual encoding takes place for the characters typed.

Password fields are frequently used on forms for entering passwords and sensitive information. A password field can use the maxlength, size, and value attributes. For example:

```
<INPUT type="password" name="Social_Security"
   maxlength="9" size="9">
```

In this example the maximum length of the information submitted by the user is 9 characters. The width of the password control is also set to 9.

THE RADIO TYPE

This type behaves like on on/off switch. The action can represent on/off, true/false, yes/no. and so on. The radio button is "active" when the switch is on and "inactive" when the switch is off. The radio-button value is submitted with the form when the radio button is active.

A form may contain multiple radio buttons with the same name. These are considered a group. On submission, only one radio button in a group sends its name/value pair. This action allows only a single radio button in a group to be selected by the user. Forms may contain several groups of radio buttons, however.

Radio buttons are similar to checkboxes, except that they are usually represented as small round circles. When a radio button is active, a "dot" is placed in the center of the image. Radio buttons can use the name, value, and checked attributes.

```
<INPUT type="radio" name="Family_Size"
value="Large" checked>
```

The checked attribute identifies this radio button as the default for the group.

THE RESET TYPE

This type allows a form's controls to be reset. When this control is activated by the user, it returns all controls on the form to the initial values specified in the control's value attributes.

The name/value pair are not submitted with the form.

```
<INPUT type="reset" value="Start Over">
```

The reset button is automatically sized to the text that is entered.

The Submit Type

This type allows a form to be submitted to the location given by the action attribute of the parent <FORM>.

Forms may contain multiple submit buttons. Only the active submit button's name/value pair are submitted with the form.

```
<INPUT type="submit" value="Enter Information">
```

The submit button is automatically sized to the text that is entered.

The Text Type

This type creates a single-line text entry box. The value submitted by a text control is the input text entered by the user.

Text fields are frequently used on forms for entering names, addresses, social security numbers, and so on. A text field can use the maxlength, size, and value attributes. For example:

```
<INPUT type="text" name="CityState" maxlength="30"
   size="15">
```

In this example the maximum length of the information submitted by the user is 30 characters. However, the width of the text control is 15. When more than 15 characters are entered, the control will scroll to accept the remaining characters.

The <BUTTON> Tag

The <BUTTON> element allows you to expand types of buttons available for use. This element uses name, value, and type attributes. The name attribute assigns a name to the button, while the value attribute assigns a value to the button. The type attribute can be submit, button, or reset. The submit value is used when submitting forms. The reset value is used to reset a form's values. The button value is used to trigger a script.

The syntax for the <BUTTON> element is:

```
<BUTTON name="ref_name" value="element_value"
   type="element_type">
```

A <BUTTON> element using a submit type whose content is an image is similar to an <INPUT> element that uses an image type. The difference is that <INPUT> renders a "flat" image while <BUTTON> renders a button with relief and an up/down motion when selected.

Here is an example of a <BUTTON> element using a submit type:

```
<BUTTON name="submit_me" value="submit" type"submit">
Send<IMG src="/graphics/doit.jpg" alt="doit">
</BUTTON>
```

In a similar manner a <BUTTON> element using the reset type is like an <INPUT> element using the reset type, but with features like those just described.

The <SELECT> and <OPTION> Tags

The <SELECT> and <OPTION> elements are used together to create a drop-down list. The <SELECT> element uses name, size, and type attributes, while the <OPTION> element uses the selected and value attributes. The name attribute assigns a name to the element and is paired with selected values when the form is submitted. The size attribute specifies the number of rows to be rendered. A scrolling mechanism should be used when the number of rows is less than the number of choices. The multiple attribute, when set, will allow multiple selections from the list. The selected attribute is used to identify a selection. The value attribute gives the value to be submitted when the <OPTION> is selected.

Here is a list, or menu, constructed of a <SELECT> element and several <OPTION> elements:

```
<SELECT size="3" name="selectpet">
 <OPTION> Cat </OPTION>
 <OPTION selected> Dog </OPTION>
 <OPTION> Horse </OPTION>
</SELECT>
```

In this example list, 3 items will be presented since the size attribute was set to 3. Dog is selected as the default choice by using the selected attribute.

The <TEXTAREA> Tag

The <TEXTAREA> element is similar to the <INPUT> element using the text type. The main difference is that a text area allows multiple lines of text information to be entered by the user. This element uses the name, rows, and cols attributes. The name attribute assigns a name to the element and is paired with selected values when the form is submitted. The rows attribute identifies the number of visible lines that are to be visible within the area. Additional lines should be permitted and a scrolling mechanism should be provided. The cols attribute identifies the number of visible columns that are to be visible within the area. Longer lines should be permitted and a scrolling mechanism should be provided.

Here is an example that sets a 10-row by 40-column text-entry area. The area initially contains one line of text.

```
<TEXTAREA name="mystory" rows="10" cols="40">
This is my story:
</TEXTAREA>
<INPUT type="submit" value"sendit">
<INPUT type="reset">
```

If no default text is used, the </TEXTAREA> can immediately follow the <TEXTAREA> element.

The <LABEL> Tag

This element is used to attach information to other control elements. The <LABEL> element uses the for attribute that associates the label with another control. For example, in a <TABLE> you might use the following:

```
<TAE>
 <TR>
  <TD>
   <LABEL for="city">City Name
   </LABEL>
  <TD>
   <INPUT type="text" name=cityname" id="city">
 <TR>
  <TD>
   <LABEL for="state">State Name
   </LABEL>
  <TD>
   <INPUT type="text" name=statename" id="state">
</TABLE>
```

The for attribute can be used to associate more than one <LABEL> with a control.

The <FIELDSET> and <LEGEND> Tags

The <FIELDSET> element is used to group related controls together. The <LEGEND> element is used to assign a caption to the <FIELDSET> element.

The <LEGEND> element uses the align attribute to specify the position of the legend with respect to the fieldset. If a value of top is used (the default), the legend is above the fieldset. A value of bottom places the legend below the fieldset. A value of left or right places the legend to the left or right of the fieldset. For example:

```
<FIELDSET>
<LEGEND align="top">Patient Identification</LEGEND>
Social Security Number:
 <INPUT name="social_security" type="text">
 </INPUT>
</FIELDSET>
```

Element Characteristics

There are several ways an active element receives focus from a user. Focus can be achieved with a mouse, keyboard tabbing, or the use of an access key–often called a shortcut or accelerator key. The use of a pointing device, such as a mouse, requires no special intervention. In this section we'll examine tabbing order and access keys. In addition, we'll examine how to disable or make elements read-only.

Tabbing Order

The tabbing order is set with the tabindex attribute. It is the order in which elements receive focus when navigated with the keyboard. The tabbing order can include nested elements. Navigation proceeds with elements with low to elements with high tabindex value. Tabindex values need not be sequential. If elements are not provided with tabindex values, they are navigated in the order in which they appear in the HTML document. Disabled elements do not appear in the tabbing order.

For example:

```
<INPUT tabindex="2" type="text" name="lastname">
<INPUT tabindex="1" type="text" name="firstname">
<INPUT tabindex="6" type="text" name="state">
<INPUT tabindex="5" type="text" name="city">
```

Here the tabbing order is 1, 2, 5 and 6 or firstname, lastname, city, and state.

Access Key

An access key is set with the accesskey attribute. The accesskey attribute assigns a single character from the document character set to act as the access key. When an access key is pressed, the identified element receives focus. For example:

```
<LABEL for="lname" accesskey="L">
Last Name
</LABEL>
<INPUT type="text" name="lastname" id="lname">
<LABEL for="fname" accesskey="F">
First Name
</LABEL>
<INPUT type="text" name="firstname" id="fname">
```

Access keys are activated under Windows by using the Alt key in conjunction with the defined accesskey. Apple systems use the Cmd key in conjunction with the defined accesskey.

Disable

When the disabled attribute is used with an element, the element will not receive focus. In addition, the element will not be present in the tabbing order, and the control's value will not be submitted with the form. The rendering of disabled elements depends upon the user agent, but most frequently the element is "grayed" to indicate that it has been disabled.

In the following example, the third element has been disabled:

```
<INPUT tabindex="2" type="text" name="lastname">
<INPUT tabindex="1" type="text" name="firstname">
<INPUT disabled tabindex="6" type="text" name="state">
<INPUT tabindex="5" type="text" name="city">
```

Read-only

When the read-only attribute is used with an element, and is set, the element prohibits changes. Elements identified as read-only receive focus but cannot be changed. The elements are included in the tabbing order, and their values are submitted with the form. For example:

```
<TEXTAREA readonly name="mystory" rows="2" cols="20">
This is my story:
</TEXTAREA>
```

A Simple Form

The following listing produces a complete form for registering a pet. The form makes use of many of the elements and attributes discussed in the previous sections. Examine the listing and see if you can determine the reason and placement of each item.

```
<HTML>
<HEAD>
<TITLE>Pet Registration</TITLE>
</HEAD>
<BODY>
<H1>Please complete the following form
<BR>to register your pet</H1>
<HR>
```

```
<H3>Information about you:</H3>
<FORM method="post"
 action="http://hoohoo.ncsa.uiuc.edu/cgi-bin/post-query">
Your last name: <INPUT type="text" name="lname"
 maxlength="25" size="18">
First name: <INPUT type="text" name="fname"
 maxlength="25" size="18">
<BR>
Social Security Number: <INPUT type="text" name="ssn"
 maxlength="11" size="11">
<HR>
<H3>Information about your pet:</H3>
<TABLE>
<TR valign="top">
<TD>Type of pet:
<BR>
<SELECT Name="PetType">
 <OPTION>Cat </OPTION>
 <OPTION selected>Dog </OPTION>
 <OPTION>Horse </OPTION>
 <OPTION>Other </OPTION>
</SELECT>
</TABLE>
<INPUT type="radio" name="sex" value="m">Male
<INPUT type="radio" name="sex" value="f">Female
Pet's breed: <INPUT type="text" name="breed"
 maxlength="20">
Please check all that apply to your pet:
<INPUT type="checkbox" name="char"
 value="e">Cropped ears
<INPUT type="checkbox" name="char"
 value="t">Docked tail
<INPUT type="checkbox" name="char"
 value="c">Good with children
<H3>Tell us something unique about your pet:</H3>
<TEXTAREA name="info" rows=10 cols=60>
</TEXTAREA>
<HR>
<H3>Thank you for your information -
 your pet will be registered.</H3>
<INPUT type="submit">
<INPUT type="reset">
</FORM>
</BODY>
</HTML>
```

This form is quite long, so Figure 11-1 shows the top portion, responsible for collecting information about the pet's owner.

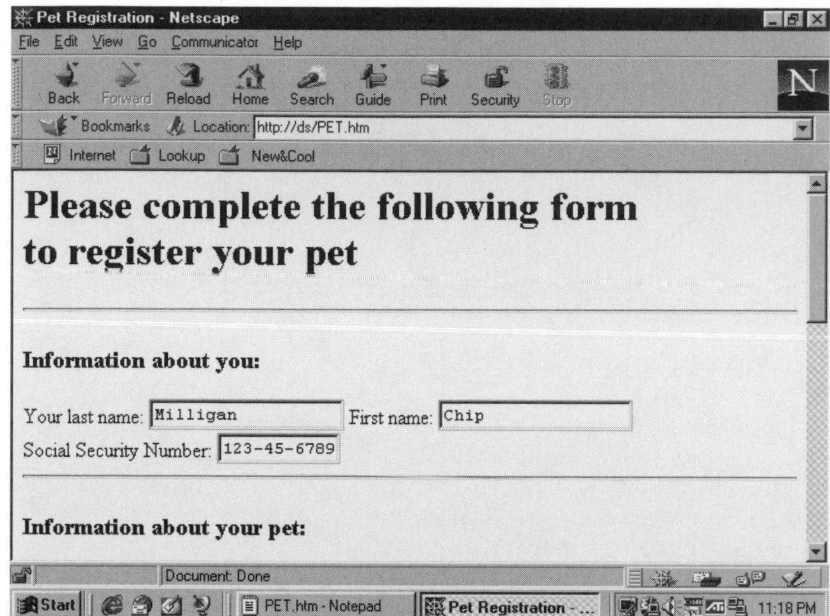

Figure 11–1: *The upper portion of the Pet Registration form, used to collect owner information*

Information regarding the pet's type, sex, and some unique characteristics is entered on the next portion of the form, shown in Figure 11–2.

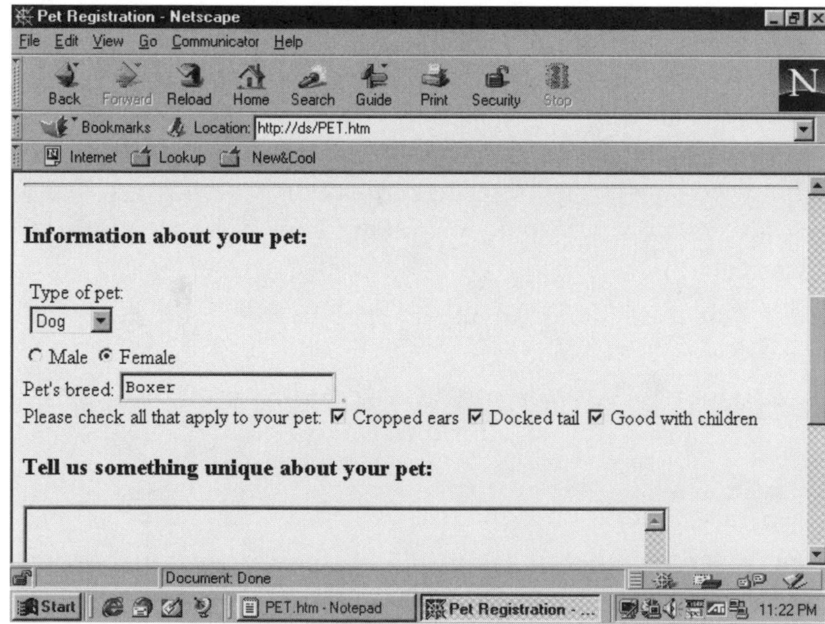

Figure 11–2: *This portion of the Pet Registration form collects specific information on your pet*

The final portion of the form, shown in Figure 11-3, allows you to enter a short but unique description of your pet.

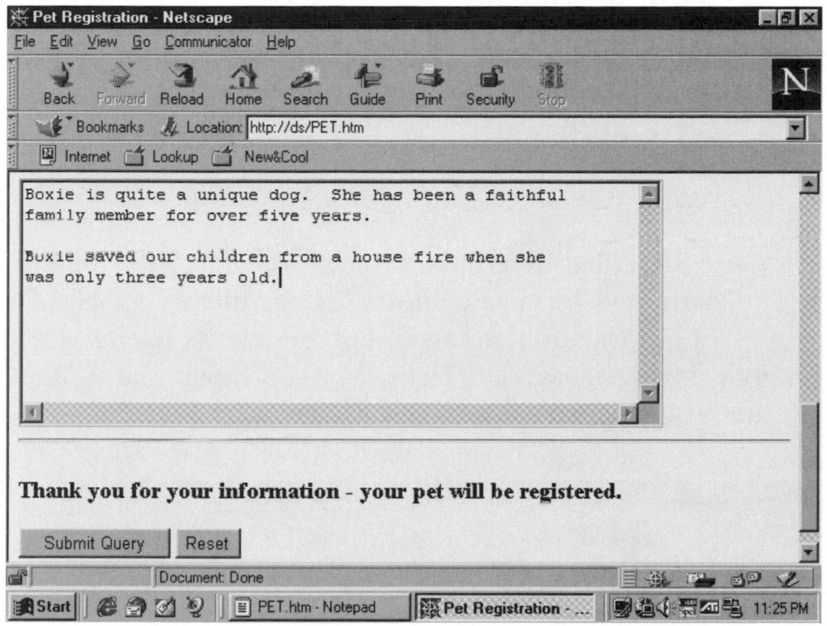

Figure 11–3: *The final portion of the form allows you to enter unique information about your pet*

As you examine the previous figures, you'll notice that the form has already been completed by a grateful pet owner. We'll examine this data shortly.

Recall that form design is just one part of the process of form creation and implementation. In order to process the form's information there must also be a server-side program. The CGI, or Common Gateway Interface, is the preferred manner of processing form data on the server side. Appendix C addresses some of the issues of CGI development.

Happily, however, there are some techniques that are easily used to test the operation of a completed form. We'll examine two in the next section.

Checking Your Form

In the previous section a complete HTML document containing a form was listed. Did you notice that two lines in that listing were set in a bold font? Just in case you missed them, here they are:

```
<FORM method="post"
 action="http://hoohoo.ncsa.uiuc.edu/cgi-bin/post-query">
```

The NCSA site identified here provides a server that will examine data from any submitted form and return the results as an HTML page. None of the information is saved, but the site is useful when checking initial form operation. Figure 11–4 shows the output returned by the NCSA server.

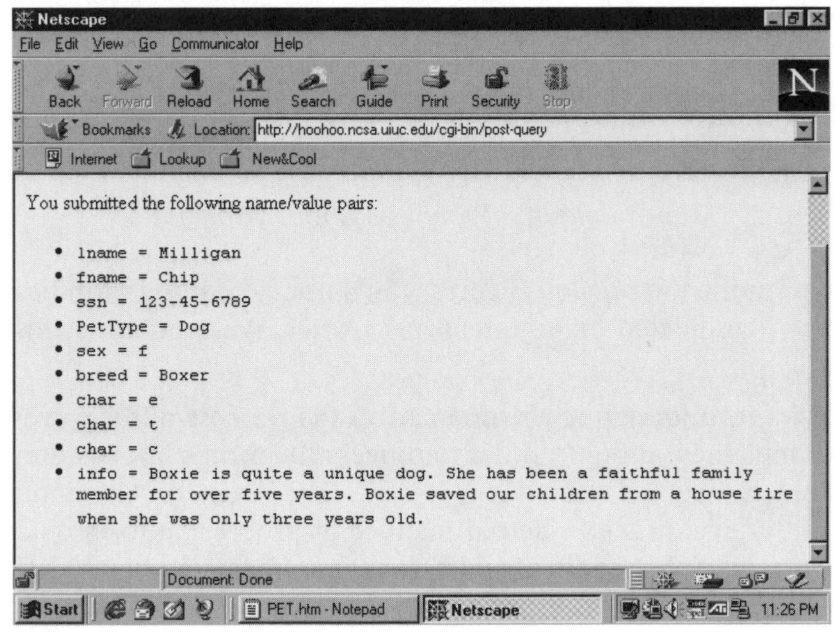

Figure 11–4: *The NCSA server is used to check our form*

If you own Microsoft FrontPage, you'll discover that during the installation the product's setup program installs a Web server named "Personal Web Server." If you save an HTML document in the home page location with the name default.htm, the Personal Web Server will allow you to also test your form. In order to do this, remove the bolded lines of text in the HTML document listing shown earlier and replace them with the following:

```
<form method="POST" action="—WebBOT-SELF—">
 <!—Webbot bot="SaveRcsults"
   startspan U-File="_private/form_results.txt"
 S-Format="TEXT/CSV"
   S-Label-Fields="TRUE" —><!—Webbot bot="SaveResults"
 endspan —>
```

Figure 11–5 shows the Personal Web Server just after the form has been loaded. The Personal Web Server will allow you to select your browser from any that you have installed.

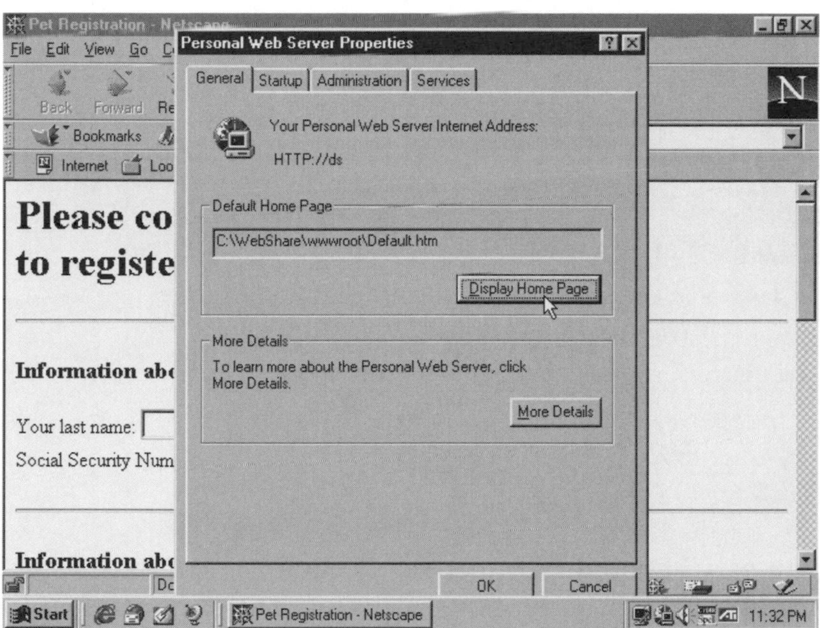

Figure 11–5: *The Microsoft Personal Web Server is used to examine and test a form*

The output provided by the Personal Web Server is similar to the output that is returned by the NCSA server, as you can see in Figure 11–6.

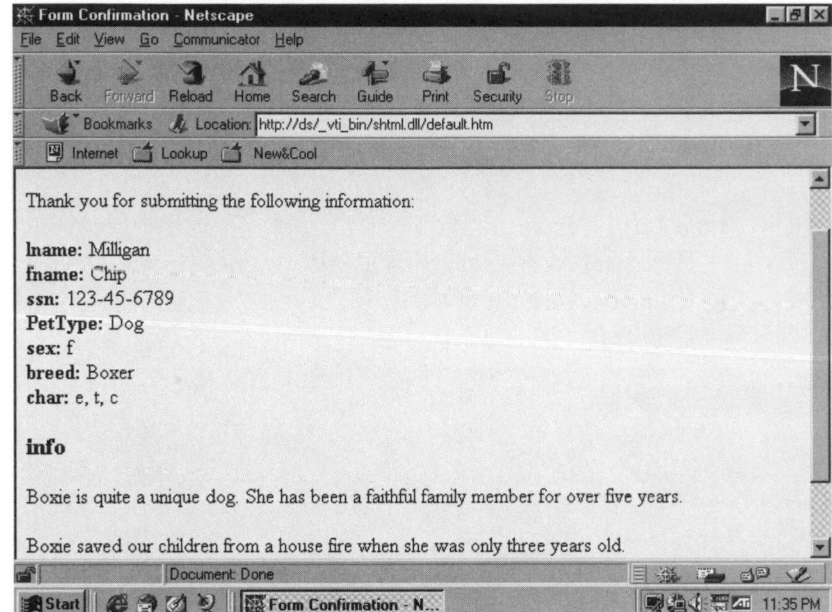

Figure 11–6: *This is the information returned by the Microsoft Personal Web Server*

Forms—One More Look

Forms are a very important component of many HTML documents. They form the backbone of most interactive exchanges of data.

In this chapter we have concentrated on form creation and implementation. However, good form design is very important for a successful user interface. Several practices are used to achieve good form design. Here are a few good points to remember.

1. Keep the form as simple and short as possible.
2. Keep related questions grouped together.
3. Do not attempt to gather unneeded information.
4. Keep the form as simple and short as possible.

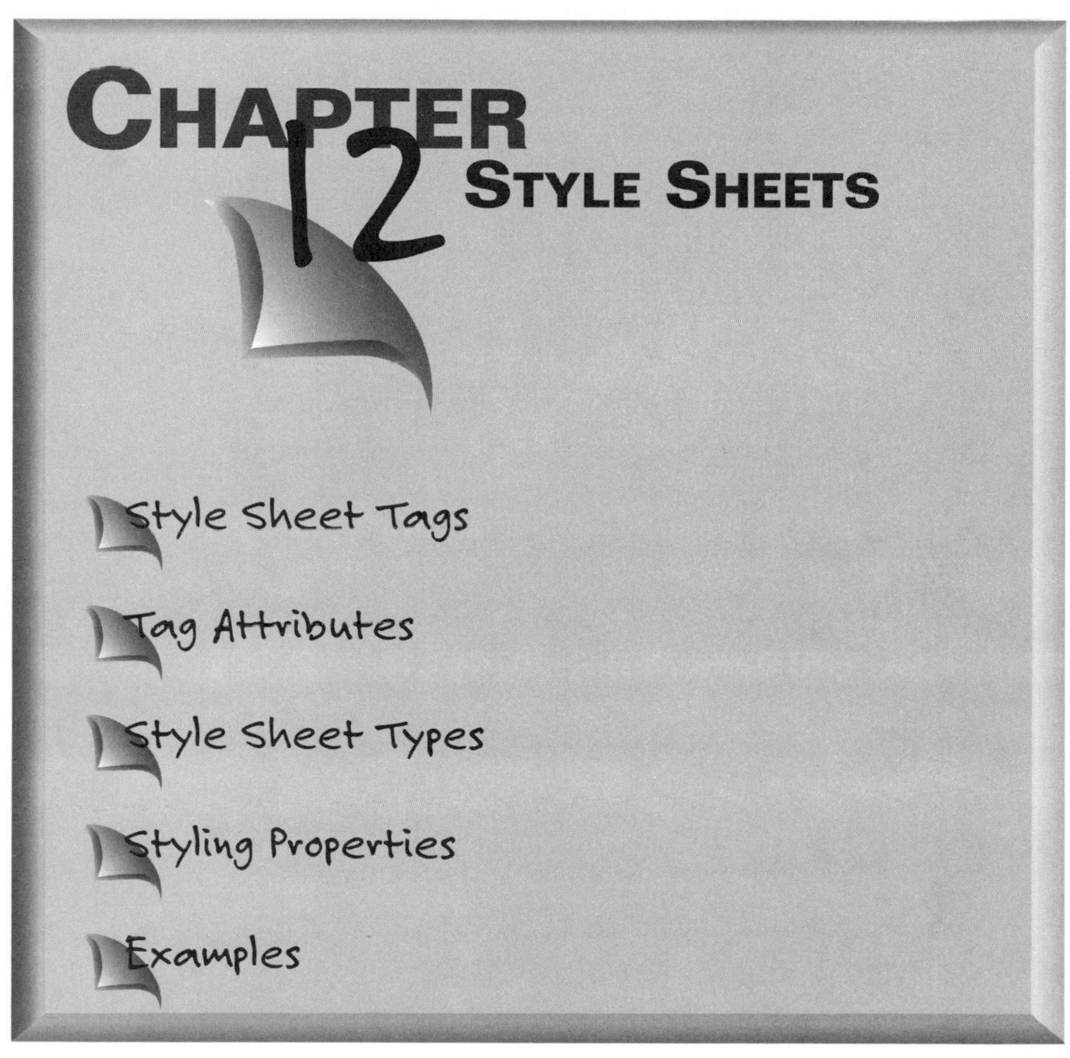

Introduction

Style sheets allow the control of both the appearance and layout of an HTML document. Microsoft Windows, probably more than any other product, has pushed HTML developers to require control over font styles and sizes, screen and text colors, and so on. Users that work in the Windows graphics environment require the same features in their Web page designs that they see in Windows.

HTML was originally conceived as a technique for presenting scientific *context*; the *presentation* aspect was chiefly ignored. Many different attempts were made to solve the presentation problem. These included using proprietary HTML extensions, converting text to images, using tables for page layout ,and so on. Unfortunately, these attempts did not produce uniform results across the industry.

HTML 3.2 first addressed this issue with the introduction of the <STYLE> tag. HTML 4.0 continues by addressing:

- Alternative styles
- Cascading style sheets
- Variations in the placement of style information
- Independence from specific style-sheet languages
- Media dependencies
- Performance concerns

In this chapter we'll examine each of these style issues and learn how HTML 4.0 style sheets bring control over the presentation aspects of HTML documents.

This Chapter's HTML Tags

Five tags are used in conjunction with document styling techniques. Each tag, together with a short description, is listed in Table 12–1. You'll see how these tags are used with the various styling options available to the developer.

Table 12–1: *New tags relating to styling*

Tag	Description
<DIV>	Used to structure documents as a hierarchy of divisions of the <BODY> element.
<LINK>	Provides a means of linking an external style sheet with the current HTML document.
<META>	Used to describe the contents of a specific document. In styling, for example, <META> can be used to set the default style sheet language for an HTML document.

<SPAN>	Used to define styling information for specific local situations. For example, italic styling could be added to local elements by wrapping them between the <STYLE> and </STYLE> elements.
<STYLE>	Allows the use of global styling within an HTML document. This element is typically contained within the <HEAD> </HEAD> elements of an HTML document.

HTML Style-Sheet Issues

In this section you'll learn how HTML 4.0 addresses each of the style-sheet issues mentioned in the introduction. HTML 4.0 completes the style-sheet work initially started in HTML 3.2.

Alternative Styles

HTML 4.0 addresses the issue of alternative styles by including provisions for user-selectable styles. For example, a user who is visually impaired might prefer a large font style and different color from that implemented by the document designers.

Cascading Style Sheets

HTML 4.0 allows the use of cascading style sheets. What this means in specific documents is that multiple style sheets are combined together. For example, a college's computer science department might style documents in a particular manner. When these documents leave the department, they may need to bc styled by the college's style guidelines rather than just those of the computer science department. Cascading style sheets provide that ability. Cascading style sheets are applied in an ordered sequence; later style sheets have a higher precedence level than earlier ones. In our example, the computer science department's style sheet has a lower precedence level than the college's style sheet.

Cascading style sheets have the advantage that individual styles can be stored and later reused.

Variations in the Placement of Style Information

HTML 4.0 allows style sheets to be placed either in the HTML document itself or in files separated from the document.

Many developers prefer to place styling instructions at the start of an HTML document. Others prefer to intermix styling elements throughout the body of the document. The disadvantage to the latter approach is that the styles are uniquely blended with the document itself.

When multiple documents are to use the same styles, it is best to separate the style sheets from the HTML document. This approach makes it easier to manage styles on a site basis, as in the college example mentioned earlier. With this approach you can use HTTP headers to set the style sheets used in any document.

Independence from Specific Style-Sheet Languages

HTML 4.0 doesn't require the use of a particular style-sheet language. While CSS (Cascading Style Sheets) is quickly becoming a standard with the major browsers, other style-sheet languages can be selected. Style sheets using JavaScript are one alternative way to include styling in HTML documents.

Media Dependencies

HTML 4.0 allows developers to produce documents that are media independent in terms of context. This flexibility permits access to Web pages through a variety of devices including computers with different operating systems, Web-TV, and so on.

Style sheets, on the other hand, usually apply to specific computers or devices. The presentation of the document is affected by the device.

Under HTML 4.0, an attempt is made to allow a specification to be included for a particular medium. Thus, a style-sheet language may specify a computer-screen resolution, inclusion of audio capabilities, and so on.

Performance Concerns

If style sheets are held external to the HTML document, performance concerns may arise involving the retrieval and loading of these style-sheet files.

Under HTML 4.0, developers can include the rendering instructions within specific HTML elements. This allows the information to be available by the time the element is rendered.

Style-Sheet Fundamentals

HTML 4.0 permits style-sheet rules to be embedded within the HTML document or in a separate style sheet file. If you are creating CCS style sheets, included as a separate file, the file will use a .css file extension.

This section will illustrate several ways in which style-sheet information may be provided to an HTML document. These examples will use cascading style sheets. Remember, though, that other style-sheet formats are allowed.

The Default Sheet Language

The <META> tag is used to set the default style-sheet language for an HTML document. This is necessary because the syntax of a style rule belongs to the style-sheet language, not to the HTML itself.

To set the default language to CSS, the following portion of code should be added to the <HEAD> element of a document. If the language isn't specifically declared, it is assumed to be CCS.

```
<HEAD>
<META name="Content-Style" content="text/css">
.
.
.
</HEAD>
```

It is also possible to set the default style-sheet language with HTTP headers. For example:

```
Content-Style: text/css
```

When two or more style-sheet specifications attempt to set the default style-sheet language, the last specification takes precedence. HTTP headers are treated as occurring before the <HEAD> element in a document.

Within an HTML document, HTML elements/attributes specify the beginning of style-sheet data. The end of style-sheet data is marked by the appropriate end tag (</>). This format is required so that HTML parsers can distinguish HTML code from style-sheet rules.

CSS Style Properties

CSS style sheets offer a wide variety of style properties that can be specified for use in an HTML document. Table 12–2 provides a list of these properties and a brief description of each.

Table 12–2: *CSS styling properties*

Property	Characteristic	Typical Values
Box	border	Allows all border values to be set, such as width style and color. For example: `border:10pt solid green`
	border-top, border-left, border-bottom, border-right	Sets the style and color of each border surrounding an element. Use *dashed*, *dotted*, *double*, *groove*, *inset*, *outset*, *none,* or *ridged* for the style. For example: `border-top:blue`

border-top-width, border-left-width, border-bottom-width, border-right-width	Sets the width of each border surrounding an element. Use *thin*, *medium*, or *thick*. Widths can also be specified in ems, percentages, points, and so on. For example: `border-top-width:12pt`
border-width	Sets all four borders at the same time. For example: `border-width:6pt 8pt 10pt 12pt`
clear	Used to place an element below any floating element on that side. Use *left*, *right*, or *center*. For example: `clear:center`
float	Used to align an element to the *left*, *right*, or *center*. Text wrapping can occur. For example: `float:right`
height	Specifies the height of the bounding box. Text boxes contain scrolling bars. Images are scaled to fit the box. A physical value is permitted, or *auto* allows automatic allocation of space. For example: `height:auto`
margin	Allows all four margins to be set at the same time. For example: `margin: 4em, 4em, 2em, 2em`
margin-top, margin-left, margin-bottom, margin-right	Specify the spacing between adjacent elements. Use a length, percentage, or *auto*. For example: `margin-top:4em;` `margin-left: 4em;` `margin-bottom:2em;` `margin-right:2em`
padding	Allows all four padding values to be set at the thc same time. For example: `padding:1cm 1cm 0.5cm 0.5cm`

Table 12–2: *CSS Styling Properties (continued)*

Property	Characteristic	Typical Values
	padding-top, padding-bottom, padding-left, padding-right	Specify the padding between the box and the given elements. Use a length, percentage, or *auto*. For example: `padding-top:1cm; padding-left: 1cm; padding-bottom:0.5cm; padding-right:0.5cm`
	width	Specifies the width of the bounding box. Text boxes contain scrolling bars. Images are scaled to fit the box. A physical value is permitted, or *auto* allows automatic allocation of space. For example: `width:auto`
Classification	display	Determines when and how a style element is used. Use *block*, *inline*, *list-item*, or *none*. For example: `display:block`
	list-style	Allows list-style -type, -image, and -position to be specified at the same time. For example: `list-style:circle url(arrow.gif) outside`
	list-style-image	Used to specify an image that will replace the normal marker. For example: `image:url(arrow.gif)`
	list-style-position	Used to specify text formatting following the list-item marker. Use *inside* and *outside*. Outside is the default and aligns additional lines with the first character of the original line. Inside aligns additional lines with the item-list marker.
	list-style-type	Used to set marker types for a list. Values can include circle,

		decimal, disc, lower-alpha, lower-roman, upper-alpha, upper-roman, and none.
	white-space	Specifies how spaces and line breaks are processed. Uses *normal, pre,* and *nowrap*. Normal–extra spaces are ignored and breaks are made with . Pre–all space is left as entered. Nowrap–wrapping done on .
Background	background	Allows multiple background characteristics to be set at once. The order is -color, -image, -repeat, -attachment, and -position.
	background-attachment	Used to determine if background image is *fixed* or can *scroll* with foreground text. For example: `background-attachment:url(scroll)`
	background-color	Specifies the background color. Specifies by color (such as red, green, blue) or by RGB value [such as RGB(255,0,0), RGB(0,255,0), RGB(0,0,255) and so on]. Hexadecimal values can be used–for example, #FF0000, #00FF00, and #0000FF.
	background-image	Specifies an image to be displayed on top of a background color. For example: `background-image:url(back.jpg)`
	background-position	Specifies an image's starting position. For horizontal, use left, center, or right. For vertical, use top, center, or bottom. Positions can also be given as percentages ranging from 0 to 100%. For example: `background-position: center center`

Table 12-2: *CSS Styling Properties (continued)*

Property	Characteristic	Typical Values
	background-repeat	Specifies if the background should be tiled. Use repeat-x to repeat the image in a horizontal line and repeat-y to repeat the image in a vertical line. For example: `background-repeat:repeat-y`
Color	color	Specifies color of text. Uses same format as background-color.
Font	font	Permits the font-size, line-height, and font-family to be set at one time.
	font-family	Name of the font family. Families such as arial, courier, roman, and so on are permitted.
	font-size	Font size specified in points, inches, centimeters, or pixels or as a percentage. Point values are the preferred method. Values are expressed, for example, as 12pt, 16pt, 36pt, and so on.
	font-style	Used to indicate a *normal*, *italic,* or *bold* font.
	font-variant	Specified as *normal* or *small-caps*. Small-caps are the size of lower-case letters.
	font-weight	Specifies the thickness of a typeface. *Normal*, *bold*, *bolder*, *light*, and so on are allowed. Values from 100 to 900 can also be used.

Measurement	absolute	Use *in*, *cm*, *mm*, *pt*, or *pc* units. These represent inches, centimeters, millimeters, points, or picas.
	percentage	Use a numeric value between 0 and 100 relative to a length unit.
	relative	Use *em*, *ex*, or *px*. The first value represents a typographic term referring to the height of a character. The second value refers to the height of the letter "x". The third represents measurements in pixels.
Text	line-height	Used to set the leading of a paragraph. Specified in points, inches, centimeters, or pixels or as a percentage
	letter-spacing	Specifies space between letters. See word-spacing below. The value, *em*, is the width of the letter "m". Extra space is added between letters with this value. For example: `letter-spacing:0.8em`
	text-align	Specifies how text is aligned. Use *left*, *right*, *center*, or *justify*. For example: `text-align:center`
	text-decoration	Allows extra text characteristics such as blinking, strike-through, and so on. For example: `text-decoration:blink`
	text-indent	Specifies text indenting. Measured in ems or inches as space added to the first line. For example: `text-indent:8em`

Table 12–2: *CSS Styling Properties (continued)*

Property	Characteristic	Typical Values
	text-transform	Used to specify capitalization. Use *capitalize* (first letter of each word), *uppercase* (all letters upper case), *lowercase* (all letters lower case), and *none* (no capitalization). For example: `text-transform:capitalize`
	vertical-align	Specifies vertical positioning. Uses basline, bottom, middle, sub, super, text-bottom, text-top, top, or a percentage. For example: `vertical-align:text-top`
	word-spacing	Specifies space between words. The value, *em*, is the width of the letter "m". The default value is 0em. Another example: `word-spacing:2em`

You'll see additional examples of CSS styling later in this chapter.

Inline Style Information

Inline style sheets are created by adding the style attribute to specific HTML tags. This style information is obtained from the default style-sheet language. CSS style declarations use a name:value format. Property declarations are separated by a semicolon.

For example, here is an inline style that sets the font family, size, and color:

```
<p style="font-family:arial; font-size=16pt; color:red">
  Setting a font's properties is easy!
</p>
```

It is also possible to use the <SPAN> or the <DIV> tags for inline styling.

```
<SPAN style="font: arial 16pt">
  Use for short blocks of text.
</SPAN>
```

```
<DIV style="font: roman 10pt">
  Use for longer blocks of text.
</DIV>
```

While inline styling is easy, especially for shorter HTML documents, its ultimate downfall is that the styling is embedded within the HTML document. This makes it nonportable, which certainly defeats the purpose of cascading style sheets.

Using the <STYLE> Tag

The <STYLE> element is typically used to style whole documents. Style-sheet rules are often placed in the document's header. When user agents don't support specific style elements, they must hide the contents of the <STYLE> element. The <STYLE> element often permits a wider variety of rules than the style attribute discussed earlier in the chapter. The <STYLE> element can be used to specify all instances of HTML elements, such as H1, H2, H3 elements and so on. The <STYLE> element can also be used to style all instances of elements belonging to a class.

An HTML document may contain several H1 and H2 elements. If we wish to place a border around every H1 and H2 element in the document, the <STYLE> element should be used.

```
<HEAD>
  <STYLE type="text/css">
    H1 {border-width:2; border:solid; text-align:center}
    H2 {border-width:1;border:dashed; text-align:left}
  </STYLE>
</HEAD>
```

The following example shows you how to style all elements in a specific class. Classes behave as a subset of a previously defined declaration. For example:

```
<HEAD>
  <STYLE type="text/css">
    #clasid H1 {border-width:2; border:solid;
    text-align:center}
  </STYLE>
</HEAD>
<BODY>
  <H1 id="classid"> This H1 element is styled. </H1>
  <H1 class="anotherclass"> This H1 element is NOT styled.
  </H1>
  <H1> This one is NOT affected either. </H1>
</BODY>
```

We'll see several of these styling techniques used in the example program given at the end of this chapter.

External Style Sheets

External style sheets exist as documents separated from the HTML document. This allows the developer/user to share the style sheets across a number of documents, sites, and locations. It also allows easy modification without affecting the HTML document.

Users are often given the choice of styling. In this case the style sheet is an *alternate* choice. If the user cannot alter a particular style or sheet, it is known as *persistent*. Default style sheets are usually used when loading a document but can allow the user to select an alternative style sheet.

The <LINK> tag is used to incorporate an external style sheet. The href attribute identifies the location of the style sheet. The rel attribute is used to indicate persistence or alternate. Set rel="stylesheet" for persistent and use rel="alternate stylesheet" for alternate. The title attribute can be used to change the style sheet from persistent to default.

Here is an example using two external style sheets.

```
<LINK href="CompSheet.css" rel="alternate stylesheet">
<LINK href="CollSheet.css" rel="stylesheet">
```

The first is an alternate style sheet that might be used by a computer science department. The second is persistent and might be used by the entire college.

If two alternate style sheets share the same title, they will both be applied when that style is activated. For example:

```
<LINK href="CollSheet1.css" title="header"
  rel="alternate stylesheet">
<LINK href="CollSheet2.css" title="header"
  rel="alternate stylesheet">
```

The <META> element can be used to set the default style for an HTML document. For example:

```
<HEAD>

<META http-equiv="Default-Style" content="header:>
</HEAD>

<LINK href="CollSheet1.css" title="header"
  rel="alternate stylesheet">
<LINK href="CollSheet2.css" title="header"
  rel="alternate stylesheet">
```

In a similar manner, a media attribute can be used to specify different media such as screen, printing, speech, and so on.

```
<LINK href="CollScreen.css" media="screen" rel="stylesheet">
<LINK href="CollPrint.css" media="print" rel="stylesheet">
```

HTML Document Styling Examples

In the following examples we'll borrow the pet-registration HTML document from the previous chapter. This document involved a form for pet registration but didn't contain any styling. In the first example, PET2.htm, we'll use both the <STYLE> element and a little inline styling. All styling information is contained within the HTML document. In the second example, PET3.htm, we'll create a cascading style sheet and save it as an external file. This external style sheet will then be brought into the HTML document. Both examples will produce identical screen results.

Styling PET2.htm

The following listing contains the whole PET2.htm document, including styling. The styling is shown in a bold font.

```
<HTML>
<HEAD>
<TITLE>Pet Registration</TITLE>
<STYLE type="text/css">
  BR {}
  H1 {border:6pt double red; text-align:center; color:red}
  H3 {border:2pt inset blue; text-align:left; color:blue}
  BODY {font-family:arial; font-size:14pt;
         font-style:italic; background: #00FFFF}
</STYLE>
</HEAD>

<BODY>
<H1><p style="font:30pt arial">
  Please complete the following form
  <BR>to register your pet</p></H1>
<HR>
<H3>Information about you:</H3>
<FORM method="post"
  action="http://hoohoo.ncsa.uiuc.edu/cgi-bin/post-
query">
Your last name: <INPUT type="text" name="lname"
  maxlength="25" size="18">
First name: <INPUT type="text" name="fname"
  maxlength="25" size="18">
<BR>
Social Security Number: <INPUT type="text" name="ssn"
  maxlength="11" size="11">
<HR>
<H3>Information about your pet:</H3>
<TABLE>
<TR valign="top">
<TD>Type of pet:
<BR>
<SELECT Name="PetType">
   <OPTION>Cat </OPTION>
```

```
    <OPTION selected>Dog </OPTION>
    <OPTION>Horse </OPTION>
    <OPTION>Other </OPTION>
  </SELECT>
  </TABLE>
  <INPUT type="radio" name="sex" value="m">Male
  <INPUT type="radio" name="sex" value="f">Female
  <BR>
  Pet's breed: <INPUT type="text" name="breed"
    maxlength="20">
  <BR>
  Please check all that apply to your pet:
  <INPUT type="checkbox" name="char"
    value="e">Cropped ears
  <INPUT type="checkbox" name="char"
    value="t">Docked tail
  <INPUT type="checkbox" name="char"
    value="c">Good with children
  <BR>
  <H3>Tell us something unique about your pet:</H3>
  <TEXTAREA name="info" rows=10 cols=60>
  </TEXTAREA>
  <HR>
  <H3>Thank you for your information -
    your pet will be registered.</H3>
  <INPUT type="submit">
  <INPUT type="reset">
  </FORM>
  </BODY>
  </HTML>
```

The first section of styling occurs with the use of the <STYLE> element. By placing the styling in the <HEAD> of the document we insure global styling throughout the document. All level-one headers will be surrounded by a red double border sized to match a 6-point font size. The text contained within the border will be centered and also red in color. In a similar manner all level-three headers will be surrounded by a blue inset border sized to match a 2-point font size. The text contained within the border will be left aligned and also blue in color. Finally, all text contained within the body of the document will be in a 14-point italic Arial font. The background of the body will be set to a light blue value.

Inline styling is used within the document to override the global styling and set the level-one header to a 30-point Arial font.

Figure 12–1 shows a portion of the results of applying these styling changes.

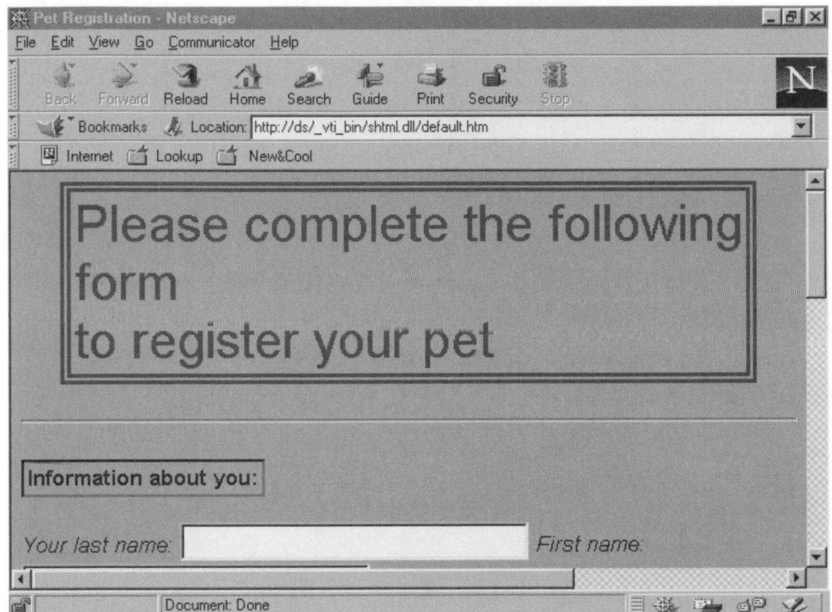

Figure 12–1: *The use of the <STYLE> element and inline styling produce interesting results*

In the next subsection we'll approach styling is a different manner.

Styling PET3.htm

This example involves the use of a cascading style sheet. The external file containing the style sheet is named mystyle.css and exists at the same location as PET3.htm. Here are the contents of the mystyle.css file. As you can see, they are virtually lifted out of the PET2.htm document. The mystyle.css file can contain any amount of styling needed for your documents.

```
<STYLE type="text/css">
  BR {}
  H1 {border:6pt double red; text-align:center; color:red}
  H3 {border:2pt inset blue; text-align:left; color:blue}
  BODY {font-family:arial; font-size:14pt;
  font-style:italic; background: #00FFFF}
</STYLE>
```

The mystyle.css file is brought into the PET3.htm file with just a small portion of code, as shown next.

```
<HTML>
<HEAD>
<TITLE>Pet Registration</TITLE>
<LINK href="mystyle.css" rel="stylesheet">
</HEAD>

<BODY>
    .
    .
    .
(remainder identical to previous PET2.htm listing)
```

Except for the <LINK> element and the absence of styling information within the PET3.htm document, the document is identical to the PET2.htm document shown in the previous subsection. The screen will produce results identical to those shown in Figure 12–1.

Before Leaving

Experiment with the various style types and attributes described in this chapter. Use the PET3.htm document and change font sizes and colors. Hey, isn't this great? You might want to apply the concept of classes to the PET3.htm document before going onto the next chapter.

Introduction

Scripts are programs that execute on a user's computer when an HTML document loads or when a particular link is activated. Client-side scripts can be included within the HTML document or loaded as a separate file. Scripts require no interaction from the server-side, yet add an interactive element to an HTML document's abilities.

A specific script language is not required by HTML, although two languages are becoming very popular: JavaScript and VBScript. Browsers must support the scripting language used, or care must be taken to hide it. For example, JavaScript works well with the Netscape Communicator (version 4.0) and the Microsoft Internet Explorer (version 4.0). However, VBScript only works with the Internet Explorer.

Scripts offer several features to HTML documents:

- Scripts can be linked to buttons, checkboxes, and so on to create interactive elements.
- Scripts can be used to load and unload files.
- Scripts can ensure that entered data conforms to the range and type specified by the developer.
- Scripts can modify the contents of an HTML document in a dynamic fashion.
- Scripts can process form data as the user enters it.

Scripts fall into two broad categories–those that execute upon loading and those that execute based upon an event. Scripts that are contained within the <SCRIPT> element are usually executed when the HTML document is loaded. If a script is to execute when a specific event occurs, it is usually assigned to an element via the intrinsic event attributes.

This Chapter's HTML Tags

Two tags are used in conjunction with the scripting techniques presented in this chapter. Each tag, together with a short description, is listed in Table 13–1. You'll see how these tags are used with the various scripting options available to you as you develop documents with JavaScript or VBScript.

Table 13–1: *New tags relating to scripting*

Tag	Description
<NOSCRIPT>	Can be used where browsers do not support scripting or a particular scripting language.
<SCRIPT>	Identifies a portion of code that the interpreter reads in the identified scripting language.

Script Fundamentals

In this section you will learn how to embed scripts within an HTML document or bring them in as an external file. You'll also learn how to specify specific scripting languages, the syntax of a script, and how to use intrinsic events with scripts.

The <SCRIPT> Tag

The <SCRIPT> tag is used to place a script within an HTML document. This element uses several attributes: type, language, and src.

The type attribute is used to specify the scripting language. It must be an Internet Media Type. There is no default scripting language. For example, thc language might be specified as:

```
language="javascript"
```

or

```
language="vbscript"
```

The language attribute is deprecated. The use of the type attribute is preferred. The src attribute uses the url to specify the location of an external script

The Script Language

Since there is not a default scripting language, an HTML document developer must identify the language used in each script. This can be done by explicitly setting a default scripting language for the entire document or by using a local declaration.

Global Declarations

A default scripting language can be identified for all scripts within a document by using the <META> element in the <HEAD> of a document. For example:

```
<HTML>
<HEAD>
<TITLE> A global scripting language declaration. </TITLE>
<META http-equiv="Content-Script-Type"
content="text/javascript"
    .
    .
    .
```

The content type can be any valid Internet Media type, such as "text/javascript" or "text/vbscript." The default scripting language can also be set with an HTTP header. For example:

```
Content-Script-Type:"text/vbscript"
```

Local Declarations

The scripting language can also be specified with each <SCRIPT> element by using the type attribute. If a default scripting language has been identified, the <SCRIPT> type attribute, when specified, overrides it.

For example, in the following listing the default scripting language is set to "text/vbscript." There is one <SCRIPT> element used whose scripting language is identified as "text/javascript." The local declaration overrides the default declaration. This example is named ScripTst.htm.

```
<HTML>
<HEAD>
<META http-equiv="Content-Script-Type"
content="text/vbscript">
</HEAD>
<BODY>
<FORM>
<INPUT type="button" name="but1" value="Yes"
  onclick="Yes();">
<INPUT type="button" name="but2" value="No"
  onclick="No();">
<SCRIPT type="text/javascript">
  <!—
    function Yes() {
      alert('Yes, the JavaScript is working!');
    }
    function No() {
      alert('No, this was not hard to do!');
    }
  <!— End of JavaScript —>
</SCRIPT>
</FORM>
</BODY>
</HTML>
```

Intrinsic Events

Research regarding intrinsic events is ongoing by members of W3C. Developers are advised to check the W3C Web site at http://www.w3.org/ for more information on developments in this area.

Intrinsic events make it possible to associate an action with an event that occurs when the user interacts with the HTML document. Table 13–2 lists intrinsic events that will take a value that is a script. The script is then executed when an event occurs for that element.

Table 13–2: *Event attributes and descriptions*

Event Attribute	Event Description
onblur	Occurs when an element loses focus. Can occur by using the mouse or keyboard tabbing.
onchange	Occurs when a control loses the input focus if its value has changed since gaining focus. Applies to <INPUT>, < SELECT>, and <TEXTAREA>.
onclick	Occurs when a mouse button is clicked over an element.
ondblclick	Occurs when a mouse button is double-clicked over an element.
onfocus	Occurs when an element receives focus. Can occur by using the mouse or keyboard tabbing. Applies to <BUTTON>, <INPUT>, <LABEL>, <SELECT>, and <TEXTAREA>.
onkeydown	Occurs when a key is pressed over an element.
onkeypress	Occurs when a key is pressed and released over an element
onkeyup	Occurs when a key is released over an element.
onload	Occurs when a window is completed loaded or all frames within a <FRAMESET>. Can be used within <BODY> and <FRAMESET>.

Table 13–2: *Event attributes and descriptions (continued)*

Event Attribute	Event Description
onmousedown	Occurs when the mouse button is pressed over an element.
onmousemove	Occurs when the mouse is moved while over an element.
onmouseout	Occurs when the mouse is moved away from an element.
onmouseover	Occurs when the mouse is moved onto an element.
onmouseup	Occurs when the mouse button is released over an element.
onreset	Occurs when a form is reset. Applies to <FORM> only.
onselect	Occurs when text is selected in a text field. Applies to <INPUT> and <TEXTAREA>.
onsubmit	Occurs when a form is submitted. Applies to <FORM> only.
onunload	Occurs when a document is removed from a window or frame. Can be used within <BODY> and <FRAMESET>.

Unless otherwise noted, most of the attributes listed in Table 13–2 apply and work with most elements.

Here is a portion of an HTML document showing a short JavaScript. In this case, intrinsic events for two buttons respond to the onmousedown event.

```
    .
    .
    .
<INPUT type="button" name="but1" value="Emergency"
  onmousedown="Stat();">
<INPUT type="button" name="but2" value="No Rush"
  onmousedown="NoStat();">
<SCRIPT type="text/javascript">
  <!-
    function Stat() {
      alert('Call Doctors!');
    }
    function NoStat() {
      alert('Call Technicians!');
    }
  <!- End of JavaScript ->
    .
    .
    .
```

You'll see additional example of the use of intrinsic events in the Javascript and VBScript examples at the end of this chapter.

The <NOSCRIPT> Tag

The <NOSCRIPT> element can be used to address those situations where a script is not executed. It is an alternate content container for non-script-based rendering.

This situation can occur when a browser does not evaluate scripts or doesn't support a particular scripting language.

```
<SCRIPT type="text/vbscript">
  (vbscript goes here)
</SCRIPT>

<NOSCRIPT>
  (alternate code for cases where script is not supported)
</NOSCRIPT>
```

Commenting Out Scripts

When the browser does not recognize a script element, it will most likely be displayed as text. JavaScript and VBScript allow script statements to be enclosed in an SGML comment. This allows those browsers that don't recognize the script to ignore the contents. For browsers that do recognize scripting the script element within the comments will be executed.

For example, in JavaScript and VBScript use "<!–" at the start of a <SCRIPT> element and "–>" at the end to hide the contents from old browsers.

For example, in the following portion of JavaScript, all of the script will be hidden from a nonsupporting browser because it is contained between "<!–" and "–>".

```
<SCRIPT type="text/javascript">
  <!–
    function Stat() {
      alert('Call Doctors!');
    }
    function NoStat() {
      alert('Call Technicians!');
    }
  <!– End of JavaScript –>
```

Scripting with JavaScript

In this section we'll examine a simple example that uses JavaScript as the scripting language.

Examine the complete listing that follows. You'll notice that the portions pertaining to scripting have been set in a bold font. This document is saved as JDate.htm.

```
<HTML>
<HEAD>
<TITLE>DATE Time Information</TITLE>
<META http-equiv="Content-Script-Type"
  content="text/javascript">
<STYLE type="text/css">
  BODY {font-family:arial; font-size:20pt;
    font-style:italic; background: #00FFFF}
</STYLE>
</HEAD>

<BODY>
<CENTER>
```

```
<FORM name="calendar">
  <INPUT type="text" name="info" size=27>
<HR>
<INPUT type="button" name="but1" value="Date"
  onclick="NewDate();">
<INPUT type="button" name="but2" value="Time"
  onclick="NewTime();">
<INPUT type="button" name="but3" value="Date/Time"
  onclick="NewDateTime();">
</CENTER>

<SCRIPT>
  <!-
    function NewDate() {
      var CurrDate = new Date();
      var month=CurrDate.getMonth()+1;
      var day=CurrDate.getDate();
      var year=CurrDate.getYear();
      DataStr = month + " / " +
                day + " / " +
                year;
      document.calendar.info.value=DataStr;
    }
    function NewTime() {
      var CurrTime = new Date();
      var hours=CurrTime.getHours();
      var minutes=CurrTime.getMinutes();
      var seconds=CurrTime.getSeconds();
      DataStr = hours + " : " +
                minutes + " : " +
                seconds;
      document.calendar.info.value=DataStr;
    }
    function NewDateTime() {
      document.calendar.info.value = Date();
    }
  <!- End of JavaScript ->
</SCRIPT>
</FORM>

</BODY>
</HTML>
```

The first thing you'll note when examining the listing is that the <META> element is used to identify the scripting language. This is accomplished with just a small portion of code:

```
<META http-equiv="Content-Script-Type"
  content="text/javascript">
```

Three buttons initially appear in the window. They allow the user to select a date, time, or date/time display. The JavaScript for retrieving this information is straightforward. Examine a portion of the script that returns the date to the window when the first button is selected:

```
<SCRIPT>
  <!–
    function NewDate() {
      var CurrDate = new Date();
      var month=CurrDate.getMonth()+1;
      var day=CurrDate.getDate();
      var year=CurrDate.getYear();
      DataStr = month + " / " +
                 day + " / " +
                 year;
      document.calendar.info.value=DataStr;
    }
```

This function is named NewDate() and takes advantage of a built in JavaScript function named Date(). Date() returns a whole string of data including day, date, and time. In order to obtain just the date, information can be parsed by using getMonth(), getDate(), and getYear(). A string is then built using these values named DataStr. Notice that the month value adds a 1 to the value returned by getMonth. This is because the indexing for months starts at zero instead of one.

The remaining two functions behave in a similar manner. Test the document in a browser such as Netscape or the Internet Explorer. If you select the Date button, your screen should appear similar to Figure 13–1.

Now, select the Time button. Your screen should take on the appearance of Figure 13–2.

No special formatting was applied to the returned time. The time format is military. You'll also notice that for minutes or seconds less than 10, the leading zero is missing. For example, a time of 13 : 8 : 6 will be displayed rather than 13 : 08 : 06.

The real surprise occurs when the Date/Time button is selected. Here the entire contents of the string, returned by calling Date(), is displayed to the screen.

JavaScript, as you can see, can easily be integrated into your HTML documents. You might want to continue your study of JavaScript by purchasing a book devoted just to that topic. Who knows what creative aspects your HTML documents will take on!

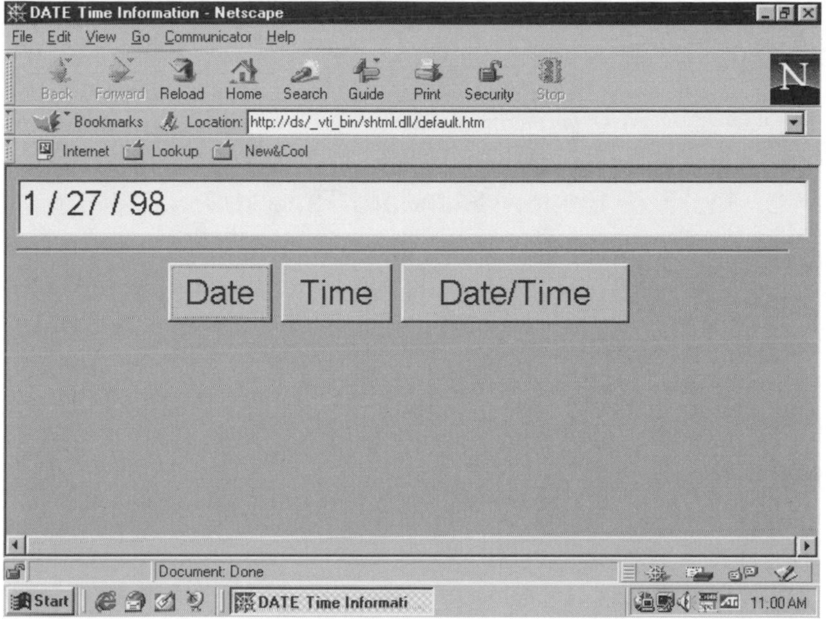

Figure 13–1: *The Date button is selected*

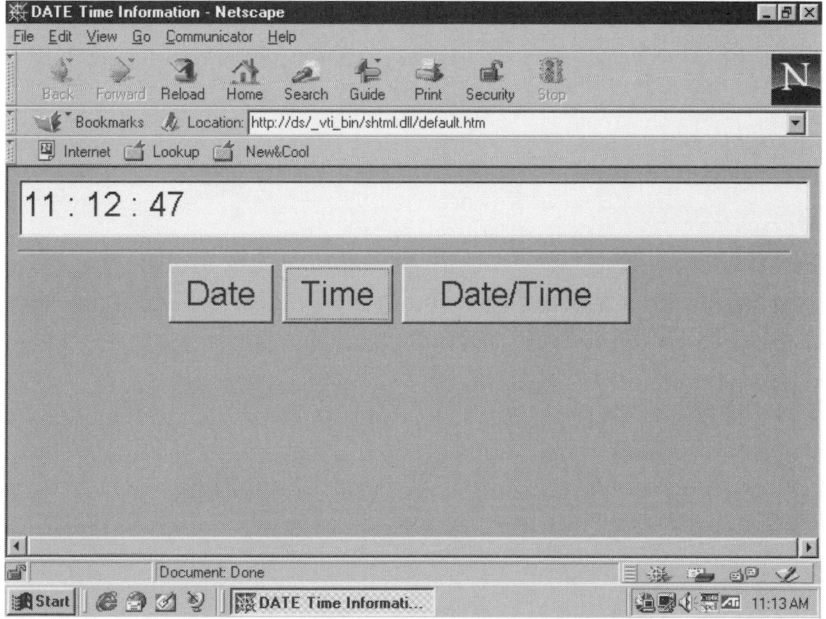

Figure 13–2: *The Time button is selected*

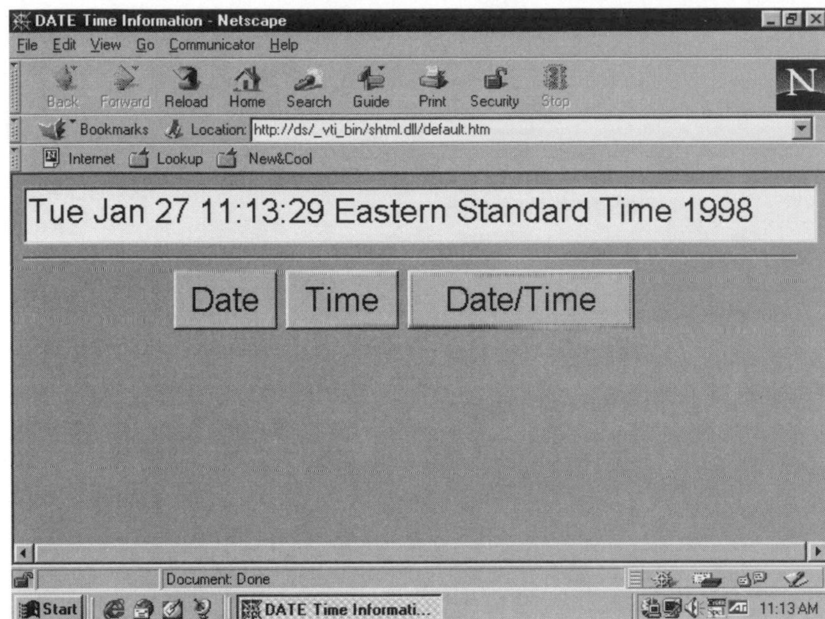

Figure 13–3: *The Date/Time button is selected*

Scripting with VBScript

In this section we'll examine a simple example that uses VBScript as the scripting language.

Examine the complete listing that follows. You'll notice that the portions pertaining to scripting have been set in a bold font. This document is saved as VBDate.htm.

```
<HTML>
<HEAD>
<TITLE>DATE Time Information</TITLE>
</HEAD>

<BODY>
<CENTER>
<FORM name="calendar">
  <INPUT type="text" name="info" size=20>
<HR>
<INPUT type="button" name="cmdbut1" value="Time">
```

```
<INPUT type="button" name="cmdbut2" value="Date">
</CENTER>

<SCRIPT language="vbscript">
  <!—
    Sub cmdbut1_OnClick
      document.calendar.info.value = Time()
    End Sub
    Sub cmdbut2_OnClick
      document.calendar.info.value = Date()
    End Sub
  <!— End of VBScript —>
</SCRIPT>
</FORM>

</BODY>
</HTML>
```

The first thing you'll note when examining the listing is that the scripting language is set within the <SCRIPT> element.

Two buttons initially appear in the window. They allow the user to select a time or date display. The VBScript for retrieving this information is straightforward and is achieved by calling the Visual Basic Time() or Date() function. For example, this small subroutine retrieves the time information requested by a user.

```
Sub cmdbut1_OnClick
  document.calendar.info.value = Time()
End Sub
```

When the Time button is clicked, the time will be displayed as shown in Figure 13–4. The time is reported in the correct format with leading zeros for minutes and seconds under ten.

Push the Date button and see the date displayed in the format shown in Figure 13–5.

VBScript is also easy to use. However, remember that VBScript is supported only by the Microsoft Internet Explorer. If your document is opened under Netscape, you will not see any returned information from button clicks. Many books are available that teach VBScript. If you are a Visual Basic programmer, you will feel right at home with VBScript.

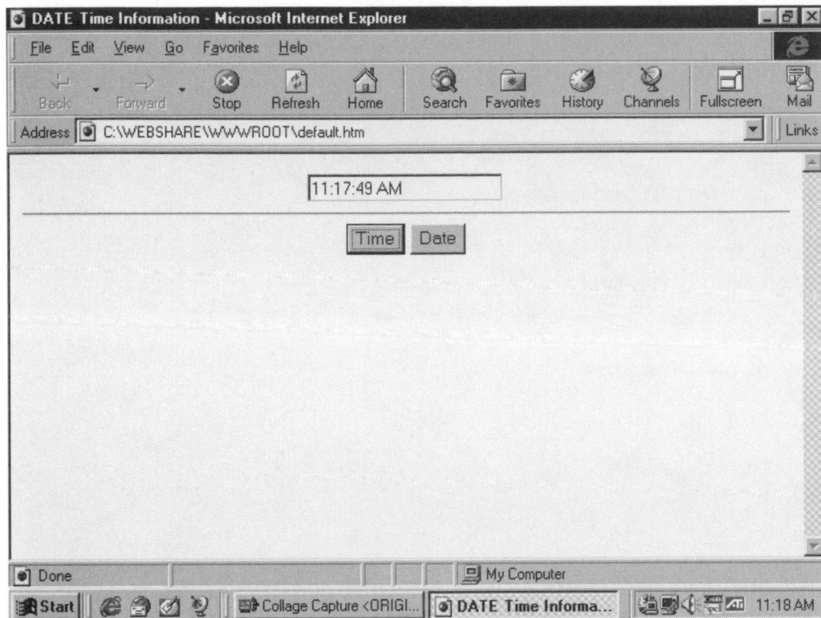

Figure 13–4: *The Time button is selected*

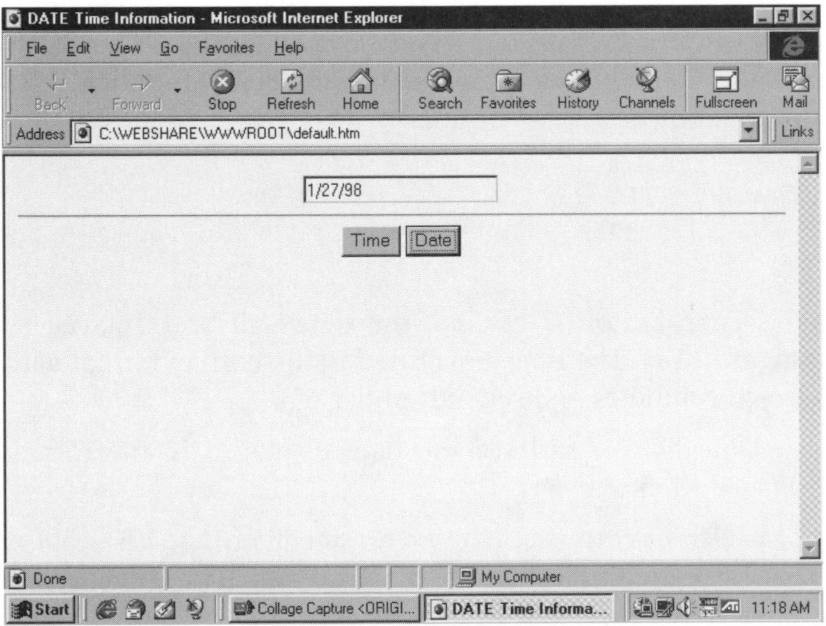

Figure 13–5: *The Date button is selected*

A Whole Lot More

This chapter has looked at several scripting examples as they relate to HTML documents. Obviously, a whole lot more can be done with JavaScript and VBScript. We encourage you to investigate further the scripting language of your choice and integrate those features into your documents.

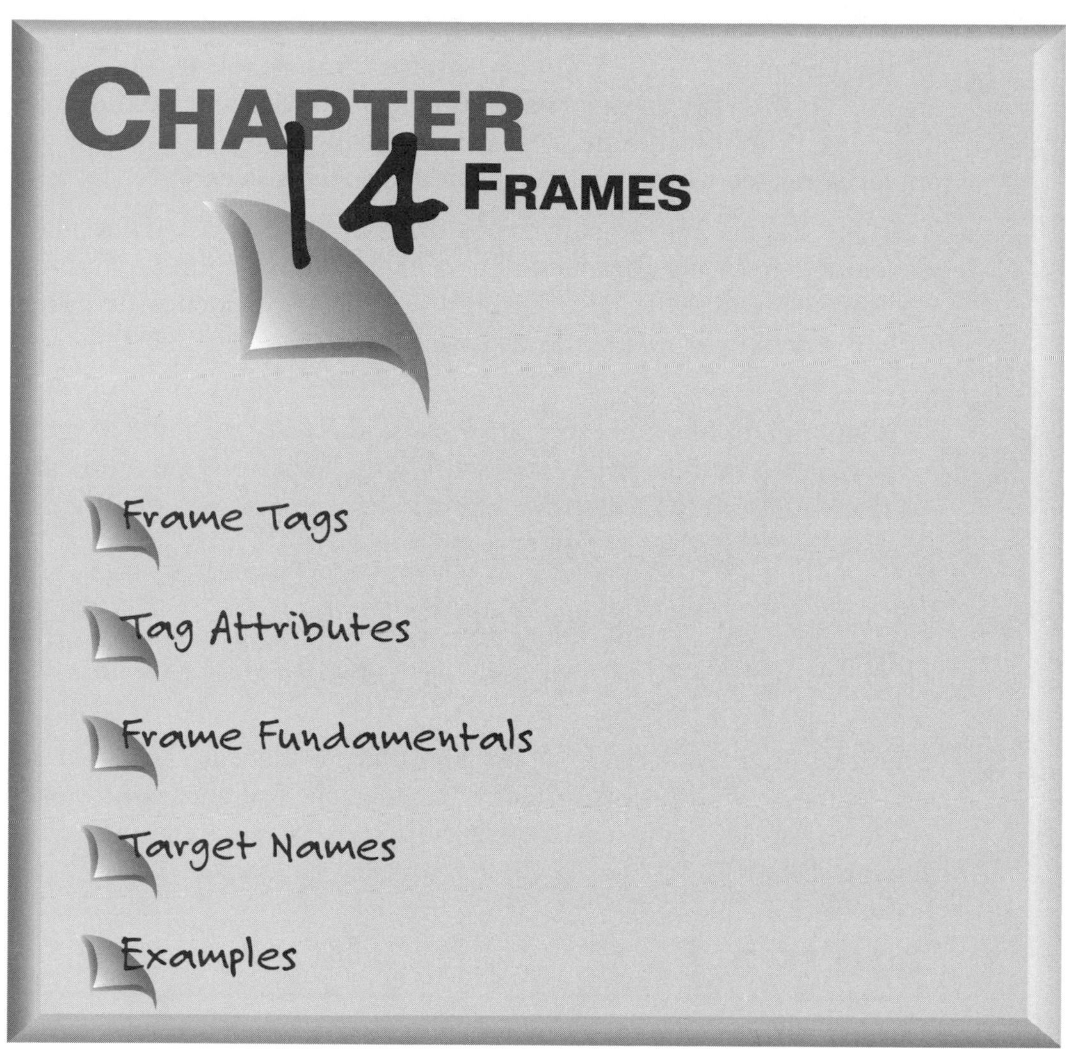

Introduction

Frames allow developers to create imaginative document views by allowing the viewing area to be divided into multiple sections. Each section can be treated independently from the others–some serving as navigation frames and others as content frames. Imagine your viewing area as being represented by a picture window. Adding frames to your document viewing areas comparable to adding panes to the picture window. Now, instead of being one big screen, your viewing area can be neatly divided and organized. For example, consider this situation:

A viewing area is divided into three frames. One frame holds an image of the company's main building. Another frame holds a navigation menu, allowing the users to make choices as to what information they will view. The third frame is used to allowing scrolling through text material related to the previous navigation-menu selection.

Inline frames are officially recognized by HTML 4.0. They allow developers to insert a frame within a block of text. Inline frames are no longer restricted to just the borders of HTML documents. Their only restriction, as compared with standard frames, is that they cannot be resized.

While not all browsers support frames, you will find that the material discussed in this chapter will work with Netscape Communicator (version 4.0) and the Microsoft Internet Explorer (version 4.0).

This Chapter's HTML Tags

Four tags are used in conjunction with frames. Table 14–1 lists the tag names together with a brief description of each. You'll learn how each of these tags can be used to create unique viewing areas in the following sections.

Table 14–1: *New tags relating to frames*

Tag	Description
<FRAME>	Specifies the contents and appearance of a single frame view
<FRAMESET>	Specifies the layout of the main window in terms of rectangular spaces
<IFRAME>	Specifies the contents and appearance of an inline frame
<NOFRAMES>	Specifies content that will be displayed when frames are not displayed (i.e., used to provide an alternate content for user agents that do not support frames)

Frame Fundamentals

In this section you will learn how to create frames, specify the number of frames in a viewing area, and set their size, resizing capabilities, scrolling capabilities, borders, and margins.

You'll see that frames are easy to create and use and should be a part of a well-defined display. Frames can make it easy for your users to navigate your site.

The <FRAMESET> Tag

Documents incorporating frames must use the <FRAMESET> tag to define the layout of all views in the window. The <FRAMESET> element is used in place of the <BODY> element. Elements normally placed in the <BODY> element cannot be placed before the first <FRAMESET> element.

The syntax for using the complete container is straightforward:

```
<FRAMESET frameset_attributes>
    .
    .
    .
</FRAMESET>
```

The HTML 4.0 attributes for <FRAMESET> include cols and rows. Table 14–2 names and describes <FRAMESET> attributes.

Table 14–2: *HTML 4.0 <FRAMESET> attributes*

Attribute	Description
cols	Layout of vertical frames. Length of each frame is expressed in a physical unit (pixels, integer) or as a percentage of the actual viewing area.
rows	Layout of horizontal frames. Length of each frame is expressed in a physical unit (pixels, integer) or as a percentage of the actual viewing area.

For example, the following code shows how <FRAMESET> can be used to create three vertical frames of approximately the same value:

```
<FRAMESET cols="33%,33%,34%">
```

In a similar manner, four horizontal rows could be created with this code:

```
<FRAMESET rows="25%,25%,25%,25%">
```

A grid can be constructed by specifying both the number of cols and number of rows. Here is the code necessary to create a grid with four columns and three rows:

```
<FRAMESET cols="25%,25%,25%,25%"
rows=""33%,33%,34%">
```

Figure 14–1 shows this layout in a screen show produced with the following HTML code:

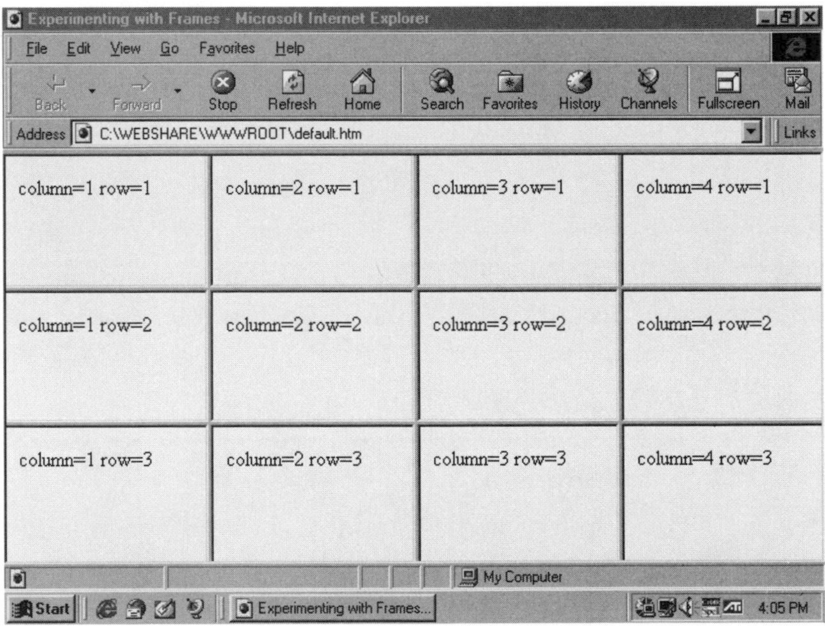

Figure 14–1: *<FRAMESET> is used to create a grid in the viewing area*

```
<HTML>
<HEAD>
<TITLE>Experimenting with Frames</TITLE>
</HEAD>

<FRAMESET cols="25%,25%,25%,25%" rows="33%,33%,34%">
  <FRAME src="c1r1.html">
  <FRAME src="c2r1.html">
  <FRAME src="c3r1.html">
  <FRAME src="c4r1.html">
  <FRAME src="c1r2.html">
  <FRAME src="c2r2.html">
  <FRAME src="c3r2.html">
  <FRAME src="c4r2.html">
  <FRAME src="c1r3.html">
  <FRAME src="c2r3.html">
  <FRAME src="c3r3.html">
  <FRAME src="c4r3.html">
</FRAMESET>

</HTML>
```

Frame sets can also be nested–for example:

```
<FRAMESET cols="25%,25%,25%,25%">
  <FRAMESET rows=""33%,33%,34%">
```

As you have probably figured out, if the cols attribute is not specified, each row will extend the entire width of the window. Likewise, if the rows attribute is not specified, each column will extend the entire length of the window. Views are divided from left-to-right for columns and top-to-bottom for rows.

The length and height values are given as percentages (using %), pixels, or a relative integer length (using an asterisk).

Consider the following example:

```
<FRAMESET cols="2*, 200,3*">
```

In this case, three columns are created. The second column is set to 200 pixels. The first and third frames divide the remaining space proportionally. The first frame will receive 40% and the third frame 60% of the remaining space. The default always adds to 100%.

When percentages are used, it is left to the browser to correctly adjust for under- and overspecifications of percentages.

The <FRAME> Tag

The <FRAMESET> element is used to define the layout of all views within a window. <FRAME> tags defining the contents and appearance of each individual view follow the <FRAMESET> tag.

The syntax for the <FRAME element> within the <FRAMESET> container is:

```
<FRAMESET frameset_attributes>
  <FRAME frame_attributes>
  <FRAME frame_attributes>
  <FRAME frame_attributes>
    .
    .
    .
</FRAMESET>
```

The attributes used with the <FRAME> element include frameborder, marginheight, marginwidth, name, noresize, scrolling, and src. Table 14–3 names and describes various <FRAME> attributes.

Here is another example. This one illustrates nesting:

```
<HTML>
<HEAD>
<TITLE>More Frames</TITLE>
</HEAD>

<FRAMESET cols="150,*,*">
  <FRAMESET rows="150,*">
    <FRAME src="image1.gif">
    <FRAME src="doc2.html">
  </FRAMESET>
  <FRAME src="doc3.html">
  <FRAME src="doc4.html">
</FRAMESET>

</HTML>
```

An image approximately 150 × 150 pixels is placed in the upper-left corner of the viewing area. This location represents the first frame. Two additional columns are specified, each to occupy one-half of the remaining horizontal viewing area. These will hold documents 3 and 4, respectively. A second row will be inserted under the first column and will occupy the remaining column length. This frame will hold the contents of document 2. Figure 14–2 shows the resulting screen.

Table 14-3: *HTML 4.0 <FRAME> attributes*

Attribute	Description
frameborder	A frame is drawn between adjacent frames. Use a value of 1 (default). A value of 0 specifies no frame.
longdesc	Provides a link to a long description of the frame. Useful for nonvisual user agents.
marginheight	Space between frame contents and top and bottom margins. Value must be > 1 pixel. Default value is determined by browser.
marginwidth	Space between frame contents and the left and right margins. Value must be > 1 pixel. Default value is determined by browser.
name	Assigns a name to the current frame.
noresize	When this attribute is present, the frame cannot be resized.
scrolling	Set to auto|yes|no. The default is auto and provides scrolling when necessary. A yes value always provides scrolling capabilities. A no value never provides scrolling capabilities.
src	Specifies the url location of the document to be contained by the frame.

Can you determine how this layout was accomplished by examining the screen and the previous listing?

The <NOFRAMES> Tag

The <NOFRAMES> tag is used to identify content that is to be viewed when frames are not displayed. The <NOFRAMES> element, also known as an *alternate context* tag, can be used in the <FRAMESET> container or in the <BODY> of a document used within a frameset.

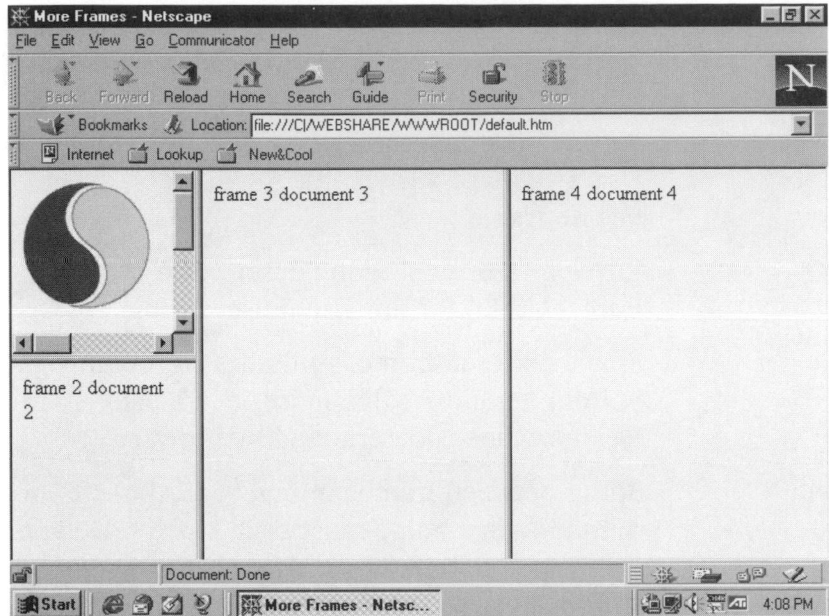

Figure 14–2: *A viewing area with multiple frames*

This document specifies a frameset with two identical rows, each occupying one-half of the viewing area each. Name this document master.html.

```
<HTML>
<HEAD>
<TITLE>A problem if frames aren't displayed</TITLE>
</HEAD>
<FRAMESET rows="50%,50%">
  <FRAME src="main,html">
  <FRAME src="document.html">
  </FRAMESET>
</HTML>
```

The first frame will incorporate a main.html document and the second will use document.html. If the browser is not displaying frames, the user will not see anything, since there is no <BODY> element in the previous listing. A better way to write this would be to restructure the master.html and main.html documents. Here is the new master.html:

```
<HTML>
<HEAD>
<TITLE>NOFRAMES to the rescue</TITLE>
</HEAD>
```

```
<FRAMESET rows="50%,50%">
  <FRAME src="main,html">
  <FRAME src="document.html">
  <NOFRAMES>
  <A href="main.html">
  </A>
  </NOFRAMES>
</FRAMESET>
</HTML>
```

Here is the new main.html:

```
<HTML>
<BODY>
<NOFRAMES>
  (place the document.html contents here)
</NOFRAMES>
  (remainder of the main.html document goes here)
</BODY>
</HTML>
```

In this situation the document.html contents are included at the top of the main.html document within a <NOFRAMES> container. The main.html and master.html are then linked when frames are not displayed.

The <IFRAME> Tag

The <IFRAME> tag is used for inserting frames within a block of text. This element allows the frame to be inserted, aligned, and so on. The syntax for <IFRAME> is similar to that of the <FRAME> element. The src attribute refers to the information to be inserted inline. Frames created with <IFRAME> cannot be resized, so this attribute is nonfunctional.

Consider this example, named Iframe.htm:

```
<HTML>
<HEAD>
<TITLE>An IFRAME Example</TITLE>
</HEAD>

<BODY>
<H1>An inline frame example!</H1>
<HR>
```

(continued)

```
<P>
Here is a regular HTML document that contains simple <BR>
text for you to view.  An inline frame will be inserted <BR>
under this text to illustrate how easy this is to do.
</P>

<IFRAME src="data.htm" width="250"
  height="150" scrolling="yes">
</IFRAME>

<P>
A small inline frame is ideal for providing instant detail <BR>
for text that the user encounters within the main document.
</P>

</BODY>
</HTML>
```

A normal HTML document is created. If frames are displayed, a paragraph of text will be displayed. Then an inline frame with additional text will be inserted. Finally, another paragraph of regular text will follow. Figure 14–3 shows the resulting screen for this example.

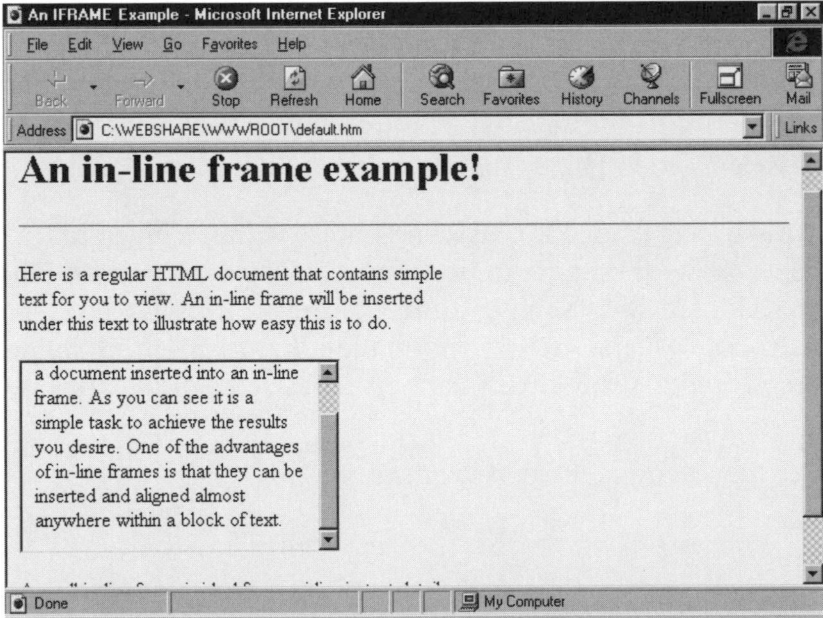

Figure 14–3: *Inserting an inline frame is simple under HTML 4.0*

Target Frame Information

If a name is assigned to a frame using the name attribute, developers can reference the frame as a target of links defined by other elements. The target attribute can be set for elements that create links (<A> and <LINK>), image maps (<AREA>), and forms (<FORM>).

Let's examine an example named Target.html.

```
<HTML>
<HEAD>
<TITLE>Illustrating the target attribute</TITLE>
</HEAD>

<FRAMESET rows="20%,30%,50%">
  <FRAME name="top" src="top.html">
  <FRAME name="middle" src="middle.html">
  <FRAME name="bottom" src="bottom.html">
</FRAMESET>

</HTML>
```

The <FRAMESET> element is used to create three frames. The first row occupies the top 20% of the viewing area, the second frame 30%, and the final frame 50%. The frames are named top, middle, and bottom, respectively. Their contents will be top.html, middle.html, and bottom.html, respectively.

The contents of the first document, named top.html, is shown next.

```
<HTML>
<BODY bgcolor="#00FFFF">

<P>
This is a portion of text that will remain fixed in
the first frame.<BR>
In the second frame you can experiment with the tar-
get attribute by<BR>
making a selection that "targets" the third frame.
</P>

</BODY>
</HTML>
```

This document will set the background color of the frame to light-blue, then print some text in the frame. The contents of this frame are fixed and will not change.

The second frame sets the background color to yellow, then identifies the bottom frame as the target. Depending on the selection, the admin.html, dept.html, or stud.html documents will replace the contents of the bottom.html. This document is named middle.html.

```
<HTML>
<BODY>
<BODY bgcolor="#FFFF00">

<A href="admin.html" target="bottom">Administrative
Structure</A>
<BR>
<A href="dept.html" target="bottom">Department
Structure</A>
<BR>
<A href="stud.html" target="bottom">Student
Structure</A>

</BODY>
</HTML>
```

The third frame uses an empty document named bottom.html.

```
<HTML>
<BODY>


</BODY>
</HTML>
```

As selections are made within the second frame, various documents will “target” the bottom frame and replace its contents.

If the Administrative Structure is selected, admin.html will replace the contents of the bottom.html frame. The following listing represents the contents of the admin.html file:

```
<HTML>
<BODY>

<P>
At this college we have:<BR>
  A President<BR>
  Vice Presidents<BR>
  Division Deans<BR>
</P>

</BODY>
</HTML>
```

If the Department Structure is selected, dept.html will replace the contents of the bottom.html frame. The following listing represents the contents of the dept.html file:

```
<HTML>
<BODY>

<P>
Within a department we have:<BR>
   A department chair<BR>
   Faculty<BR>
   Full and part-time adjunct faculty<BR>
   Tech. Assistants
</P>

</BODY>
</HTML>
```

Finally, if the Student Structure is selected, stud.html will replace the contents of the bottom.html frame. The following listing represents the contents of the stud.html file:

```
<HTML>
<BODY>

<P>
Among the student body, we have:<BR>
   Full time students<BR>
   Part time students
</P>

</BODY>
</HTML>
```

Figure 14–4 shows the initial viewing area.

Figure 14–5 shows the viewing area and the updated contents of the third frame when the Department Structure is selected in the middle frame.

The contents of the bottom frame are changed, because they are targeted by items in the second frame.

Four special target names can be used in place of a specific target: _blank, _parent, _self, and _top. Table 14–5 names and describes these special target names.

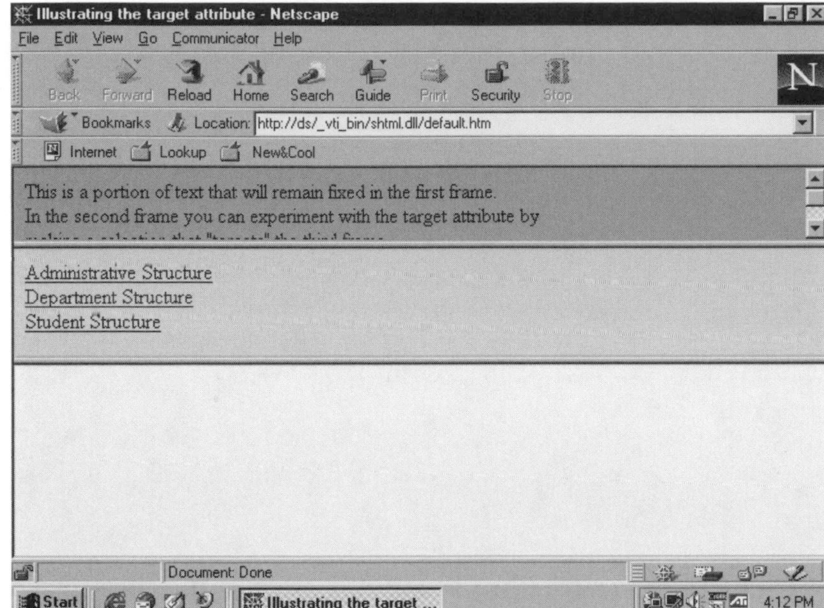

Figure 14–4: *The initial viewing area of the target example*

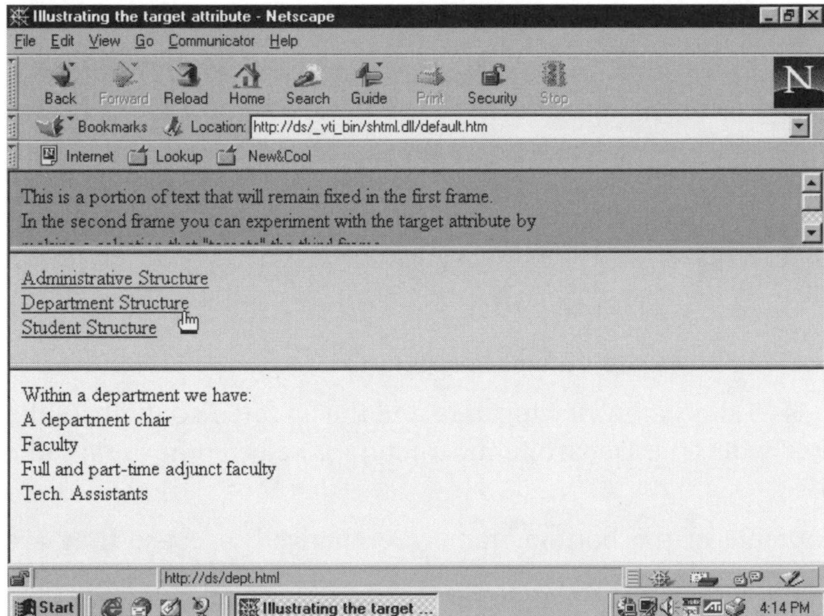

Figure 14–5: *The new contents of the bottom frame*

Table 14–4: *Special target names*

Target Name	Description
_blank	Displays contents in a new, empty window that replaces the framed windows. This window has no name. Selecting the browser's "Back" button returns the user to the frame windows.
_parent	Displays contents in the immediate <FRAMESET> parent of the document. If the frame has no parent, then this behaves like _self.
_self	Displays contents in the same frame where the link is located. _self is typically the default.
_top	Displays contents in a new full-sized viewing area.

In the previous example, if the contents of this portion of the middle.html document were changed from:

```
<A href="dept.html" target="bottom">Department
Structure</A>
<BR>
```

to:

```
<A href="dept.html" target="_self">Department
Structure</A>
<BR>
```

the results of this change would be as shown in Figure 14–6.

As you can see, the contents of the middle frame are replaced, since _self identifies the target as the frame containing the link.

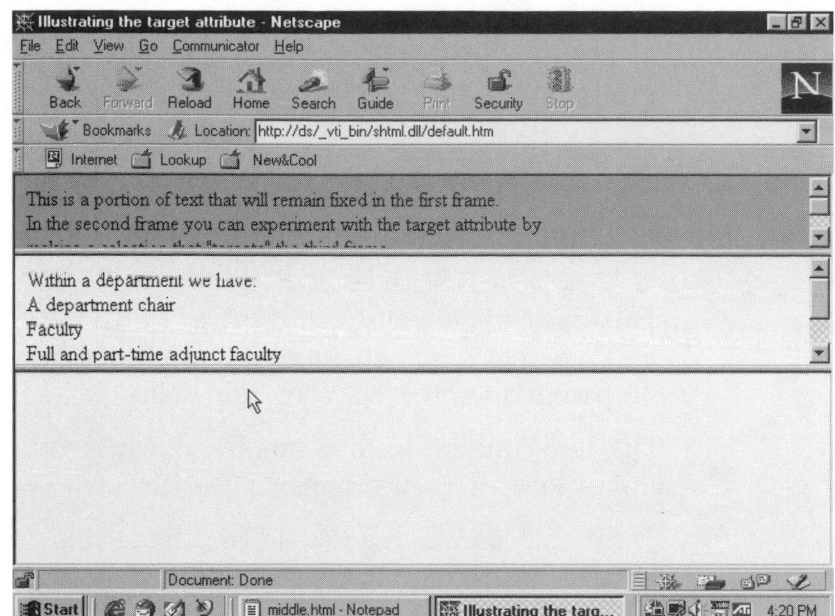

Figure 14–6: *Changing the target to _self produces interesting results*

Just Before Leaving

We have covered a detailed topic with as many examples as we thought were practical. However, you've got to try working with frames to really get a feel for their use.

Why not create a document with three frames. In one frame, place an image or favorite picture. In the second, use a list that is linked to the third frame. If an item in the second list is selected, change the contents in the third frame to reflect the choice.

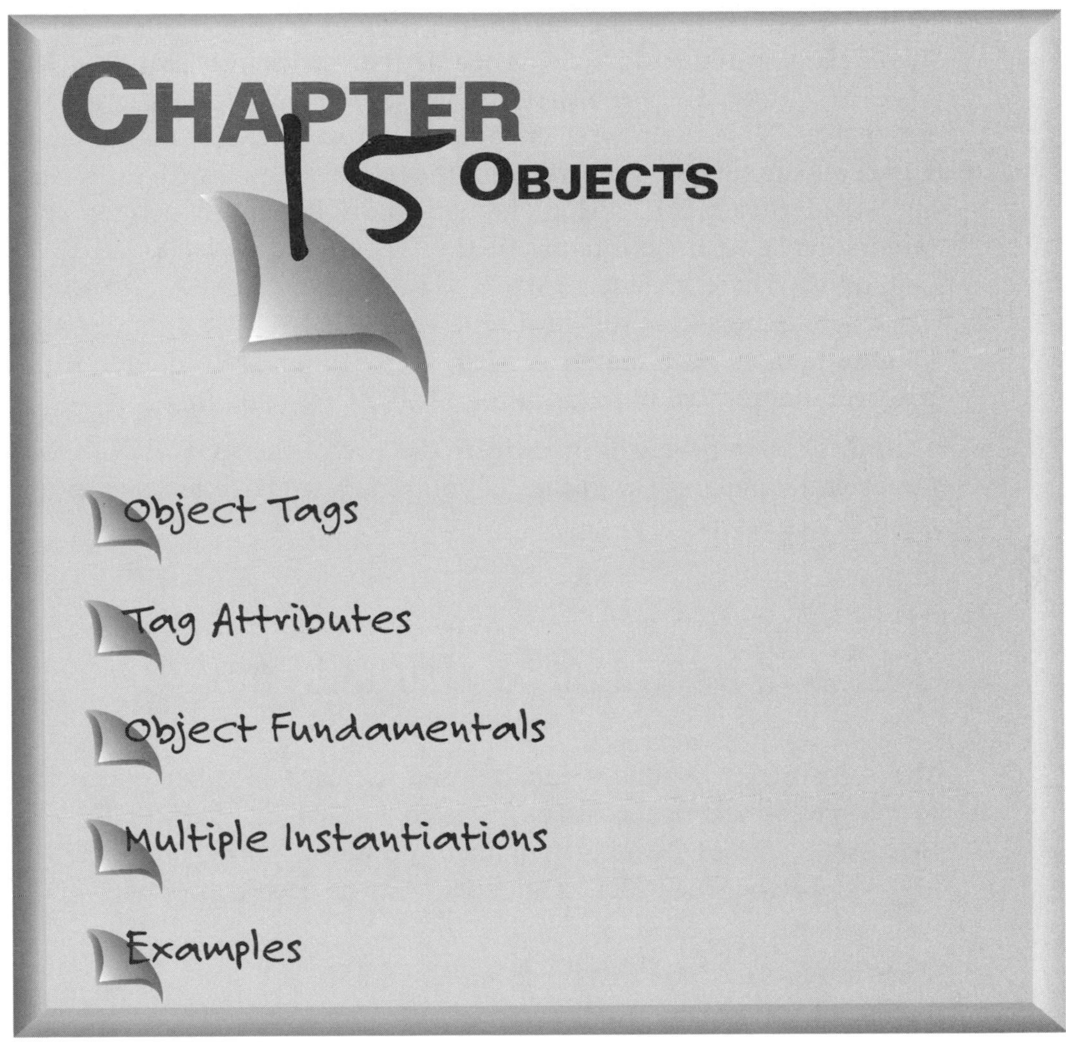

Introduction

One of HTML's weaknesses is that the number of tags and containers has been fixed from one version to another. Simply put, that means that developers desiring extended HTML capabilities have had no means of extending HTML outside of proprietary elements. Proprietary elements usually mean chaos for developers trying to implement applications for multiple browsers, even when the choice is limited to just the Microsoft Internet Explorer or the Netscape Navigator.

The World Wide Web Consortium (W3C) has solved this problem by officially introducing the <OBJECT> container in HTML 4.0. The <OBJECT> container is a first, and good, attempt at making HTML extensible. When a browser encounters an <OBJECT> container in an HTML document, it knows that it is about to deal with an image, applet, another HTML document, and so on. Previously defined containers can also handle many of the types handled by <OBJECT> containers. These include <IMG>, <IFRAME>, <MAP>, and so on. These containers can still be used. The <OBJECT> container also handles applets. As a matter-of-fact, the <APPLET> container, itself, has been deprecated in favor of the <OBJECT> container.

In this chapter we will investigate the use of the <OBJECT> container and compare it with that of containers we have learned to use in earlier chapters.

This Chapter's HTML Tags

The <OBJECT> container can be used in place of other containers which have already been discussed, such as <IMG>, <APPLET>, and <IFRAME>. All of the other containers are still supported under HTML 4.0, save for the <APPLET> container that has been deprecated.

Table 15–1: *Tags related to <OBJECT>*

Tag	Description
<OBJECT>	Subsumes and expands the tasks available with other containers. Offers an all-purpose solution to object inclusion in documents. Allows extendability.
<PARAM>	Used in conjunction with the <OBJECT> container for providing initial values for objects at run-time.

In the sections of this chapter that follow we'll investigate the versatility of the <OBJECT> container and compare its use to that that of containers you have already learned about.

Object Fundamentals

In this section we'll investigate the syntax and parameters associated with the <OBJECT> and <PARAM> elements and look into how they relate to other familiar containers.

The <OBJECT> Tag

The <OBJECT> tag is presented by HTML 4.0 as a generic solution to object inclusion for new and old media types. The use of the <OBJECT> element usually involves specifying source code, initial values, and any necessary run-time data. Images, for example, may include hyperlinks.

The <OBJECT> element uses a large number of attributes, which are listed and described in Table 15-2.

Table 15-2: *Attributes used by the <OBJECT> element*

Attribute	Description
align	Specifics the objects location in the viewing area. Use bottom to align the bottom of the element with the current baseline. Bottom is the default. Use middle to vertically align the center of the object with the current baseline. Use top to vertically align the object with the top of the current text line. Use left or right to align the image with the current left or right margin, respectively.
archive	Specifies a space separated archive list.
border	Specifies the border width placed around the object. The browser sets the default.
class	Specifies a documcntwide identifier.
classid	Specifies the location of an object's implementation with a URL.

Table 15–2: *Attributes used by the <OBJECT> element (continued)*

Attribute	Description
codebase	Specifies the base path used to resolve a relative URL given by classid. The default is the base URL of the current document.
codetype	Specifies the Internet Media Type of data used by the object specified by classid. The default value is that specified by the type attribute. The use of codetype avoids loading information for unnecessary media types.
data	Specifies a URL for the location of the object's data.
declare	A Boolean attribute used to make the <OBJECT> definition a declaration only. This requires that the object be instantiated by another <OBJECT> definition that refers to this declaration.
dir	Specifies text direction.
export	Specifies export shapes to parent.
height	Specifies the height of an object in pixels.
hspace	Specifies the amount of space to the left and right of an object. No default is specified.
id	Specifies the object for the viewing area. It can also be used to locate other objects or hyperlinks.
lang	Specifies language information.
name	This attribute is used with forms. The name identifies objects in a <FORM> container to be submitted.
onclick	Specifies an action relating to a mouse click (push/release).
ondblclick	Specifies an action relating to a mouse double click (push/release).
onkeydown	Specifies an action relating to a key-down event.

onkeypress	Specifies an action relating to a key-press (down/release) event.
onkeyup	Specifies an action relating to a key-release event.
onmousedown	Specifies an action relating to a mouse-button push.
onmousemove	Specifies an action relating to the movement of the mouse.
onmouseout	Specifies an action related to moving the mouse out of the area.
onmouseover	Specifies an action related to moving the mouse into the area.
onmouseup	Specifies an action relating to a mouse-button release.
shapes	Used with client-side image maps. For example:

```
<OBJECT data="my.jpg" shapes>
 <A href=myshape.html shape=rect coords="0,0,150,150">
</OBJECT>
```

standby	Specifies a message that a browser may display while loading the object's implementation and data. For example:

```
standby="loading file" or standby="please wait!"
```

style	Specifies inline style information.
tabindex	Specifies keyboard tabbing navigation.
title	Specifies element titles.
type	Specifies the Internet Media Type of data used by the object specified by data. The use of type avoids loading information for unnecessary media types. If no value is specified, the browser must attempt to identify the media type. For example:

```
type="image/gif" or type="video/avi"
```

Table 15–2: *Attributes used by the <OBJECT> element (continued)*

Attribute	Description
usemap	Specifies a URL used with a client-side image map.
vspace	Specifies the amount of space above and below an object. No default is specified.
width	Specifies the width of an object in pixels.

Most common data types are rendered by built-in mechanisms provided by the browser. These data types may include, but are not limited to; avi, gif, HTML, jpeg, mov, mpeg, plain, and wav. When the data type isn't supported, the browser can seek an external application for support. The <OBJECT> element allows an object to be rendered internally, externally, or by a program identified by the developer.

Three pieces of information are needed, either singly or together:

- The object's implementation. In other words, what is the location of the object's code?
- The data to be rendered. For example, if the object renders color data, the location of that data must be indicated.
- Initial values, where applicable, for the object's use at run-time. This is typically done via the <PARAM> element.

Browsers interpret an <OBJECT> element by rendering either the object or the object's contents.

Consider this example, which attempts to load a Java applet:

```
<OBJECT codetype="application/octet-stream"
  classid="java:program.start" width="400"
  height="300">
Click mouse here to view images in a Java applet
</OBJECT>
```

Here a Java applet is rendered in the viewing area with a width of 400 pixels and a height of 300 pixels.

Here is the syntax for bringing an ActiveX object to the vicwing area:

```
<OBJECT classid="clsid:884C8FEF-iEF8-11CE-A4DC-080072E12601"
  data="http://www.hereitis.com/ole/myobject.stm">

  This object is not currently supported
</OBJECT>
```

<OBJECT> containers can also be nested. For example, the following example first attempts to load a Perl application. If this cannot be rendered, a JPEG image, on the local hard disk, will be rendered.

```
<OBJECT title="Great shapes"
  classid="http://www.mysite.pic/myprogram.pl">
    <!— Otherwise, try this image —>
  OBJECT data="cllipse.jpg">

    <!— Otherwise, display this text —>

    An ellipse shape.
  </OBJECT>
</OBJECT>
```

In this example, a browser will attempt to render the first <OBJECT> element possible. The first attempt will be to execute *myprogram.pl*. If this cannot be done, an attempt will then be made to display an image of an ellipse (ellipse.jpg).

The first <OBJECT> element specifies a program that has no data or initial values. The second <OBJECT> element will rely on the browser to handle the image type, since no location is defined. Alternative text is provided for situations where both <OBJECTS> fail to be rendered.

Here is a complete example that will attempt to load a JPEG satellite weather image from the specified location:

```
<HTML>
<HEAD>
<TITLE>Viewing JPEG Weather Images</TITLE>
</HEAD>
<BODY>

<OBJECT
  data="ftp://explorer.arc.nasa.gov/pub/Weather/
              GOES-8/jpg/vis/4km/9711211644.jpg"
  type="image/jpeg" align=center
```

(continued)

```
   standby="Weather image loading"
   height="400" width="400" title="Weather">

   <!— If not, try this one —>
   <OBJECT data="c:\temp\9711211644.jpg"
     type="image/jpeg" align=center
     standby="Alternate weather image loading"
     height="400" width="400" title="earth">
   </OBJECT>
</OBJECT>

</BODY>
</HTML>
```

If thc first object cannot be rendered, an attempt will be made to load the same JPEG image previously stored on the local hard disk. Figure 15–1 shows the viewing area for one attempt.

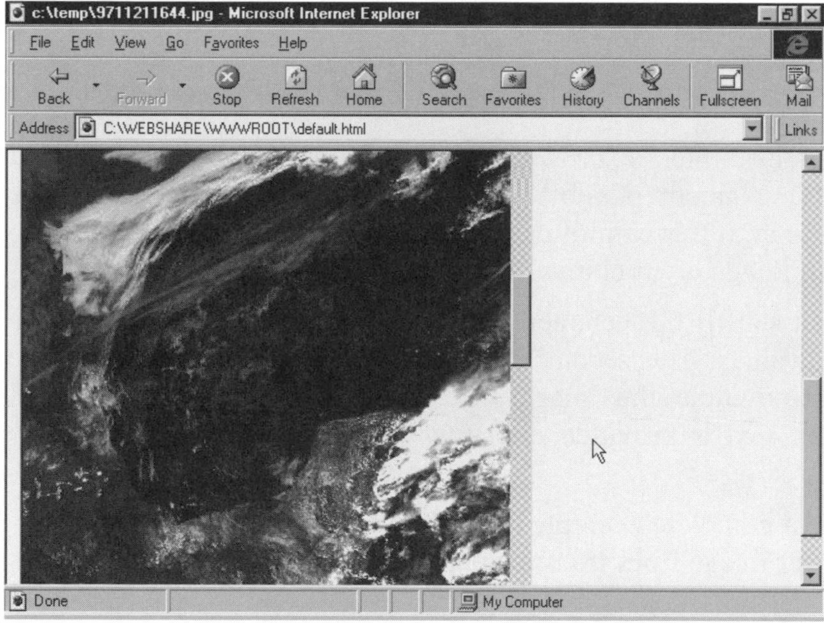

Figure 15–1: *The original object is rendered, so the JPEG image from the hard disk is not accessed*

It is possible for data to be supplied inline or from an external source. Inline sources are typically faster but limited in the amount of data. External sources are slower but offer vast resources of data.

Multiple Instantiations

When a document can contain more than one instance of the same object (multiple instantiations), it is possible to separate the object declaration from its instantiations. This has the advantage of a single retrieval of a object, even when it is reused several times.

When the declare attribute is set in the <OBJECT> element, the object will not be executed when read by the browser. The use of the declare attribute requires that the id attribute also be set to a unique value. All future instantiations will refer to this id attribute value.

The following example borrows part of the previous weather-satellite example to show the syntax for multiple instantiation.

```
<HTML>
<HEAD>
<TITLE>Multiple Instantiations</TITLE>
</HEAD>
<BODY>

<OBJECT declare
  id="jpeg-image"
  data="c:\temp\9711211644.jpg"
  type="image/jpeg"
  standby="Please Wait - Loading JPEG Image"
  height="400" width="400" title="Earth">
  An Earth picture from a weather satellite.
</OBJECT>

A weather disturbance in the <A href="#jpeg-image">
Gulf of Mexico.</A>

</BODY>
</HTML>
```

Figure 15–2 shows the image that is rendered when the HTML document is loaded.

Multiple mouse clicks on the “Gulf of Mexico” text produce multiple instantiations. Notice the address shown in Figure 15–3 as compared to that in Figure 15–2.

If a browser doesn’t support the declare attribute, it must render the contents of the <OBJECT> declaration.

Figure 15–2: *The original image object is loaded*

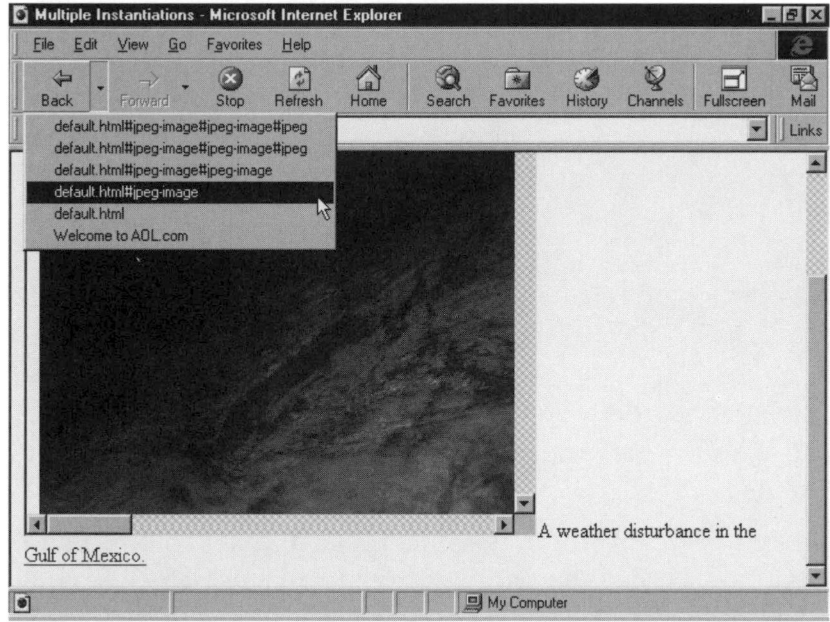

Figure 15–3: *An instantiation of the original object*

The <PARAM> Tag

The <PARAM> tag is used in conjunction with the <OBJECT> tag to specify initial values to be used by an object at run time. Any number of <PARAM> tags may follow an <OBJECT> tag. Names and values are passed to the object on its standard input. The <PARAM> tag uses the attributes listed and described in Table 15-3.

Table 15-3: *Attributes used by the <PARAM> element*

Attribute	Description	
id	Specifies a documentwide id.	
name	Specifies the run-time parameter name. The object must know the parameter name.	
type	Specifies the Internet Media Type of data used by the object specified by value attribute when valuetype is set to "ref." This specifies the type of values found at the URL.	
value	Specifies the value of a run-time parameter specified by name. The object determines the meaning of the value.	
valuetype	Specifies the value type as data, ref, or object.	
	data:	passes the specified value to the object's implementation as a string. Embedded character and/or numeric character entities are resolved. This is the default.
	ref:	passes the URL specified by value where run-time values are stored.
	object:	passes a fragment URL specified by value that identifies an object declaration in the same document. Use the id attribute.

Here is a portion of code to illustrate the use of the <PARAM> element. Here the <PARAM> tags specify initial values and the height and width of the rendered object.

```
      .
      .
      .

<OBJECT
  classid="http://www.mylocation.com/jpgviewer"
  standby="Loading a mountain">
<PARAM name="init_values"
   value="./Shel09_1.jpg"
   valuetype="ref">
<PARAM name="height" value="200">
<PARAM name="width" value="200">
</OBJECT>
      .
      .
      .
```

The standby attribute is set here to warn the user of a possible delay in seeing the render object.

<IMG> or <OBJECT> Tag

In Chapter 6 you learned how to use the <IMG> tag to render a graphics image in the viewing area. The syntax is fairly simple–for example:

```
<IMG src="ftp://explorer.arc.nasa.gov/pub/Weather/
          GOES-8/jpg/vis/4km/9711211644.jpg">
```

An equivalent example using the <OBJECT> element takes on this form:

```
<OBJECT
data="ftp://explorer.arc.nasa.gov/pub/Weather/
      GOES-8/jpg/vis/4km/9711211644.jpg"
      type="image/jpg">
```

Why use <OBJECT>, when rendering images with <IMG> requires less code? The answer is that all file types, even if they are not HTML files types, can be treated as objects.

The use of <OBJECT> in place of <IMG> also eliminates the dialog that occurs when you attempt to link to a file type not known by the system. The system does not have to deal with the returned MIME type. The burden rests with the browser and associated helper applications.

<IFRAME> or <OBJECT> Tag

In Chapter 14 we investigated the use of the <IFRAME> tag. HTML 4.0 actually allows you to accomplish the same feats with the <OBJECT> element. Here is the <IFRAME> example from the previous chapter.

```
<HTML>
<HEAD>
<TITLE>An IFRAME Example</TITLE>
</HEAD>

<BODY>
<H1>An in-line frame example!</H1>
<HR>

<P>
Here is a regular HTML document that contains simple <BR>
text for you to view. An in-line frame will be inserted <BR>
under this text to illustrate how easy this is to do.
</P>

<IFRAME src="data.html" width="250"
  height="150" scrolling="yes">
</IFRAME>

<P>
 A small in-line frame is ideal for providing instant <BR>
detail for text that the user encounters within the main <BR>
document.

</P>

</BODY>
</HTML>
```

Recall that the <IFRAME> element allows a document to be inserted into another document. The inserted document, named data.html, will remain independent of the initial document.

With just a little work this example can be modified to use the <OBJECT> tag. The following listing shows the necessary changes.

```
<HTML>
<HEAD>
<TITLE>An OBJECT tag replaces the IFRAME tag</TITLE>
</HEAD>

<BODY>
<H1>An in-line frame example!</H1>
<HR>

<P>
Here is a regular HTML document that contains simple <BR>
text for you to view.  An in-line frame will be inserted <BR>
under this text to illustrate how easy this is to do.
</P>

<OBJECT data="c:\data.html" width="250"
  height="150" scrolling="yes">
</OBJECT>

<P>
A small in-line frame is ideal for providing instant <BR>
detail for text that the user encounters within the main <BR>
document.
</P>

</BODY>
</HTML>
```

Figure 15-4 shows the object as rendered to the viewing area.

Just as in the case of using the <IFRAME> element, the embedded document is rendered within another document but remains independent of that document.

Image Maps Revisited

In Chapter 10 you learned how to build both client-side and server-side image maps. The image was rendered with the <IMG> element and the map was identified with the <MAP> element. Then each area of the map was set using the <AREA> element.

It is possible to specify a client-side image map using the <OBJECT> container. Server-side maps are specified in the conventional manner presented in Chapter 10.

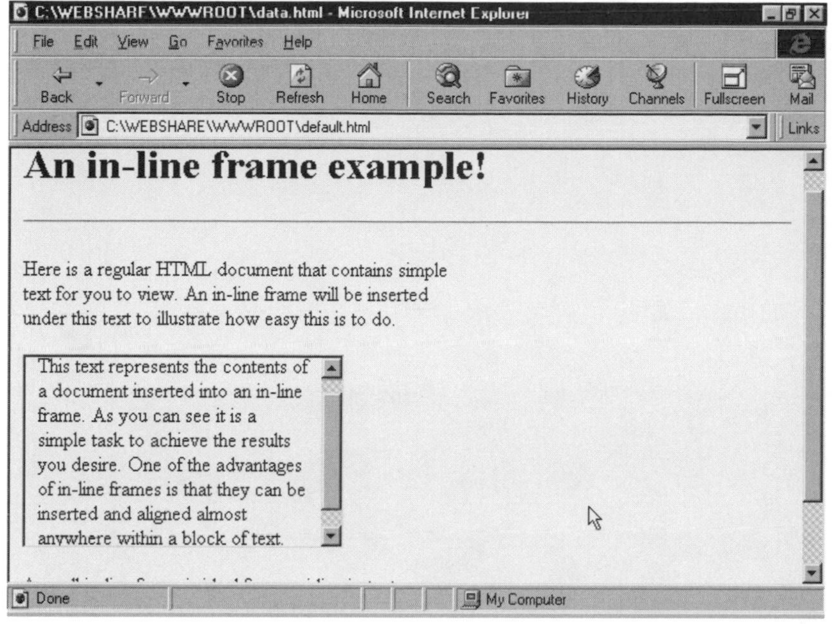

Figure 15–4: *Use <IFRAME> or <OBJECT> to embed a document in another*

To use a client-side map specified with the <OBJECT> container, the shapes attribute must be set and the image map defined within the container.

Here is a short example, from Chapter 10, that builds a client-side image map in the conventional manner.

```
<HTML>

<HEAD>
<TITLE>Client-side imagemap</TITLE>
</HEAD>
<BODY>

<IMG src="ImgMap1.jpg" usemap="#firstmap">
<P>You want to go where today?<BR>
<MAP name="firstmap">
<AREA href="http://www.microsoft.com/office/"
  shape="rect"
  coords="0, 0, 210, 137">
<AREA href="http://www.microsoft.com/word/"
  shape="rect"
  coords="211, 0, 420, 137">
<AREA href="http://www.microsoft.com/excel/"
  shape="rect"
```

(continued)

```
  coords="0, 138, 210, 275">
<AREA href="http://www.microsoft.com/access/"
  shape="rect"
  coords="211, 138, 420, 275">
</MAP>

</BODY>
</HTML>
```

Figure 15–5 shows how this client-side map is rendered.

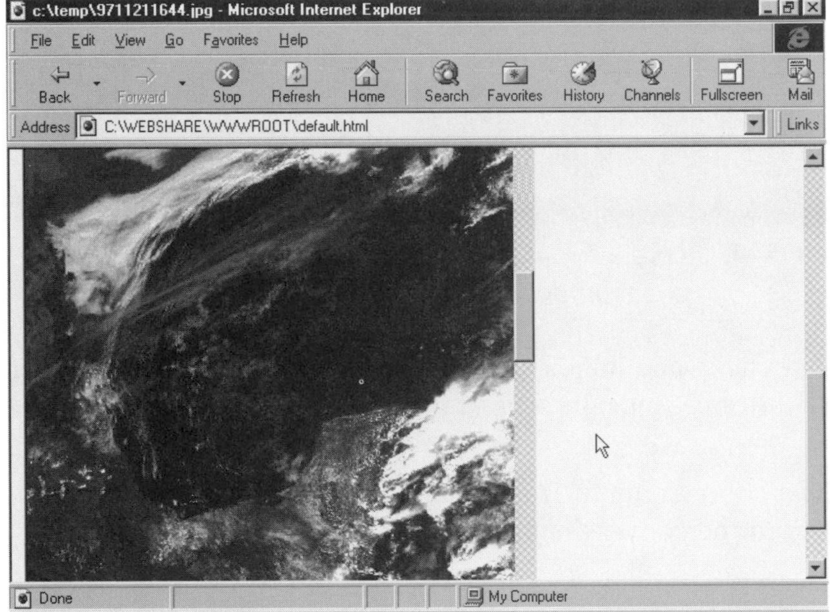

Figure 15–5: *A client-side image map using <IMG>, <MAP>, and <AREA> elements*

The previous example can be modified to use the <OBJECT> tag. The following listing shows the necessary changes.

```
<HTML>

<HEAD>
<TITLE>Client-side imagemap with OBJECT</TITLE>
</HEAD>

<BODY>
<OBJECT data="ImgMap1.jpg" firstmap>
<P>You want to go where today?<BR>
<A href="http://www.microsoft.com/office/"
```

```
shape="rect"
  coords="0, 0, 210, 137"></A>
<A href="http://www.microsoft.com/word/" shape="rect"
  coords="211, 0, 420, 137"></A>
<A href="http://www.microsoft.com/excel/"
shape="rect"
  coords="0, 138, 210, 275"></A>
<A href="http://www.microsoft.com/access/"
shape="rect"
  coords="211, 138, 420, 275"></A>
</OBJECT>

</BODY>
</HTML>
```

The shapes attribute notifies the <OBJECT> element that an image map is to be defined. The image map is defined within the <OBJECT> container, with each region of the map being specified using the <A> container. Each <A> element then uses the shape attribute to specify the unique region.

As of this writing, neither Internet Explorer (version 4.71) nor Netscape Communicator (version 4.04) fully supports client-side maps included in this manner. We're sure this is a temporary problem that will be addressed with the release of HTML 4.0 by the W3C standards committee.

Before You Leave

Perhaps you are thinking, "Gee, I can already do most of this stuff with containers that are better supported than <OBJECT> and <PARAM>." We agree with you! However, the future rests with the new <OBJECT> container, for all of the reasons mentioned in this chapter. In the future, you will see containers such as <IMG>, <MAP>, and so on used less, in less in favor of the <OBJECT> container. Now is the time to get started using the <OBJECT> container as you develop new documents.

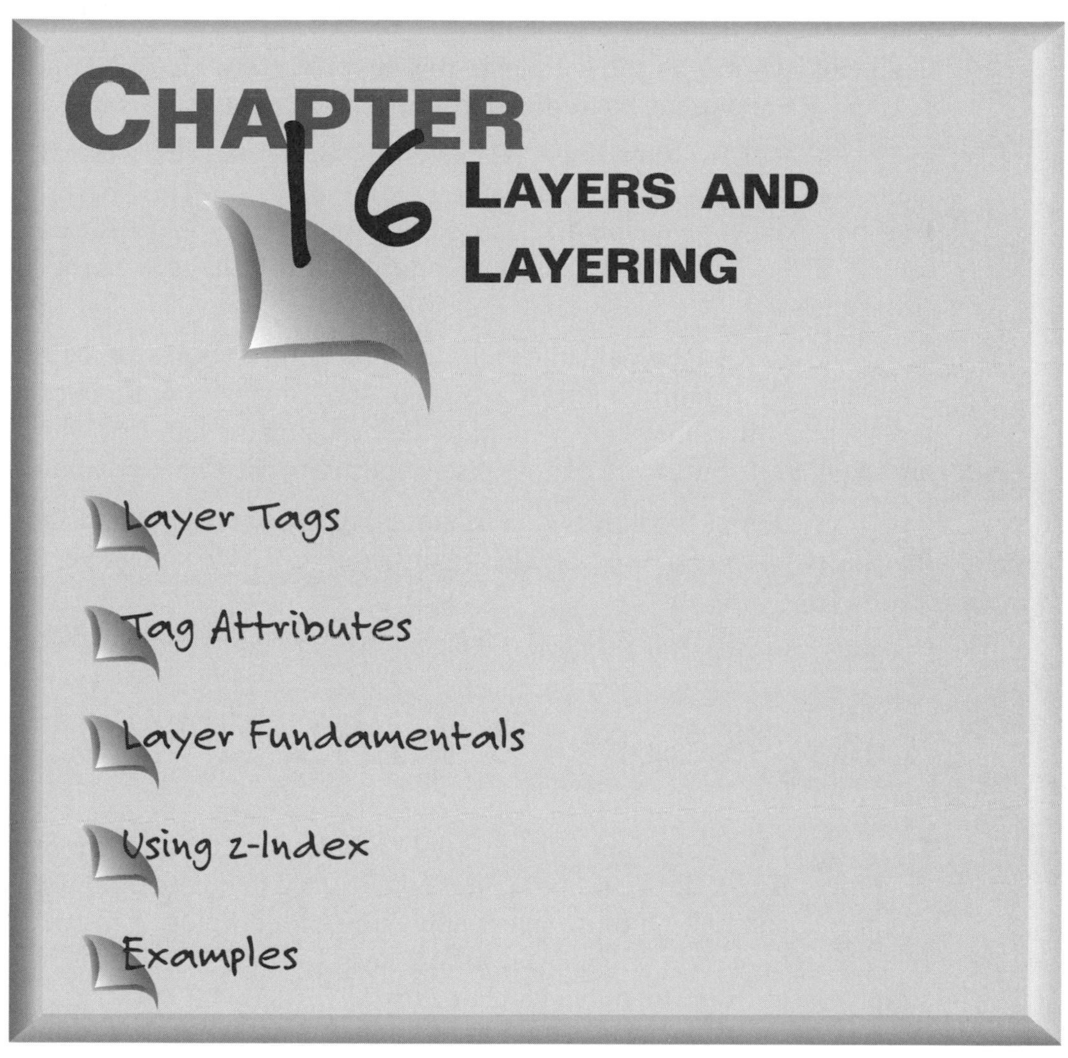

Introduction

Netscape first introduced the formal use of the <LAYER> and <ILAYER> containers. Layers have not been included by the W3C group at the time of this writing and thus are not a part of the proposed HTML 4.0 standard. However, the concept and the capabilities of layers demand they be introduced in almost any HTML book.

Let's start by separating the concept of layering from the <LAYER> container. Layering just means placing one thing over another. An Oreo cookie is layered: cookie bottom, white stuff in the middle, and a cookie top. The concept is simple enough. All browsers permit some degree of layering, as you will see in this chapter. Here <LAYER> and </LAYER> represent the top and bottom of the cookie.

The <LAYER> container is currently supported by Netscape Communicator, version 4.0 and later. As of this writing, The Microsoft Internet Explorer, version 4.72, does not support the <LAYER> container. If the W3C group doesn't endorse it, it will be exclusively Netscape's tag.

The <LAYER> container can be use to control portions of the viewing area. If multiple layers are used, some may show their contents while others may choose to hide theirs. Using the left, top, width, and height attributes you can precisely specify each layer's position.

In this chapter we'll first look at some layering concepts and then investigate the use of the <LAYER> container and a close relative, the <ILAYER> container.

This Chapter's HTML Tags

The <LAYER> container can be used to create outflow layers in a document. The <ILAYER> container can be used to create inflow layers in a document. Outflow layers allow you, the developer, to specify the exact location of the layer. Inflow layers, on the other hand, are simply offset from the previous tag or text.

Table 16–1: *The <LAYER> and <ILAYER> tags*

Tag	Description
<LAYER>	Allows an out-flow layer to be added to a document and precisely positioned.
<ILAYER>	Allows an in-flow layer to be added to a document. Its placement follows a previous tag or text.

In the sections of this chapter that follow we'll investigate the versatility of the <OBJECT> container and compare its use to containers you have already learned about.

Layer Fundamentals

In the upcoming sections we'll investigate the syntax and parameters associated with layering and the <LAYER> and <ILAYER> containers. You'll see that you are already familiar with many "layering" concepts.

Layering without the <LAYER> Tag

Text and images can be layered in a very simple fashion. In the first example, we'll use the <DIV> container to place two portions of text in the viewing area. One portion of text is shown in green and the other in blue.

Here is the code for this example, named Layer1.html.

```
<HTML>
<HEAD>
<TITLE>zIndex with text</TITLE>
<STYLE type="text/css">
  H2 {border: 4pt double; text-align: center;
       font: 60pt arial}
</STYLE>
</HEAD>
<BODY>
<H1><CENTER>Text zIndex Demo</CENTER></H1>

<DIV id="text1" style="position: absolute; top: 120px;
  left: 60px; color: red; z-index: 2">
<H2>The Text1 box</H2>
</DIV>
<DIV id="text2" style="position: absolute; top: 160px;
  left: 100px; color: blue; z-index: 1">
<H2>The Text2 box</H2>
</DIV>

</BODY>
</HTML>
```

As you study this example, notice that styling concepts from Chapter 12 have been used to set the <H2> border style, text alignment, and font size.

The <DIV> tag allows the document to be divided into a number of divisions, with each division containing, for example, its own text.

The style attribute sets the absolute position for the *top* and *left* of the text as well as for the font color and size.

In this example the text was made to overlap to illustrate the concept of layering. As a matter-of-fact, by using the z-index attribute, you can decide which layer appears on top. As you face the viewing area, the *y* axis of the screen is represented by the vertical coordinate of the viewing area, the *x* axis of the screen by the horizontal coordinate. The *z* axis is an imaginary line starting at the viewing area and moving toward your eyes. Positions on the *z* axis with low values appear closer to the screen. Positions on the *z* axis with high values appear closer to your eyes. Thus, in the previous example, the red text is closer to the screen than the blue text. When you view the figure, the blue text will overlap the red text. In other words, the red text layer is on top of the blue text layer. You can experiment and change the z-order around and place the red text on top of the blue text simply by changing the z-index value.

While the use of z-indexing adds the concept of 3D to the viewing area, it does not correct for perspective. So regardless of the z-order numbers, the text or image will always be drawn to the same size. If you want to give a proper perspective to the shape of text, you will have to adjust the size of the text or image yourself.

Figure 16–1 shows the viewing area for this example.

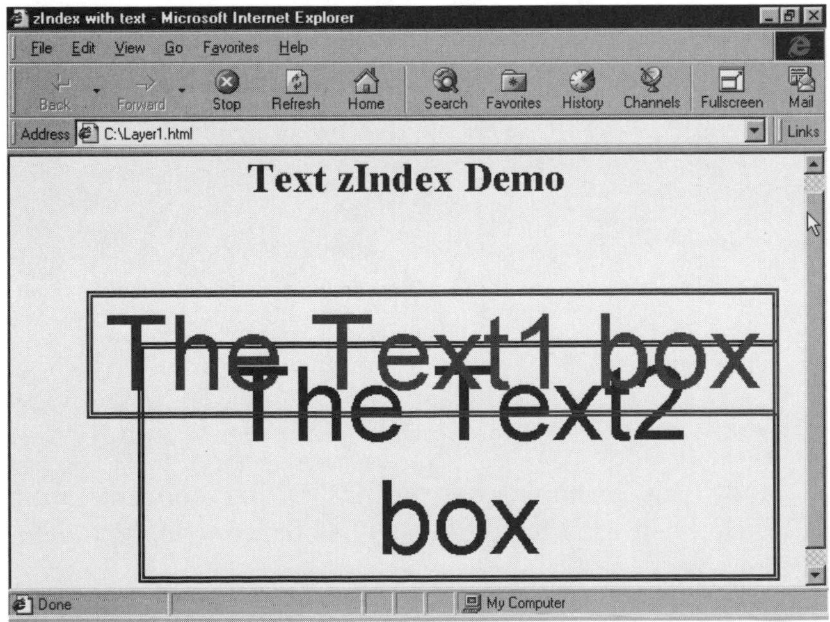

Figure 16–1: *Layering is achieved with the <DIV> container and z-indexing*

Unfortunately, the lack of color in book illustrations makes it difficult to see which layer is actually on the top. You'll just have to take our word for it–or better yet, try the example yourself.

In the second example, we'll use the <IMG> container to place three images in the viewing area. The images in this example are simply rectangles filled with specific colors. However, you can chose to use artwork or photographs if you desire.

Here is the code for this example, named Layer2.html.

```
<HTML>
<HEAD>
<TITLE>zIndex with shapes</TITLE>
</HEAD>
<BODY>
<H1><CENTER>Image zIndex Demo</CENTER></H1>

<IMG src="ybox.jpg" id=yellowshape
  style="container: positioned;
  position: absolute; top: 50;
  left: 50; height:100; width:200;
  z-index: 2">
<IMG src="bbox.jpg" id=blueshape
  style="container: positioned;
  position: absolute; top: 80;
  left: 80; height:100; width:200;
  z-index: 1">
<IMG src="rbox.jpg" id=redshape
  style="container: positioned;
  position: absolute; top: 110;
  left: 110; height:100; width:200;
  z-index: 3">

</BODY>
</HTML>
```

The <IMG> tag allows three images to be placed in the viewing area. The images were created and saved in the JPEG files format with the Microsoft Image Composer.

As you examine the code, you will see that the style attribute is used to set the absolute position of the image by specifying the *top*, *left*, *height*, and *width* values. You'll also notice that the z-index value has been set for each shape.

Based on the knowledge of z-ordering from the previous example, can you predict which shape will be in the top, middle, and bottom positions? Well, for this example, the red shape will be on top, closest to your eye, and the blue shape will be on the bottom, nearest the screen. Remember that higher z-orders move the shape closer to your eye while lower z-orders move the shape closer to the screen.

Figure 16–2 shows the screen's viewing area for this example.

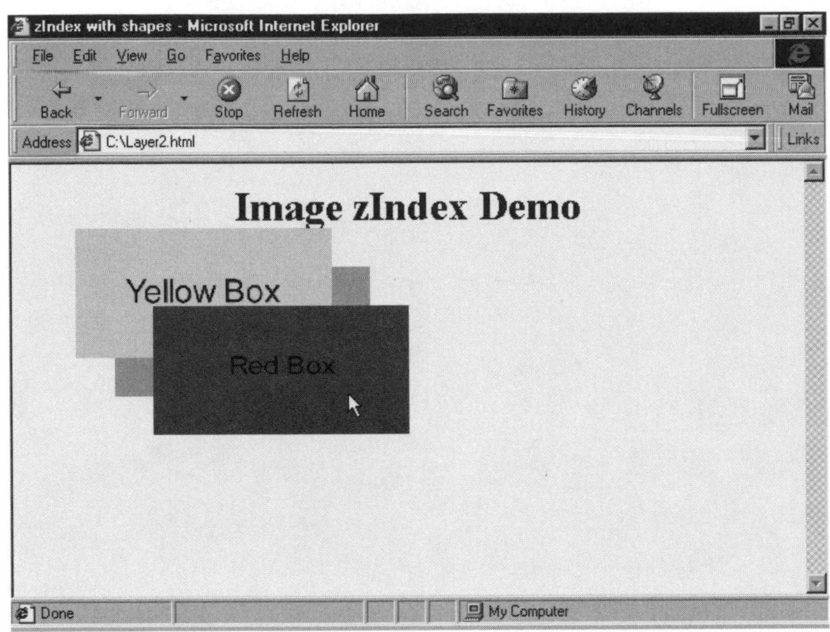

Figure 16–2: *Layering is achieved with the <IMG> tag and z-ordering*

When we tried this example, we found that the Microsoft Internet Explorer rendered the document's contents correctly, but Netscape Navigator did not.

Both of the previous examples illustrate that it is possible to work with layers within a normal document, using familiar tags. In the remainder of this chapter we'll investigate how the <LAYER> and <ILAYER> containers provide a new dimension to WEB page design.

The <LAYER> and <ILAYER> Tags

The <LAYER> and <ILAYER> tags allow a number of attributes to be set for each layer created.

Table 16-2 lists the attributes, properties, and a short description for each. These values are identical for both <LAYER> and <ILAYER> elements except where noted.

Table 16–2: *Attributes used by the <LAYER> and <ILAYER> elements*

Attribute	Properties	Description
above	Use name of any layer.	Specifies the present layer is above the given layer name.
background	Use any desired URL.	Specifies a background image to be displayed.
below	Use name of any layer.	Specifies the present layer is below the given layer name.
bgcolor	Use the hexadecimal format #RRGGBB	Specifies the background color for the layer.
clip	Use: clip.left, clip.right, clip.top, clip.bottom, clip.height, and clip.width	Specifies a clip rectangle with left, right, top, and bottom values. Values in pixels are the default. Information within the clip rectangle in a given layer is visible in the viewing area.
left	Specify an integer value representing the distance.	For <LAYER> this value specifies the layer's left-edge measured from the left-edge of the viewing area. Units measured in pixels are the default. For <ILAYER> this value specifies the left offset from the last tag or text.
name	Use any valid string.	Specifies a name that is referenced by a script language such as JavaScript or VBScript.
parentLayer	Use any valid string.	Specifies the layer in which the named layer is contained.

Table 16–2: *Attributes used by the <LAYER> and <ILAYER> elements (continued)*

Attribute	Properties	Description
siblingAbove	Use any valid string.	Specifies the current layer is above the given layer.
siblingBelow	Use any valid string.	Specifies the current layer is below the given layer.
src	SRC="URL"	SRC is a URL that the layer is pointing to. The contents of the HTML file will be the layer.
top	Specify an integer value representing the distance.	For <LAYER> this value specifies the layer's top-edge measured from the top-edge of the viewing area. Unit defaults are pixels. For <ILAYER> this value specifies the top offset from the last tag or text.
visibility	Use:show, hide, or inherit	Specifies if the layer is visible using show, hide or inherit. Inherit uses the visibility attribute of the parent.
width	Specify an integer value representing the width.	Specifies the width of the layer. Widths specified in pixels are the default.
zindex	Specify an integer value representing the z-index.	Specifies the z-index value of layer display. Using an imaginary line from the viewing area to the user's eye, higher values place the layer closer to the user, while lower numbers place the layer closer to the viewing area.

In addition to the attributes and properties, certain methods (functions) are available for each layer. Table 16–3 provides a list and short description of each of these methods.

Table 16–3: *Methods available for <LAYER> and <ILAYER> tags*

Method	Parameter	Description
visibility()	Use "show," "hide," or "inherit."	Specifies the layer's visibility.
offset()	Use any integer value to specify the x,y offset.	Specifies the layer's left and top offset. Pixels values are the default. Offset can be to the left (negative numbers), to the right (positive numbers), up (negative numbers), or down (positive numbers).
moveAbove()	Use any valid string for the layer name.	Specifies that the present layer is to be placed above the identified layer.
moveBelow()	Use any valid string for the layer name.	Specifies that the present layer is to be placed below the identified layer.
moveTo()	Use any integer value to specify the x,y position.	Specifies the position to place a layer by using the upper-left starting position of the layer.
resize()	Use any integer value to specify the width, height values.	Specifies the new size of a resized layer. The width and height values are given in pixels by default.

In the previous programming example we layered three differently colored rectangles using the <IMG> tag. In the next example we'll create a similar (but not identical) example using the <LAYER> element. This example is named Layer3.html.

```
<HTML>
<HEAD>
<TITLE>z-Indexing with layers</TITLE>
</HEAD>
<BODY>
<H1><CENTER>z-Index with Layers Demo</CENTER></H1>

<LAYER name="red" left=50 top=50 width=200 height=100
  visibility=show bgcolor="#FF0000" z-index=1>
</LAYER>
<LAYER name="green" left=80 top=80 width=200 height=100
  visibility=show bgcolor="#00FF00" z-index=3>
</LAYER>
<LAYER name="blue" left=110 top=110 width=200 height=100
  visibility=show bgcolor="#0000FF" z-index=2>
</LAYER>

</BODY>
</HTML>
```

In this example, the <LAYER> element is used to create three identically sized colored rectangles. The first rectangle is set at a position starting at a viewing position of 50, 50 pixels. The second rectangle is started at 80, 80 and the third at 110, 110. The visibility attribute of each rectangle is set to *show*. If z-ordering weren't used, the rectangles would be layered in the order they are specified: red, green, and blue. However, z-index numbers rearrange this ordering to green, blue, and red. Figure 16–3 is a screen shot of the viewing area. The green rectangle is the top layer in this figure.

To further your understanding of <LAYER> and <ILAYER> attributes, why not take the time to modify the visibility and z-index attributes. It is always fun to try to predict results before you execute the example.

Animation with Layers

Layers lend themselves to animation techniques because they can be sized to almost any shape and because they can be precisely placed in any viewing area. In the next example we'll create a small blue rectangular layer and then move it about in a 640 × 480 pixel viewing area. This example is named Layer4.html.

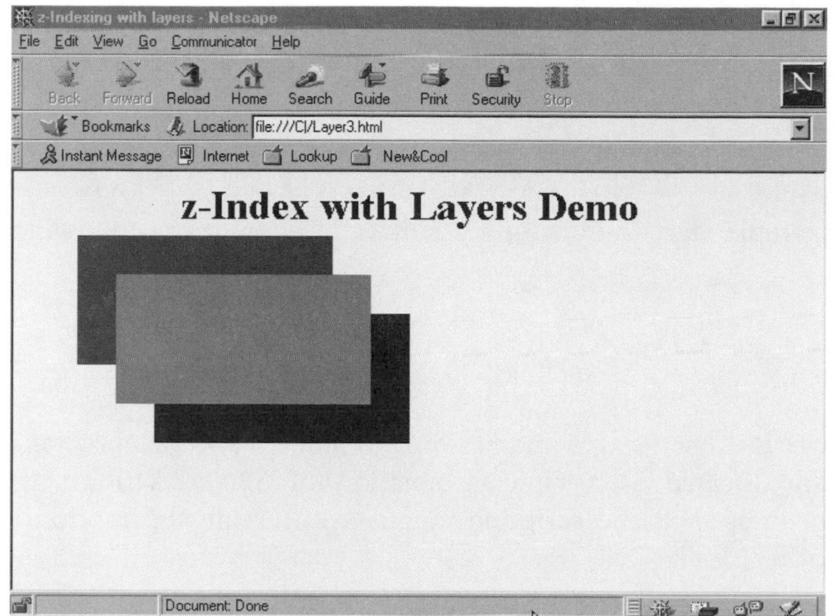

Figure 16–3: *The <LAYER> element is used to create three distinctive layers*

```
<HTML>
<HEAD>
<TITLE>Bouncing Shape Demo</TITLE>
</HEAD>
<BODY rgcolor="#FFFF00">
<H1><CENTER>Layer Animation</CENTER></H1>

<LAYER name="shape" top=240 left=320 height=15
  width=15 bgcolor=#0000FF></LAYER>
<SCRIPT language="JavaScript">
function motion() {
  yPos=yPos+yStep;
  xPos=xPos+xStep;
  if (xPos>640) {xStep=-xStep}
  if (xPos<0) {xStep=-xStep}
  if (yPos>480) {yStep=-yStep}
  if (yPos<0) {yStep=-yStep}
  document.layers["shape"].top=yPos;
  document.layers["shape"].left=xPos;
  setTimeout ("motion()", 5);
}

xStep=2;
yStep=2;
xPos=320;
yPos=240;
```

(continued)

```
motion();
</SCRIPT>

</BODY>
</HTML>
```

This example starts by creating a simple layer with the following codc:

```
<LAYER name="shape" top=240 left=320 height=15
  width=15 bgcolor=#0000FF></LAYER>
```

The layer is named *shape* and is simply a blue 15 (15 pixel rectangle initially located at a viewing position of 320 × 240 pixels. JavaScript is used as the scripting language to create the motion() function.

```
<SCRIPT language="JavaScript">
function motion() {
  yPos=yPos+yStep;
  xPos=xPos+xStep;
  if (xPos>640) {xStep=-xStep}
  if (xPos<0) {xStep=-xStep}
  if (yPos>480) {yStep=-yStep}
  if (yPos<0) {yStep=-yStep}
     .
     .
     .
```

The layer (object) will bounce about in a viewing area set to the size of a VGA 640 × 480 screen. If the object approaches a left-right or top-bottom boundary, the step position is reversed to send the object in the opposite direction. Each time the function is executed, the position of the layer is changed by specifying new *top* and *left* positions.

```
      .
      .
      .
  document.layers["shape"].top=yPos;
  document.layers["shape"].left=xPos;
  setTimeout ("motion()", 5);
}
```

The JavaScript setTimeout() function is used to pace the movement of the object. The time interval is set to 5 milliseconds. Experiment with this value to speed up or slow down the movement.

The final portion of code shows how the initial values for the layer are set.

```
xStep=2;
yStep=2;
xPos=320;
yPos=240;
motion();
</SCRIPT>
```

The initial object position agrees with the position at which the object was drawn, using the <LAYER> element. The step size is set to 2 for both the horizontal and vertical increments. If this value is increased, the motion will appear to speed up but will be coarser. If the value is decreased to 1, the motion will appear to slow down but will be smoother.

Figure 16–4 shows a screen shot of the layer shortly after the motion began.

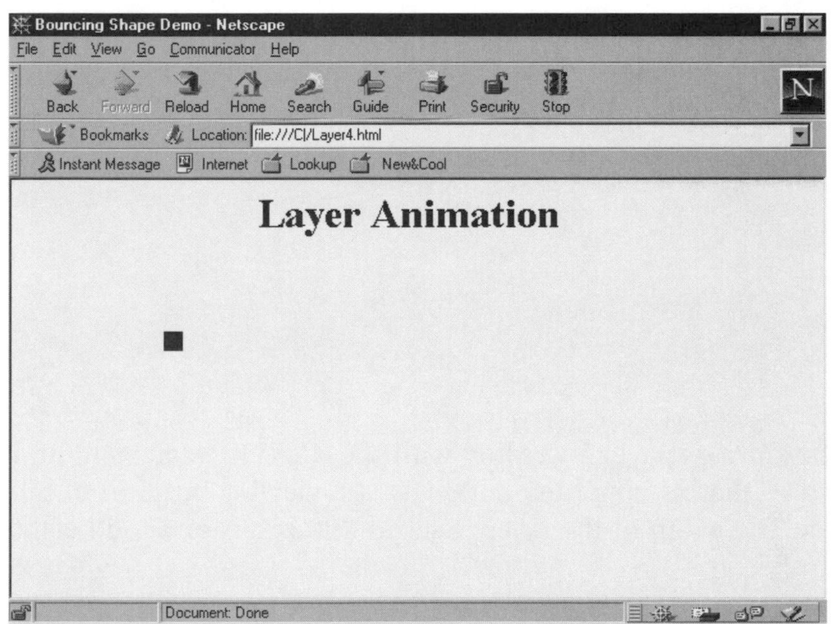

Figure 16–4: *Layers can be moved about in the viewing area, producing simple animation*

The next step for this example, if you are so inclined, is to replace the colored rectangle with an image. How about inserting a flying saucer?

Clipping and Relative Positioning

In the final example on layers we'll demonstrate how to create a clipping rectangle using the <LAYER> element, then demonstrate how <ILAYER> positions layers relative to the last text or image displayed.

Examine the following code, named Layer5.html.

```
<HTML>
<HEAD>
<TITLE>Using LAYER and ILAYER together</TITLE>
</HEAD>
<BODY>
<H1><CENTER>LAYER and ILAYER Demo</CENTER></H1>

More than one LAYER or ILAYER can be used in a
document to create dramatic effects.

<LAYER name="gray" left=50 top=250 width=200 height=50
  visibility=show bgcolor="#C0C0C0" clip="0, 0, 100, 60">
  Such as the text enclosed in this clipping rectangle.
</LAYER>

As you know with ILAYER, positioning is relative
to the last text or image in the viewing area.

<ILAYER name="yellow" width=50 height=20
  visibility=show bgcolor="#FFFF00">
  Use this type of layering to produce dramatic effects.
</ILAYER>

There is no limit to what you can do with layers!

</BODY>
</HTML>
```

In this example a layer is created with the <LAYER> element and positioned so that its upper-left corner is at a viewing position of 50, 250 pixels. The width of the layer is set to 200 pixels and the height to 100 pixels.

```
<LAYER name="gray" left=50 top=250 width=200 height=100
  visibility=show bgcolor="#C0C0C0" clip="0, 0, 100, 60">
  Such as the text enclosed in this clipping rectangle.
</LAYER>
```

A clipping rectangle is created with the dimensions shown in the previous portion of code. As you view Figure 16–5, you'll notice that not all of the text is displayed. The clipping rectangle displays only that portion of text within the clipping area.

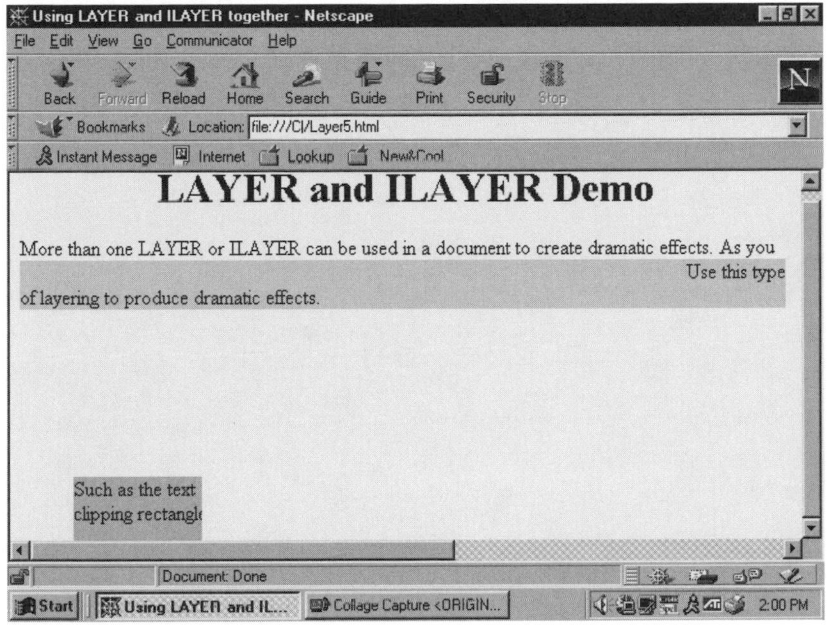

Figure 16–5: *The grayed box, in the lower portion of the screen, shows text in the visible clipping region.*

The <ILAYER> element places layers relative to the last text or image that was displayed. The following portion of code creates a yellow layer and places it immediately after the previous text.

```
<ILAYER name="yellow" width=50 height=20
  visibility=show bgcolor="#FFFF00">
  Use this type of layering to produce dramatic effects.
</ILAYER>
```

The text contained within the <ILAYER> container will appear within the yellow layer. Examine Figure 16–5 once again to see how this layer is placed within the viewing area.

What Now?

In this chapter you learned that layering can be achieved in a variety of ways. The <LAYER> and <ILAYER> containers, when used with the Netscape browser, allow additional dramatic effects.

You can gain additional experience with both layer containers by experimenting with shapes, images, and various container attributes.

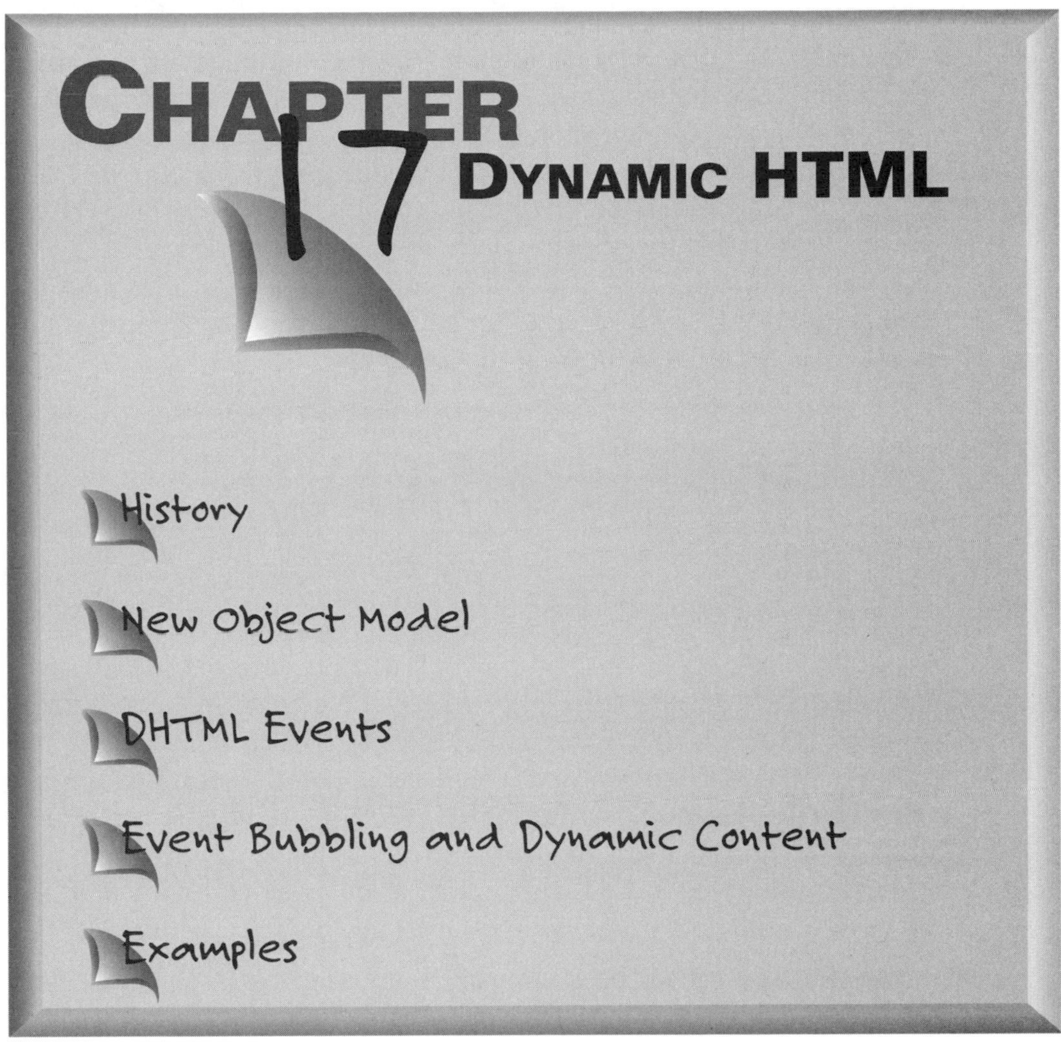

Introduction

It is almost a misnomer to include a chapter titled "Dynamic HTML" when, in fact, the HTML 4.0 standard includes all of the essential components of what has become known as Dynamic HTML.

In this chapter we'll look briefly at the circumstances surrounding the introduction of Dynamic HTML, see why Dynamic HTML is needed, and then identify the components of Dynamic HTML that have already been discussed in this book. We'll then cement the chapter together by presenting short concise examples that illustrate these various concepts.

In short, HTML specifies the information and the content for a Web page. This information includes forms, headings, links, tables, and so on. Cascading style sheets are used to determine how the information is displayed. Dynamic HTML combines the information and content along with the presentation through a new object model that allows dynamic interaction. For example, a developer can use HTML to specify text for the viewing area. A cascading style sheet can be used to control the font size, color, and so on for the presentation. Dynamic HTML can be used to update the contents of the text at any point, with no interaction from the server.

A Brief History of Dynamic HTML

From its inception in 1991 till now, HTML has affected literally millions of people, businesses, corporations, and educational institutions. Almost anyone who has been involved with Web page design has encountered HTML tags and containers. For the nonprogrammer these often appear as a nonstructured collection of cryptic commands designed without much thought or reasoning. To a seasoned programmer, however, HTML appears as a maturing standard that can serve as a stable programming base well into the next century.

HTML has basically been a means of creating static, platform independent Web pages. No doubt, your first encounter with HTML was to create a simple Web page for others to view.

Microsoft pioneered the introduction of Dynamic HTML starting with version 4 of the Internet Explorer.

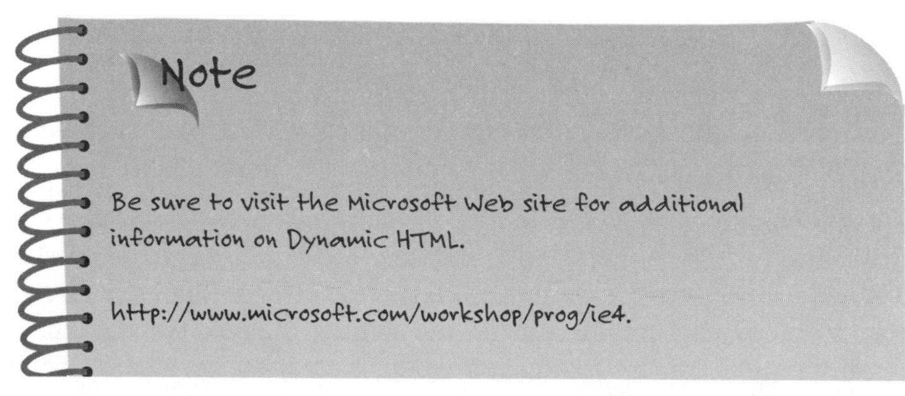

Note
Be sure to visit the Microsoft Web site for additional information on Dynamic HTML.
http://www.microsoft.com/workshop/prog/ie4.

Netscape is in close pursuit as the W3C (World Wide Web Consortium) finishes the HTML 4.0 standard. With Dynamic HTML it is possible to use applets, scripts, and ActiveX objects to modify HTML code, thus making the document *dynamic* rather than *static*.

The introduction of forms (Chapter 11), and the required server-side scripting, has pushed the demand for more interactivity in HTML. Dynamic HTML takes full advantage of cascading style sheets (Chapter 12) to format document content dynamically, without placing an additional burden on the server. Scripting languages (Chapter 13) such as JavaScript and VBScript help provide the interactive component to HTML. You have already learned that frames (Chapter 14), objects (Chapter 15), and layers (Chapter 16) play a key role in making documents more vital, dynamic, and interactive.

The various objects discussed in the previous paragraph are great additions to HTML, even when taken one at a time. However, they are even better when used collectively. Dynamic HTML binds all of these concepts together in the new object model. Hang onto your seatsóyou are really going to find this material exciting!

This Chapter's HTML Tags

No new HTML elements are introduced in this chapter. We will work with elements and containers that you have become familiar with over the past 16 chapters. One thing that you'll notice almost immediately is that you already have all the tools you need to begin developing Dynamic HTML documents.

An Introduction to the New Object Model

HTML documents, to this point, have been rather static. From beginning to end, HTML tags have described how text and images are placed in a document. They have provided very little leeway for true interactivity. Dynamic HTML changes all of this by treating a document as a series of objects. Each portion of text and each image in a document, for example, can be considered as a separate element. Dynamic HTML considers each of these elements as programmable.

The Dynamic HTML Object Model provides four important features:

- Access to all page elements
- Changing the text on the page
- Full event model
- Instant page update

In other words, the Dynamic HTML object model exposes each and every HTML element in a Web page, including its attributes and CSS (Cascading Style Sheets) properties. Using the scripting language of their choice, Web Developers can access and manipulate all elements of a Web page–tags, attributes, images, objects, and text–creating, moving, and modifying these elements when and as needed. Dynamic HTML also provides full support for keyboard, mouse, and focus events on all page elements.

You have already learned–in Chapter 12, for example–that text styles can be altered dynamically. In this section we'll consider a simple Dynamic HTML example that lets us dynamically alter a font property.

Dynamically Altering a Property

Here is a simple example that will allow the user to click the mouse on a line of text. When the mouse button is depressed, the font size is dynamically changed to 60 points. When the mouse button is released, the font size is set to 12 points. The user can interact with the document, but this places no additional burden on the server. This example is named DHtml1.html.

```
<HTML>
<HEAD>
<TITLE>Dynamic HTML Example #1</TITLE>
</HEAD>

<BODY bgcolor=#C0C0C0>
<P id="doit"
  onmousedown="bigger()"
  onmouseup="smaller()">
  Click on me to read this line!</P>

<SCRIPT language="JavaScript">
function bigger() {
  document.all.doit.style.fontSize="60pt";
}

function smaller() {
  document.all.doit.style.fontSize="12pt";
}
</SCRIPT>
</BODY>

</HTML>
```

Figure 17–1 shows the viewing area before the mouse button is depressed.

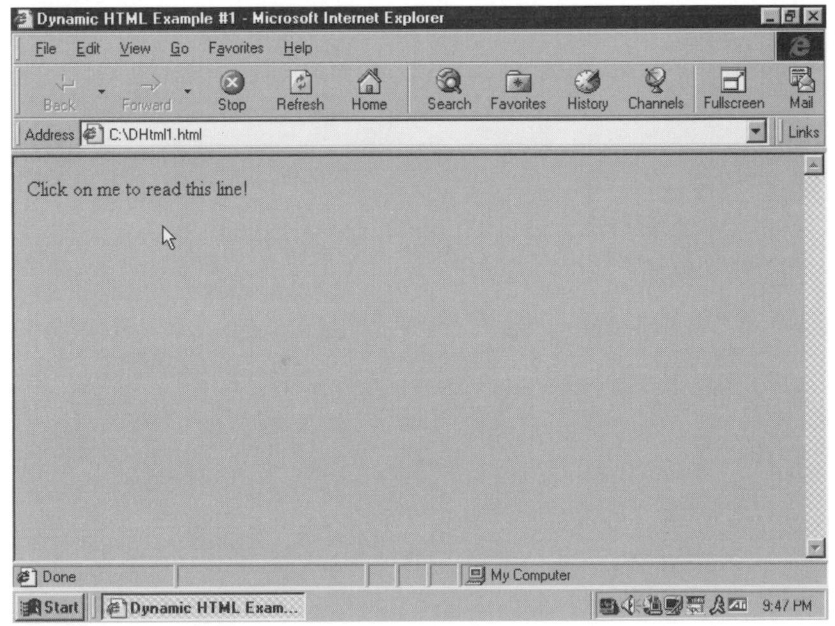

Figure 17–1: *Before the mouse button is depressed, the text is normal size*

Figure 17–2 shows the dynamic change in text size when the mouse is depressed over the line of text.

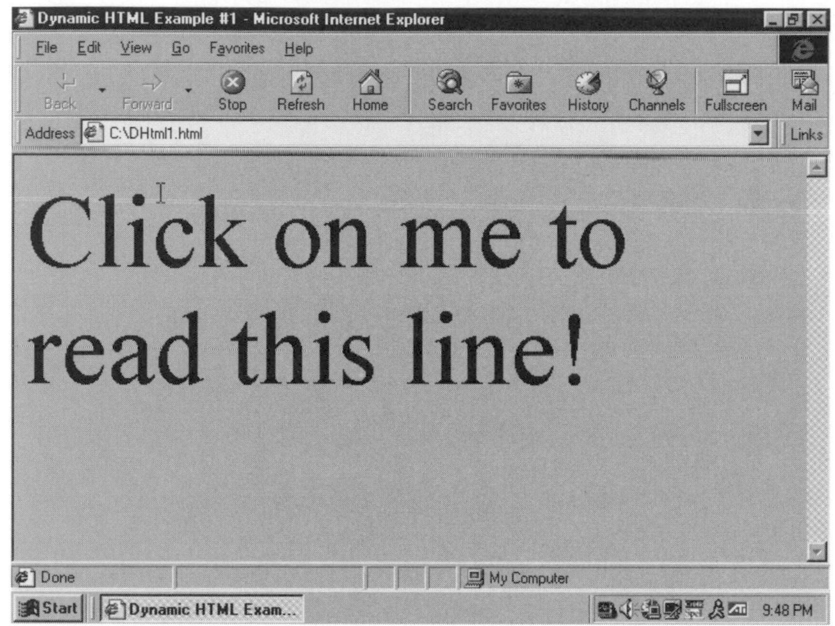

Figure 17–2: *The font size is changed when the mouse is depressed over the text*

This simple program uses all of the key components of an object-oriented program: events, methods, and properties.

Events

Many of Dynamic HTML's events have been presented in earlier chapters. Table 17–1 presents an alphabetized list of events for your reference.

Table 17–1: *Events used with the Dynamic HTML document object*

onabort	onfocus	onmouseup
onafterupdate	onhelp	onreadystatechange
onbeforeupdate	onkeydown	onreset
onblur	onkeypress	onrowenter
onbounce	onkeyup	onrowexit
onchange	onload	onscroll
onclick	onmousedown	onselect
ondblclick	onmousemove	onstart
onerror	onmouseout	onsubmit
onfinish	onmouseover	onunload

In the previous example, the *onmousedown* or *onmouseup* event triggers a call to a JavaScript portion of code that is responsible for changing the font size.

```
    .
    .
    .
<P id="doit"
  onmousedown="bigger()"
  onmouseup="smaller()">
  Click on me to read this line!</P>
    .
    .
    .
```

When the user slides the mouse over the text being displayed in the viewing area and depresses a mouse button, an onmousedown event is generated. A different event, onmouseup, occurs when the mouse button is released.

METHODS

Methods (functions) are generally written to respond to specific events. In this example the bigger() method is called when the onmousedown event is generated. When the mouse button is released, the smaller() method is called by an onmouseup event. Each of the methods just mentioned is called in order to change a font property–namely, the font size.

PROPERTIES

Size is just one of many font properties that can be set with a small portion of JavaScript or VBScript.

```
     .
     .
     .
function bigger() {
  document.all.doit.style.fontSize="60pt";
}
     .
     .
     .
```

Just a note on the program syntax shown in the previous portion of code: later in this chapter we will investigate the hierarchical relationship between various objects, including the windows and document objects.

In this example, the fontSize property was accessed with the syntax:

```
document.all.doit.style.fontSize="60pt";
```

Here *document* represents the Dynamic HTML document object and *all* the all collection of elements. More on those terms shortly. The paragraph id attribute, *doit*, has be used to instantiate the paragraph as a dynamic object. So the style attribute, *style*, and the font property that is to be changed must follow this value. However, this property could also be changed with the following line of code. Perhaps the most correct form of syntax is:

```
window.document.all.doit.style.fontSize="60pt";
```

You'll learn shortly that the window object contains information regarding the browser window, while the document object contains information regarding the current document. This syntax insures that the property will be changed for the current window and the document that it contains. To access the all collection of the document, use the *all* keyword.

Animation Effects

You have just seen how font properties can be dynamically altered with Dynamic HTML. In the previous chapter you learned that layers can be styled in terms of size, color, position, and so on. Animation was achieved, using Dynamic HTML concepts, by creating a layer and then dynamically changing its position with the JavaScript setTimeout() function.

The key word in Dynamic HTML is *dynamic*, and the animation technique presented in Chapter 16 certainly qualifies.

Before we continue with additional examples, we need to investigate object hierarchy. In the next section you'll learn how various Dynamic HTML objects relate to one another.

Object Hierarchy

Earlier in this chapter you learned that the windows object in Dynamic HTML is the parent of all document objects. Actually, the window object contains information regarding the browser and has numerous child objects, as shown in Table 17-2.

Table 17–2: *The child objects of the window object*

Parent	**Child1**
window	document event frames history location navigator screen

Of the seven child objects, we are most interested in the document object. This object, as you will recall, contains information regarding the current document being displayed by the window object.

The Document Object

It is the document object that Dynamic HTML addresses directly. The document object also has child objects. Table 17–3 shows the hierarchical breakdown of the document object into its corresponding child objects.

Table 17–3: *The document object's child objects (collections)*

Child1	**Child2 (collections)**
document	all anchors applets body embeds filters forms frames images links plug-ins scripts selection style sheets

As you can see, the study of Dynamic HTML is quite vast. In this chapter we'll limit our discussion to the document object.

Document-Object Collections

Another new term Dynamic HTML uses that you should understand is *collection*. A collection holds Dynamic HTML elements together. These elements can be forms, frames, images, links, and so on. As an example, consider this book. A collection could be considered the book's binding that holds the chapters (objects) of the book together.

In Dynamic HTML *all* is a collection. The all collection holds all of the elements making up the document. Collections are accessible via three methods: item(number), item(string), and tags(name-of-tag).

You could query for all of the elements in a document that use the <A> tag by writing:

```
document.all.tags("A")
```

An individual element could be returned from a collection by writing the following:

```
document.all.item("new_element")
```

As you may have guessed, the elements we have been discussing are elements you have been using along with HTML. The difference now is that they can be handled as objects! Dynamic HTML elements contain a common set of properties. These properties include classname, document, id, left, parentelement, right, style, tagname, and top. We have used these properties extensively in previous chapters, so we won't put you through another explanation.

Event Bubbling

Event bubbling is a Dynamic HTML concept that allows an event started in one element to "bubble" upward in the HTML document's hierarchical order until an element is found to handle it. Every event will bubble or migrate to the top, so it is possible that a number of event handlers will be called.

Consider the example shown near the start of this chapter. Here is the code, once again.

```
<HTML>
<HEAD>
<TITLE>Dynamic HTML Example #1</TITLE>
</HEAD>

<BODY bgcolor=#C0C0C0>
<P id="doit"
  onmousedown="bigger()"
  onmouseup="smaller()">
  Click on me to read this line!</P>

<SCRIPT language="JavaScript">
function bigger() {
  document.all.doit.style.fontSize="60pt";
}

function smaller() {
  document.all.doit.style.fontSize="12pt";
}
</SCRIPT>
</BODY>

</HTML>
```

Recall that if the mouse button is depressed while the pointer is over the displayed text, the font size is enlarged. The processing of this event takes place within the <P> element. Now, stripping unnecessary information away from the previous code, let's add a little indenting and another <P> element. The previous listing will now take on this form.

```
<HTML>
      <HEAD>
            <TITLE>
            </TITLE>
      </HEAD>

      <BODY>

            <P>
            </P>

            <P>
            </P>

            <SCRIPT>
            </SCRIPT>
      </BODY>

</HTML>
```

If an event takes place within either <P> element, it can be handled there. However, it will also bubble through the <BODY> element and can possibly be handled there. Finally, it will bubble to the <HTML> element. In a similar fashion, an event taking place in the <BODY> element can be handled there, then bubbled through to the <HTML> element and possibly handled again.

Any element can handle events for any objects contained within the element's structure. Because of this feature, elements can be grouped. For example, imagine that this document has two different lines of text, each contained within a separate <P> element. Instead of binding each of them separately, you know the event will bubble to the next level. So the event binding is placed in the <BODY> element, as shown in the following example. This example is named DHtml2.html.

```
<HTML>
<HEAD>
<TITLE>Dynamic HTML Example #2</TITLE>
</HEAD>

<BODY id="doit" onmousedown="bigger()"
  onmouseup="smaller()" bgcolor=#C0C0C0>

<P>Click on me to read this line!</P>

<P>Or click on me for similar results!</P>

<SCRIPT language="JavaScript">
function bigger() {
  document.all.doit.style.fontSize="60pt";
}

function smaller() {
  document.all.doit.style.fontSize="12pt";
}
</SCRIPT>
</BODY>

</HTML>
```

Figure 17–3 shows the results that you'll obtain by clicking on either of the lines of text. When you examine the previous listing, you'll probably agree that event bubbling can make coding much simpler.

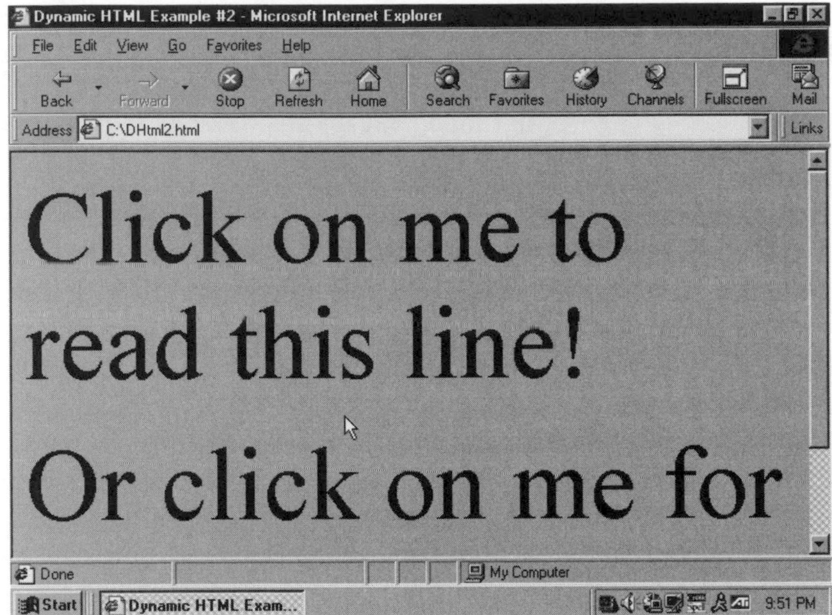

Figure 17–3: *Event bubbling makes event binding a simpler task*

Dynamic Content

Dynamic HTML allows the developer to dynamically change the tags or content of a page without additional interaction from the server. Dynamic content allows a page's content to be changed by the user, perhaps by clicking the mouse, or as a timed event using the system timer.

The ability to dynamically change the contents of a Web page results from the use of the TextRange object.

The TextRange Object

The TextRange object allows the user to dynamically change the contents of a Web page. TextRange objects can be created with the createTextRange() method. For example:

```
var ChangeThis = document.body.createTextRange();
```

An alternative method is to use rangeFromElement() in the following manner:

```
var ChangeThat = document.body.rangeFromElement(italic);
```

In this piece of code the range is the identified italic text in the document.

Once the range of the object has been defined, numerous methods can be used to change the contents of the page. Table 17–4 lists and describes TextRange properties.

Table 17–4: *TextRange properties*

Properties	Description
htmlText	Returns the tags surrounding the selected text that is to be changed.
text	Returns the actual text contained between the selected tags.

The TextRange properties provide the boundaries and the content you are about to work with.

It is possible to work with collections of elements, too. Consider a TextRange based upon the <BODY> tag. Every element contained between <BODY> and </BODY> is included in the range and makes up the collection of elements.

Table 17–5 lists and describes several TextRange methods.

These methods are useful in selecting and establishing TextRange objects.

Several methods associated with TextRange objects permit the developer to move the range, rather than the contents of the range. Table 17–6 lists and describes several of these methods.

Table 17–5: *TextRange methods*

Methods	Description
compareEndPoints()	–1 means objects share less than common endpoints. 0 means objects share common endpoints. +1 means objects share greater than common endpoints.
createTextRange()	Use <BODY>, <BUTTON>, <INPUT TYPE=TEXT>, and <TEXTAREA> to set a text range for text that can be dynamically changed.
duplicate()	Creates a duplicate of the contents of the specified TextRange.
isEqual()	Compares contents of two TextRange objects for equality.
inRange()	Determines if one TextRange object is within another TextRange object.
parentElement()	Returns the parent element of the given range.
scrollIntoView()	Scrolls the given range into view.
setEndPoint()	Sets one endpoint for a TextRange object based upon the endpoint of another TextRange object.

Table 17–6: *TextRange movement methods*

Method	Description
move()	Moves the range of text, not the text.
moveEnd()	Moves the ending point of the range of text.
moveStart()	Moves the starting point of the range of text.
pasteHTML()	Inserts text into a range of text.

The TextRange object movement is controlled by a number of unique units, as shown in Table 17-7.

Table 17-7: *Object movement units*

Unit	Description
character	Count by characters. Index specifies the number.
story	Used to move to the paragraph specified by the index.
sentence	Used to move to the sentence specified by the index.
word	Count by words. Index specifies the number.

Next you'll learn how these concepts are put together, as we look at a simple yet practical example.

Dynamically Replacing Document Text

To illustrate the concept of dynamically changing text in a Dynamic HTML document, consider the following example named DHtml3.html.

```
<HTML>
<HEAD>
<TITLE>Dynamic HTML Example #3</TITLE>
</HEAD>

<BODY onmousedown="altertext()">
<P>Here is a little text that we'll work
  with to illustrate how we can use Dynamic
  HTML to change text in a document.  This
  example uses a TextRange object to alter
  the original page of information.</P>
</BODY>

<SCRIPT language="JavaScript">
function altertext() {
  var changeit = document.body.createTextRange();
  changeit.move("Word", 4);
  changeit.text="paragraph of ";
}
</SCRIPT>

</HTML>
```

The <BODY> tag identifies an event, onmousedown, that will call the JavaScript function altertext() when the mouse is clicked on any portion of the original paragraph of text.

The altertext() function creates a TextRange for the body of the document. Note that the body of this document contains the original paragraph of text.

The move() method is used to count over four words in the paragraph; then the text() method inserts "paragraph of" into the original document.

Figure 17–4 shows the document before the mouse is depressed.

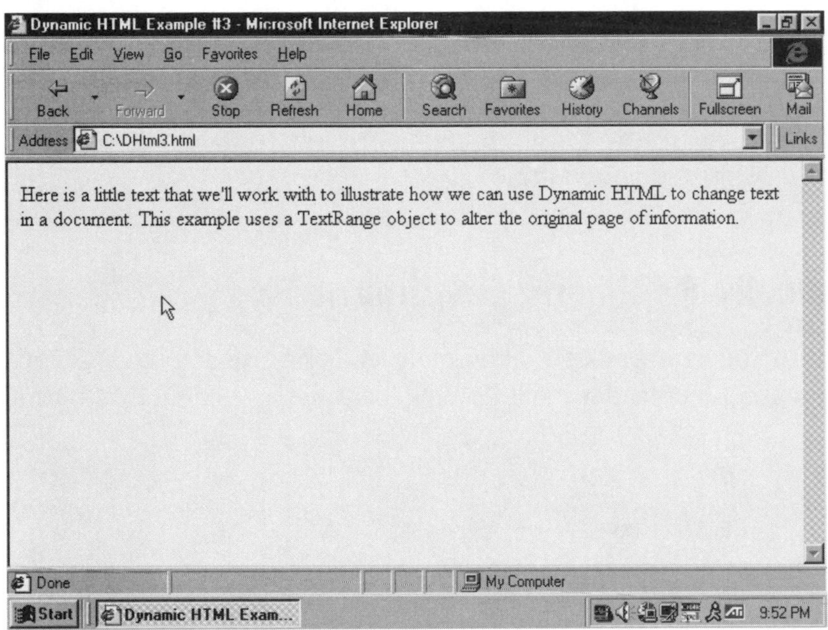

Figure 17–4: *The original document's text*

Figure 17–5 shows the small portion of text that has been inserted into the original paragraph. Can you find it?

Can you imagine the possibilities that this Dynamic HTML feature can give to your documents? Maybe you would like to create documents with real-time clocks, calendars, and graphics that change in real time!

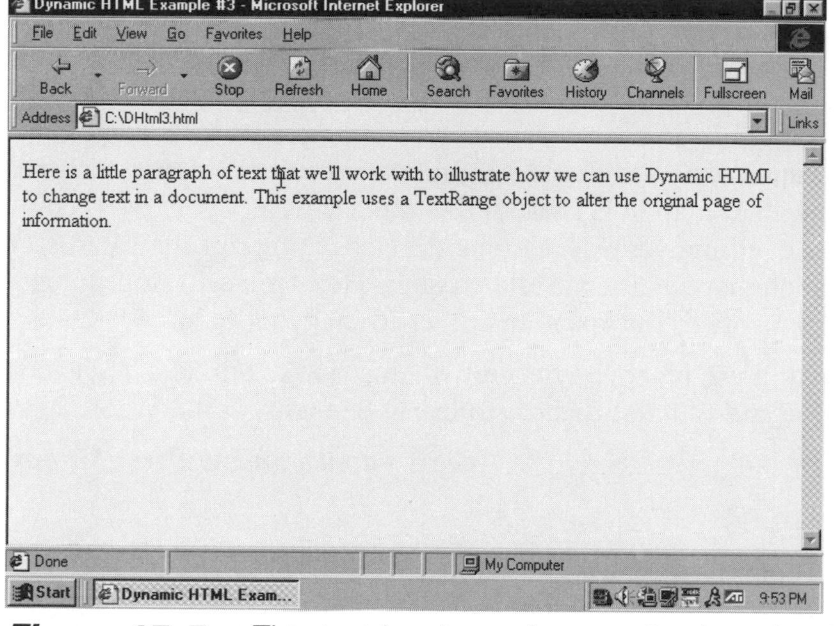

Figure 17–5: *This text has been dynamically altered with the depression of the mouse button*

Dynamic Data Binding

Data binding can be defined as a process that connects data, usually from a different source, to an HTML document. If you have programmed with forms, you have probably been involved with writing CGI scripts that allow an HTML client-side document to communicate with the server side. This process is called *server-side data binding*.

Client-side data binding, in effect, relieves the server from much of the burden required under conventional practices. With client-side data binding a client-side *data source* can be identified and retrieved by the *data consumer*, the HTML document, without the need to access the server.

What Do You Mean— "That's All?"

In this chapter you have seen the important concepts and features available with Dynamic HTML. If this topic interests you, we recommend you continue your development by checking out the Microsoft Web location given earlier in the chapter. Here you will find the latest developments in this exciting and ever-changing field.

You may have reached the end of this book, but you have not reached the end of what there is to learn. See you on the Web!

–Chris Pappas and William Murray

Appendix A
HTML 4.0 Elements

The following table contains the elements approved for HTML 4.0. You will also find information reflecting the elements supported by the Microsoft Internet Explorer and Netscape.

Table A–1: *HTML 4.0 Elements*

Element	Internet Explorer	Netscape	Start Tag	End Tag	Description
A	yes	yes	yes	yes	Anchor
ACRONYM	yes	yes	yes	yes	Acronym
ADDRESS	yes	yes	yes	yes	Author information
APPLET	yes	yes	yes	yes	Java applet
AREA	yes	yes	yes	no	Client-side image map area
B	yes	yes	yes	yes	Bold font
BASE	yes	yes	yes	no	Document base URL

Table A-1: *HTML 4.0 Elements (continued)*

Element	Internet Explorer	Netscape	Start Tag	End Tag	Description
BASEFONT	yes	yes	yes	no	Font size
BDO	yes	yes	yes	yes	BiDi override
BIG	yes	yes	yes	yes	Large text style
BLOCKQUOTE	yes	yes	yes	yes	Block quotation
BODY	yes	yes	opt.	opt.	Document body
BR	yes	yes	yes	no	Line break
BUTTON	yes	yes	yes	yes	Pushbutton
CAPTION	yes	yes	yes	yes	Table caption
CENTER	yes	yes	yes	yes	Alignment (center)
CITE	yes	yes	yes	yes	Citation
CODE	yes	yes	yes	yes	Code fragment
COL	yes	no	yes	no	Table column
COLGROUP	yes	no	yes	opt.	Table column (group)
DD	yes	yes	yes	opt.	Definition description
DEL	yes	yes	yes	yes	Deleted text
DFN	yes	yes	yes	yes	Instance definition
DIR	yes	yes	yes	yes	Directory
DIV	yes	yes	yes	yes	Generic language or style container
DL	yes	yes	yes	yes	Definition list
DT	yes	yes	yes	opt.	Definition term
EM	yes	yes	yes	yes	Emphasis (similar to bold)
FIELDSET	yes	yes	yes	yes	Form control group

Element	Internet Explorer	Netscape	Start Tag	End Tag	Description
FONT	yes	yes	yes	yes	Font (local)
FORM	yes	yes	yes	yes	Form (interactive)
FRAME	yes	yes	yes	no	Frame (sub-window)
FRAMESET	yes	yes	yes	yes	Subdivision of window
H1	yes	yes	yes	yes	Heading (style 1)
H2	yes	yes	yes	yes	Heading (style 2)
H3	yes	yes	yes	yes	Heading (style 3)
H4	yes	yes	yes	yes	Heading (style 4)
H5	yes	yes	yes	yes	Heading (style 5)
H6	yes	yes	yes	yes	Heading (style 6)
HEAD	yes	yes	opt.	opt.	Document head
HR	yes	yes	yes	no	Horizontal rule
HTML	yes	yes	opt.	opt.	Document root element
I	yes	yes	yes	yes	Italic font style
IFRAME	yes	yes	yes	yes	Inline sib-window
IMG	yes	no	yes	no	Embedded image
INPUT	yes	yes	yes	no	Form control
INS	yes	yes	yes	yes	Inserted text
ISINDEX	yes	yes	yes	no	Single line prompt
KBD	yes	yes	yes	yes	User entered text
LABEL	yes	yes	yes	yes	Field label text
LEGEND	yes	yes	yes	yes	Fieldset legend
LI	yes	yes	yes	opt.	List item
LINK	yes	no	yes	no	Link

Table A-1: *HTML 4.0 Elements (continued)*

Element	Internet Explorer	Netscape	Start Tag	End Tag	Description
MAP	yes	yes	yes	yes	Client-side image map
MENU	yes	yes	yes	yes	Menu list
META	yes	yes	yes	no	Meta information
NOFRAMES	yes	yes	yes	yes	Container for non-frame-based rendering
NOSCRIPT	yes	no	yes	yes	Container for non-script-based rendering
OBJECT	yes	yes	yes	yes	Embedded object
OL	yes	yes	yes	yes	Ordered list
OPTION	yes	no	yes	opt.	Selectable choice
P	yes	yes	yes	opt.	Paragraph
PARAM	yes	yes	yes	no	Property value
PRE	yes	yes	yes	yes	Preformatted text
Q	yes	yes	yes	yes	Inline quote
S	yes	yes	yes	yes	Strike-through (text style)
SAMP	yes	yes	yes	yes	Program output, scripts and so on
SCRIPT	yes	yes	yes	yes	Script statement
SELECT	yes	yes	yes	yes	Option selector
SMALL	yes	yes	yes	yes	Small text style
SPAN	yes	no	yes	yes	Generic language or style container

Element	Internet Explorer	Netscape	Start Tag	End Tag	Description
STRIKE	yes	yes	yes	yes	Strike-through text
STRONG	yes	yes	yes	yes	Strong emphasis
STYLE	yes	no	yes	yes	Style information
SUB	yes	yes	yes	yes	Subscript
SUP	yes	yes	yes	yes	Superscript
TABLE	yes	yes	yes	yes	Table
TBODY	yes	no	opt.	opt.	Table body
TD	yes	yes	yes	opt.	Table data cell
TEXTAREA	yes	yes	yes	yes	Text field (multiline)
TFOOT	yes	no	yes	opt.	Table footer
TH	yes	yes	yes	opt.	Table header cell
THEAD	yes	no	yes	opt.	Table header
TITLE	yes	yes	yes	yes	Document title
TR	yes	yes	yes	opt.	Table row
TT	yes	yes	yes	yes	Monospaced font style (teletype)
U	yes	yes	yes	yes	Underlined text style
UL	yes	yes	yes	yes	Unordered list
VAR	yes	yes	yes	yes	Instance of a variable or program argument

Additional information on tags, elements and containers can be found in each chapter of this book.

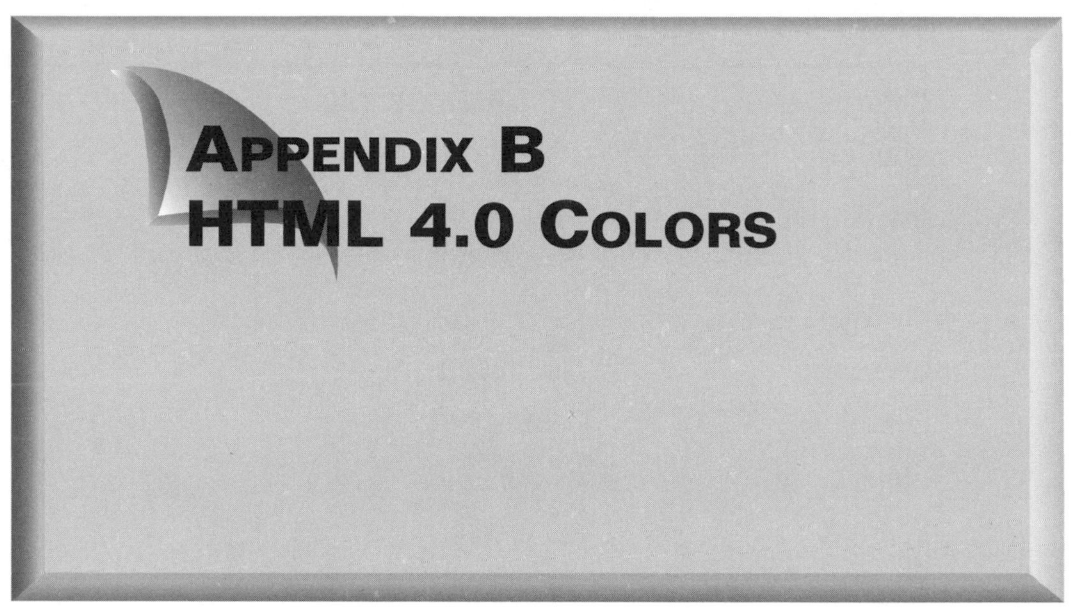

Appendix B HTML 4.0 Colors

Document colors can often be specified by name or by a hexadecimal number giving the Red, Green, and Blue (RGB) mix. The attribute value type "color" (%Color) refers to color definitions as specified in [SRGB].

For example, the color red can be specified by name or by the hexadecimal number #FF0000. Likewise, green can be specified by name of by the hexadecimal number #00FF00. Altering the RGB values can create color mixes. For example, Fuchsia can be formed by name or by the hexadecimal number #FF00FF.

Each RGB color is represented by a hexadecimal number that varies from 00 to FF or from 0 to 255 decimal. That means that there are $256 \times 256 \times 256 = 16{,}777{,}216$ possible color combinations that can be used if your equipment is capable of rendering those colors.

Table B-1 shows a list of standard HTML color names and their equivalent hexadecimal values.

The W3C group suggests that even though colors add significant amounts of information to documents and make them more readable they should be used with caution. The use of HTML elements and attributes for color has been deprecated in favor of style sheets.

Table B-1: *Color names and hexadecimal values*

Color Name	Hexadecimal Value
Aqua	"#00FFFF"
Black	"#000000"
Blue	"#0000FF"
Fuchsia	"#FF00FF"
Gray	"#808080"
Green	"#008000"
Lime	"#00FF00"
Maroon	"#800000"
Navy	"#000080"
Olive	"#808000"
Purple	"#800080"
Red	"#FF0000"
Silver	"#C0C0C0"
Teal	"#008080"
White	"#FFFFFF"
Yellow	"#FFFF00"

Problems related to the use of colors include:

- Colors can vary from one computer platform to another.
- Users that are colored challenged cannot view or read certain combination of colors..
- Background and foreground colors, that are not well chosen, add confusion to document readability.
- Also, when practical, adopt common conventions to minimize user confusion. In addition, if you use a background image or set the background color, then be sure to set the various text colors as well.

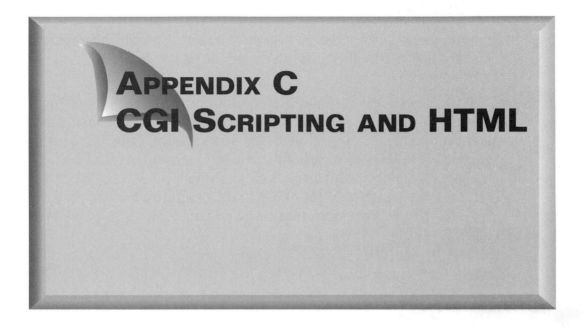

Appendix C
CGI Scripting and HTML

Introduction

You learned in Chapter 11 that communications between a client-side HTML document and a server-side program require uploading an application to the server. In this manner, information can be sent from the HTML document to the server. Once the server receives the information and processes it, the information can be collected in a database, for example, for future reference.

Server-side applications of this sort are written according to Common Gateway Interface (CGI) requirements. These applications handle the communications linkage between the client and server sides.

Two languages are emerging as the de facto languages for CGI scripts: Perl and C/C++. The example we have included in this chapter is a C programming example, but you should also consider scripting in Perl. There are a number of Perl compilers available free on the Web for your use.

You will also recall, from Chapter 11 that the GET and POST request methods must be processed differently. We strongly recommend the POST method, and our example in this appendix assumes this method.

There are whole books devoted to the topic of CGI scripting. These books cover a wide range of topics including communication problems, scripting tips and techniques and so on. One of the best books we have seen dealing with both Perl and C scripting is *CGI How-To* by Asbury, Mathews, Sol and Greer, published in 1996 by The Waite Group Press (ISBN 1-57169-028-X). You'll want to consider a book such as this if your scripting needs require complex parsing or database needs.

Web Servers

If you have been developing HTML documents, you realize that many are just client-side documents that allow browsing through various pages of text, images, sounds and so on.

Your internet provider may allow you to create a personal Web page on the server, with no additional monthly charge. When this is possible, you'll be given your own site address and your friends and relations can connect to this address to view your home page. Basically, you create your HTML document on your computer then upload the document to the server. What is missing here is the ability to upload CGI scripts.

If you are interested in obtaining information from users viewing your HTML document, such as information returned by a form that you have created, you will probably have to establish a commercial account. You will have to pay monthly charges to open and maintain a commercial account, but with it comes the ability to collect data from users. If you work for a large corporation or educational institution, you'll find that this ability already exists. Find someone in the computer center that can assist you with creating an account and uploading your CGI scripts.

If you want to simply test a form as you develop it you can access the NCSA site discussed in Chapter 11. Use the following code in your HTML document.

```
<FORM method="post"
  action="http://hoohoo.ncsa.uiuc.edu/cgi-bin/post-query">
```

This site provides a server using a script that will examine data from any submitted form and return the results as an HTML page. None of the information is saved, but the site is useful when checking initial form operation.

Personal Web Servers

If you don't have easy access to a server for uploading and testing CGI scripts, we highly recommend a personal Web server. A personal Web server allows you to create a server that can be accessed by a single computer or a small group of computers on an intranet.

Microsoft FrontPage will install a Personal Web Server during installation. If you save an HTML document in the home page location with the name default.htm, the Personal Web Server will allow you to communicate with a CGI script. The CGI script is compiled and placed in the cgi-bin subdirectory of the Personal Web Server. All you will need to do is specify this location in your HTML document.

A Simple Example

In the following example, we'll borrow the pet registration document developed in Chapter 11. Then we'll write a CGI script in C that will allow us to intercept data returned by the form when the submit button is clicked. Believe us when we tell you that CGI scripting can become much more complicated than our simple example. The reason is that the form often returns information that can be intercepted as a command-line argument by the script. The data received is in the form of a single string that must be parsed and decoded. Decoding is required because the string contains "+" symbols instead of spaces. Also, "&" symbols are used to separate key-value pairs. Other special symbols are also used. Figure C-1 shows a string of raw data rcturned by the pet registration form in key-value form.

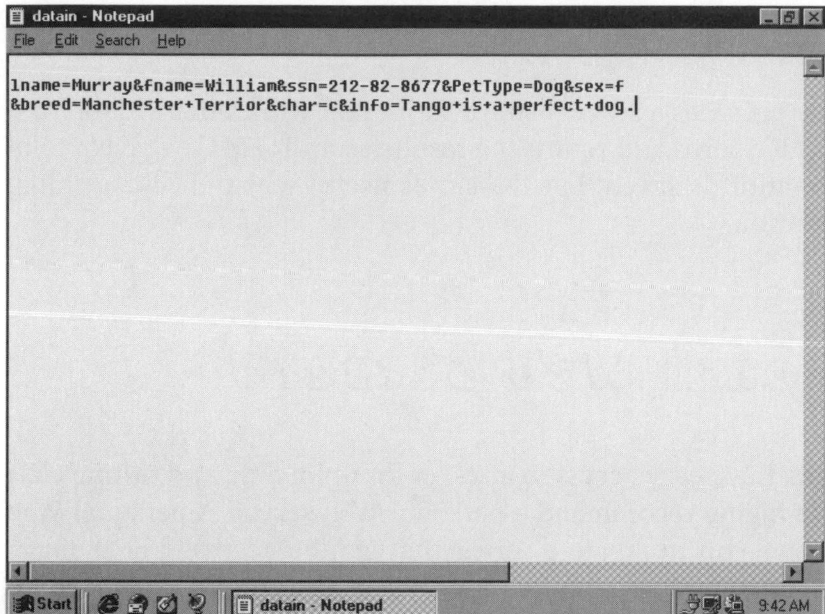

Figure C–1: *Form information is returned as a long string with special symbols representing spaces and key-value separators*

The following example will show you how to intercept this string and perform some simple parsing and decoding.

The HTML Document

The following listing contains the HTML pet registration document developed in Chapter 11. A small change has been made to the form submission line. This change is printed in a bold font. The action method indicates that the script file, DataIn.exe, is located the Server's cgi-bin subdirectory.

Name this file default.htm if you are using the Microsoft Personal Web Server.

```
<HTML>
<HEAD>
<TITLE>Pet Registration</TITLE>
</HEAD>
<BODY>
<H1>Please complete the following form
<BR>to register your pet</H1>
```

```
<HR>
<H3>Information about you:</H3>
<FORM method="post"
  action="http:/cgi-bin/DataIn.exe">
Your last name: <INPUT type="text" name="lname"
  maxlength="25" size="18">
First name: <INPUT type="text" name="fname"
  maxlength="25" size="18">
<BR>
Social Security Number: <INPUT type="text" name="ssn"
  maxlength="11" size="11">
<HR>
<H3>Information about your pet:</H3>
<TABLE>
<TR valign="top">
<TD>Type of pet:
<BR>
<SELECT Name="PetType">
  <OPTION>Cat </OPTION>
  <OPTION selected>Dog </OPTION>
  <OPTION>Horse </OPTION>
  <OPTION>Other </OPTION>
</SELECT>
</TABLE>
<INPUT type="radio" name="sex" value="m">Male
<INPUT type="radio" name="sex" value="f">Female
Pet's breed: <INPUT type="text" name="breed"
  maxlength="20">
Please check all that apply to your pet:
<INPUT type="checkbox" name="char"
  value="e">Cropped ears
<INPUT type="checkbox" name="char"
  value="t">Docked tail
<INPUT type="checkbox" name="char"
  value="c">Good with children
<H3>Tell us something unique about your pet:</H3>
<TEXTAREA name="info" rows=10 cols=60>
</TEXTAREA>
<HR>
<H3>Thank you for your information -
  your pet will be registered.</H3>
<INPUT type="submit">
<INPUT type="reset">
</FORM>
</BODY>
</HTML>
```

As you examine the listing, notice several names that will be used as key names when information is returned. For example, lname, fname, ssn and so on are used as key names. You might have noticed them in Figure 1, embedded in the string.

The CGI script developed in the next section will intercept this string of data, parse it and remove embedded "+" and "&" symbols.

The CGI Script

The C program presented in this section has been made as simple as possible in order to focus on the minimum CGI script code needed to intercept and parse data returned by the HTML document. The script file assumes a POST data return and performs no real error checking.

Name this CGI script file DataIn.c. When you compile the application, make sure the executable (.exe) is located in the cgi-bin subdirectory.

```
/* DataIn.c is an application that serves as a
*  CGI script for intercepting, parsing and
*  removing '+' and '&' symbols before
*  printing key-value pairs.
*/

#include <stdio.h>
#include <stdlib.h>
#include <string.h>

void GetInfo(char **);

void main(int argc, char *argv[])
{
  char *info;
  char searchTokens[] = "+&";
  char *startOfNextToken;

  /*required CGI header*/
  printf("Content-type: text/plain\n\n\n");

  printf("Parsed key-value pairs:\n\n\n");

  GetInfo(&info);
  startOfNextToken = strtok(info, searchTokens);
  while (startOfNextToken != NULL) {
    printf(" %s\n", startOfNextToken);
    startOfNextToken = strtok(NULL, searchTokens);
  }
}

void GetInfo(char **tempStr)
{
```

```
    char *infoStr;
    int infoLen;
    int i;

    infoLen = atoi(getenv("CONTENT_LENGTH"));
    infoStr = (char *) malloc(sizeof(char) * (infoLen + 1));

    i = 0;
    while(i < infoLen)  {
      infoStr[i++] = fgetc(stdin);
    }
    infoStr[i] = '\0';

    *tempStr = infoStr;
}
```

A call to the GetData() function returns a string of key-value pairs that is parsed using the strtok() function. The strtok() function allows the string to be scanned for '+' and '&' characters. As the original string is scanned, a substring named *startofNextToken*, is created. This string represents the characters from the previous token to the next token. In other words, all of the characters from the previous '+' or '&' symbol to the next. A **while** loop controls the number of times a substring is created and printed.

The GetInfo() function contains a number of interesting features. First, the getenv() function obtains the length of the information passed to the application via *argc* and *argv*. This information is used to determine the size of a memory buffer for the string. The standard malloc() function is used for this purpose. The string of information is built, one character at a time, using a **while** loop and the fgetc() function.

Figure C–2 shows the resulting output with the same data as used in Figure C–1.

An interesting challenge would be to now save this information in a simple database. The database could be updated each time a new user enters data.

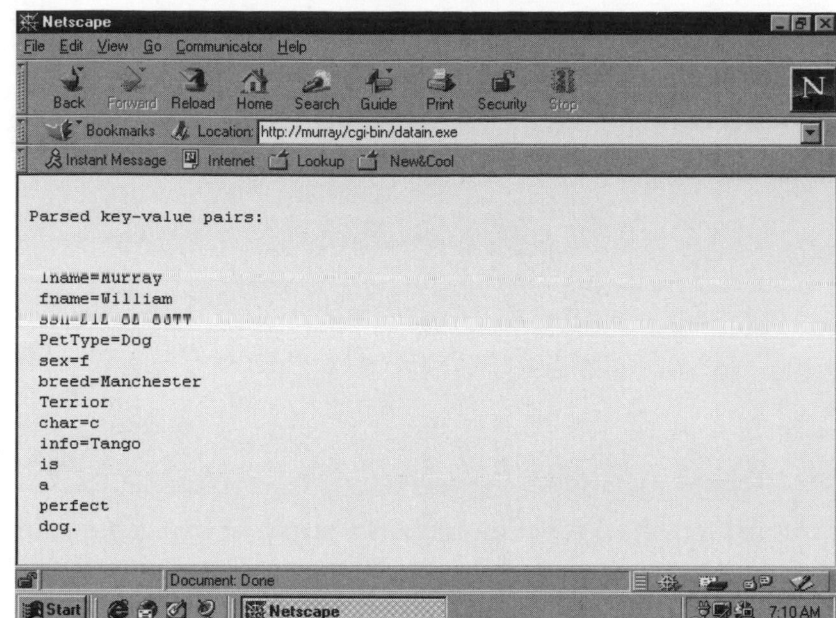

Figure C–2: *A CGI script parses a string of data returned by the HTML form*

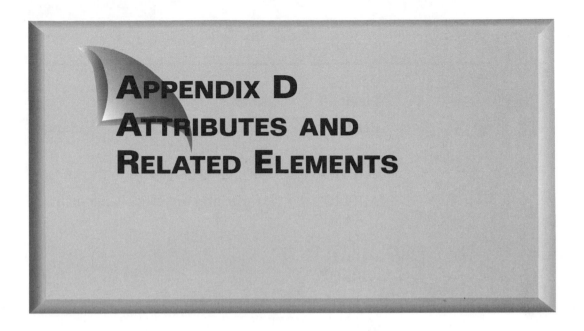

Appendix D Attributes and Related Elements

Most elements use or require several attributes. Many of these attributes are shared in common between elements. The W3C group's information on the relationship between parameters and elements is shown in Table D-1.

Table D–1: *Attribute and element relationships*

Attribute Name	Related Elements	Note
abbr	TD TH	Abbreviation used for header.
accept-charset	FORM	Character sets that are supported.
accept	INPUT	MIME types available for file uploading.
accesskey	A AREA BUTTON INPUT LABEL LEGEND	Key character accessibility.

Table D–1: *Attribute and element relationships (continued)*

Attribute Name	Related Elements	Note
action	FORM	Provides information for the server-side form handler.
align	CAPTION	Alignment is relative to the table.
	APPLET IFRAME IMG INPUT OBJECT	Horizontal or vertical alignment.
	LEGEND	Alignment is relative to field set.
	TABLE	Aligns table position relative to window.
	DIV H1 H2 H3 H4 H5 H6 P	Provides text or general alignment information.
	COL COLGROUP TBODY TD TFOOT TH THEAD TR	
	HR	
alink	BODY	Use with bgcolor, text, link, vlink, and alink.

Attribute Name	Related Elements	Note
alt	APPLET INPUT	Provides alt information.
	AREA IMG	
archive	OBJECT	Archive list separated with spaces.
	APPLET	Archive list separated with commas.
axes	TD TH	Header cells id list.
axis	TD TH	List of groups of related headers.
background	BODY	Document background (texture tile).
bgcolor	TABLE	Cell background color.
	TR	Row background color.
	TD TH	Cell background color
	BODY	Background color.
border	OBJECT	Link border width.
	IMG	
	TABLE	Sets frame width for table.
cellpadding	TABLE	Spacing within a cell.
cellspacing	TABLE	Spacing between cells.
char	COL COLGROUP TBODY TD TFOOT TH THEAD TR	Indicates the alignment char. For example: char='*'

Table D–1: *Attribute and element relationships (continued)*

Attribute Name	Related Elements	Note
charoff	COL COLGROUP TBODY TD TFOOT TH THEAD TR	Provides the offset for the alignment character.
charset	A DIV LINK SCRIPT SPAN	Provides character encoding of a linked resource.
checked	INPUT	Used by radio buttons and check boxes.
cite	BLOCKQUOTE Q	The URL for the source document.
	DEL INS	Provides information for the reason for the change.
class	Excluded elements: BASE BASEFONT FRAME FRAMESET HEAD HTML IFRAME META PARAM SCRIPT STYLE TITLE	Provides a list of classes separated by spaces.

Attribute Name	Related Elements	Note
classid	OBJECT	Provides the implementation id.
clear	BR	Indicates the text flow control.
code	APPLET	The class file for applet.
codebase	APPLET	Provides the base URL for applet (optional).
	OBJECT	Provides an additional URL when required by some systems.
codetype	OBJECT	Provides the code internet content type.
color	BASEFONT FONT	Provides an RGB color value in hexadecimal. For example green is "#00FF00"
cols	FRAMESET	When not specified, defaults to one column.
	TABLE	Used for immediate display mode
	TEXTAREA	Provides column information.
colspan	TD TH	Specifies the number of columns spanned by a cell.
compact	DIR MENU	Provides compact information .
	DL OL UL	Indicates the reduced inter-item spacing.
content	META	Related information.
coords	AREA	Provides a list of values separated by commas.
	A	Used with OBJECT SHAPES
data	OBJECT	References an object's data
datetime	DEL INS	Indicates an ISO date format (when changed)

Table D–1: *Attribute and element relationships (continued)*

Attribute Name	Related Elements	Note
declare	OBJECT	Declares but doesn't instantiate the flag.
defer	SCRIPT	UA may defer execution of script
dir	Excluded elements: APPLET BASE BASEFONT BDO BR FONT FRAME FRAMESET HR IFRAME PARAM SCRIPT	Indicates the direction for text.
	BDO	Provides directionality.
disabled	BUTTON INPUT LABEL OPTGROUP OPTION SELECT TEXTAREA	Indicates that the control is not available in this context.
enctype	FORM	Provides form enctype information.
face	BASEFONT FONT	Provides a list of font names separated by commas.
For	LABEL	Used to match field ID values.
Frame	TABLE	Specifies which part of a table frame to include.

Attribute Name	Related Elements	Note
Frameborder	FRAME IFRAME	Allows frame borders to be requested.
headers	TD TH, and so on	Id's for header cells
Height	IFRAME OBJECT	Provides the height value.
	TD TH	Indicates cell height.
	IMG	Provides the height (in pixels).
	APPLET	
Href	A LINK	The URL for a linked resource.
	AREA	Acts as a hypertext link.
	BASE	Provides Href information.
hreflanf	A DIV LINK SPAN	Language code.
Hspace	OBJECT	Provides the horizontal gutter.
	APPLET IMG	
http-equiv	META	Indicates a HTTP response header name.
Id	Excluded elements: BASE HEAD HTML META SCRIPT STYLE TITLE	Provides a unique document-wide id.

Table D–1: *Attribute and element relationships (continued)*

Attribute Name	Related Elements	Note
Ismap	IMG	Used with server-side image maps.
label	OPTION OPTGROUP	Used for hierarchical menus.
Lang	Excluded elements: APPLET BASE BASEFONT BR FONT FRAME FRAMESET HR IFRAME PARAM SCRIPT	Provides a language value.
Language	SCRIPT	Indicates the script language name (predefined).
link	BODY	Provides link information.
longdesc	IMG FRAME IFRAME	Used as a link to a long description.
marginheight	FRAME IFRAME	Provides margin heights (pixels).
marginwidth	FRAME IFRAME	Provides margin widths (pixels).
maxlength	INPUT	Indicates the maximum characters for text fields.
media	STYLE	Use with the given media.
	DIV LINK SPAN	Use when rendering on the given media.

Attribute Name	Related Elements	Note
method	FORM	Indicates the method used to submit the form.
multiple	SELECT	The default is a single selection.
name	MAP TEXTAREA	Provides name information.
	APPLET	Allows multiple applets to locate each other.
	SELECT	Provides the field name.
	BUTTON	Allows a submit button for scripting or forms.
	FRAME IFRAME	Identifies the name of the frame for targeting.
	A	Indicates a link end.
	INPUT OBJECT	Allows submission as part of a form.
	PARAM	Used to identify the property's name.
	META	Used to identify the Meta information name.
nohref	AREA	The region has no action associated with it.
noresize	FRAME	Permits frames to be resized by the user.
noshade	HR	Indicates no shade.
nowrap	TD TH	Turns off word wrapping.
object	APPLET	Identifies a serialized applet file.
Onblur	A AREA BUTTON INPUT LABEL SELECT TEXTAREA	The identified element has lost the focus.

Table D–1: *Attribute and element relationships (continued)*

Attribute Name	Related Elements	Note
Onchange	INPUT SELECT TEXTAREA	The element's value was changed.
Onclick	Excluded elements: APPLET BASE BASEFONT BDO BR FONT FRAME FRAMESET HEAD HTML IFRAME ISINDEX META PARAM SCRIPT STYLE TITLE	Indicates that a mouse (pointer) button was clicked.
ondblclick	Excluded elements: APPLET BASE BASEFONT BDO BR FONT FRAME FRAMESET	Indicates that a mouse (pointer) button was double clicked.

Attribute Name	Related Elements	Note
ondblclick *(continued)*	HEAD HTML IFRAME ISINDEX META PARAM SCRIPT STYLE TITLE	
onfocus	A AREA BUTTON INPUT LABEL SELECT TEXTAREA	Indicates that the element has the focus.
onkeydown	Excluded elements: APPLET BASE BASEFONT BDO BR FONT FRAME FRAMESET HEAD HTML IFRAME ISINDEX META PARAM SCRIPT STYLE TITLE	Indicates that a key (keyboard) was depressed.

Table D–1: Attribute and element relationships (continued)

Attribute Name	Related Elements	Note
onkeypress	Excluded elements: APPLET BASE BASEFONT BDO BR FONT FRAME FRAMESET HEAD HTML IFRAME ISINDEX META PARAM SCRIPT STYLE TITLE	Indicates that a key (keyboard) was depressed and released.
onkeyup	Excluded elements: APPLET BASE BASEFONT BDO BR FONT FRAME FRAMESET HEAD HTML IFRAME ISINDEX META PARAM	Indicates that a depressed key (keyboard) was released.

Attribute Name	Related Elements	Note
onkeyup *(continued)*	SCRIPT STYLE TITLE	
onload	FRAMESET	Indicates that all of the frames have been loaded.
	BODY	Indicates that the document has been loaded.
onmousedown	Excluded elements: APPLET BASE BASEFONT BDO BR FONT FRAME FRAMESET HEAD HTML IFRAME ISINDEX META PARAM SCRIPT STYLE TITLE	Indicates that a mouse (pointer) button was depressed.
onmousemove	Excluded elements: APPLET BASE BASEFONT BDO BR FONT FRAME FRAMESET HEAD	Indicates that the mouse (pointer) was moved within the given area.

Table D-1: *Attribute and element relationships (continued)*

Attribute Name	Related Elements	Note
onmousemove *(continued)*	HTML IFRAME ISINDEX META PARAM SCRIPT STYLE TITLE	
onmouseout	Excluded elements: APPLET BASE BASEFONT BDO BR FONT FRAME FRAMESET HEAD HTML IFRAME ISINDEX META PARAM SCRIPT STYLE TITLE	Indicates that the mouse (pointer) was moved away from the given area.
onmouseover	Excluded elements: APPLET BASE BASEFONT BDO BR FONT	Indicates that a mouse (pointer) was moved onto the given area.

Attribute Name	Related Elements	Note
onmouseover *(continued)*	FRAME FRAMESET HEAD HTML IFRAME ISINDEX META PARAM SCRIPT STYLE TITLE	
onmouseup	Excluded elements: APPLET BASE BASEFONT BDO BR FONT FRAME FRAMESET HEAD HTML IFRAME ISINDEX META PARAM SCRIPT STYLE TITLE	Indicates that a depressed mouse (pointer) button was released.
onreset	FORM	Indicates that the form has been reset.
onselect	INPUT TEXTAREA	Indicates that text has been selected.
onsubmit	FORM	Indicates that the form has been submitted.

Table D–1: *Attribute and element relationships (continued)*

Attribute Name	Related Elements	Note
onunload	FRAMESET	Indicates that all frames have been removed.
	BODY	Indicates that the document has been removed.
profile	HEAD	Indicates the dictionary of meta information.
prompt	ISINDEX	Gives a prompt message.
readonly	TEXTAREA	Provides text area information.
	INPUT	Used for both text and passwords.
rel	A LINK	Indicates forward link types.
rev	A DIV LINK SPAN	Indicates reverse link types.
rows	FRAMESET	When not specified, the default is one row.
	TEXTAREA	Provides text area information.
rowspan	TD TH	Indicates the number of rows spanned by a cell.
rules	TABLE	Indicates the number of rulings between rows and columns.
scheme	META	Allows the selection of the form of content.
scope	TD TH, etc.	Scope covered by header cells.

Attribute Name	Related Elements	Note
scrolling	FRAME IFRAME	Allows the inclusion of a scroll bar.
selected	OPTION	Provides selection information.
shape	AREA	Used to control the interpretation of coordinates.
	A	Used with OBJECT SHAPES
shapes	OBJECT	Indicates that the object has shaped hypertext links.
size	HR FONT	Specified size. For example, size="+2" or size=6
	INPUT	Indicates input specific to each type of field.
	BASEFONT	Indicates the base font size.
	SELECT	Indicates that rows are visible.
span	COLGROUP	Specifies the default number of columns in a group.
	COL	Specifies the number of columns spanned by a group.
src	SCRIPT	The URL for an external script.
	INPUT	Used for fields containing images.
	FRAME IFRAME	Indicates the source of the frame's content.
	IMG	The URL of image to be embedded.
standby	OBJECT	The message that will be displayed during loading.
start	OL	Indicates the starting sequence number.

Table D–1: *Attribute and element relationships (continued)*

Attribute Name	Related Elements	Note
style	Excluded elements: BASE BASEFONT FRAME FRAMESET HEAD HTML IFRAME META PARAM SCRIPT STYLE TITLE	Indicates the style information.
summary	TABLE	Gives the purpose or structure for output.
tabindex	A AREA BUTTON INPUT OBJECT SELECT TEXTAREA	Indicates the tabbing order position.
target	AREA BASE LINK	Indicates the location of the rendered linked resource.
	A	Indicates where to render a resource.
	DIV FORM SPAN	Indicates where to render the result.
text	BODY	Text information for the body of the document.

Attribute Name	Related Elements	Note
title	STYLE	Provides an advisory title.
	FRAME FRAMESET IFRAME	Provides an advisory title (anchors).
	Excluded elements: BASE BASEFONT FRAME FRAMESET HEAD HTML IFRAME META PARAM SCRIPT STYLE TITLE	Provides expanded advisory title information.
type	OBJECT	Indicates the internet content type for data.
	LINK	Provides the advisory internet content type.
	INPUT	Indicates what type of control is needed.
	LI	Indicates a list item style.
	OL	Indicates the numbering style.
	UL	Indicates a bullet style.
	BUTTON	Indicates use as a form's submit or reset button.
	SCRIPT	Indicates the content type for the script language.
	PARAM	Provides the media type information.

Table D–1: *Attribute and element relationships (continued)*

Attribute Name	Related Elements	Note
type *(continued)*	A DIV STYLE SPAN	Indicates the content type for the style language.
usemap	OBJECT	Provided the image map reference.
	IMG INPUT	Indicates the use of a client-side image map.
valign	COL COLGROUP TBODY TD TFOOT TH THEAD TR	Provides information for vertical alignment in cells.
value	OPTION	Indicates the default will be to element content.
	BUTTON	Indicates that information is passed to the server when submitted.
	PARAM	Provides the property value.
	INPUT	Required by radio buttons and checkboxes.
	LI	Provides a reset to the sequence number.
valuetype	PARAM	Indicates how a value is to be interpreted.
version	HTML	Provides a constant value.
vlink	BODY	Provides link information.

Attribute Namc	Related Elements	Note
vspace	OBJECT	Indicates the vertical gutter.
	APPLET IMG	
width	HR	Provides width information.
	IFRAME OBJECT	Provides the width information.
	TD TH	Width for a given cell.
	IMG	Provides the width information (pixels).
	APPLET	
	COL	Provides the width information for columns.
	COLGROUP	Provides the default width for enclosed columns.
	TABLE	Provides the table width relative to the window.
	PRE	Provides width information.

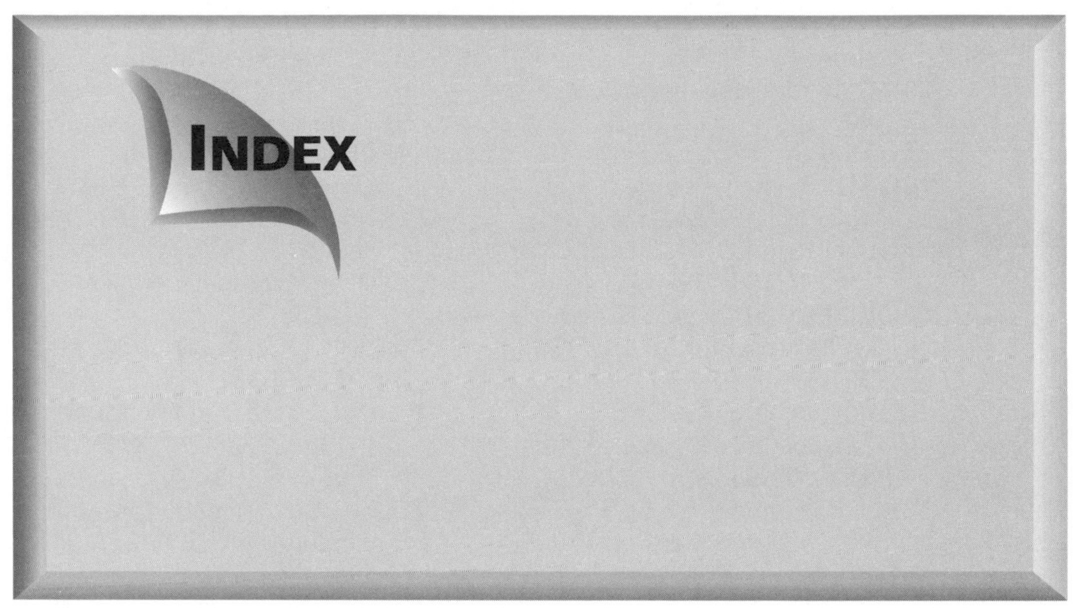
INDEX

A

B

C

F

G

H

I

J

L

M

Q

R

S

T

U

V

W

Z